The Grain of the Voice

INTERVIEWS 1962–1980

Roland Barthes

The Grain of the Voice

INTERVIEWS 1962–1980

Translated by Linda Coverdale

Hill and Wang • New York

A division of Farrar, Straus and Giroux

Translation copyright © 1985 by Farrar, Straus and Giroux, Inc.
Originally published in French as Le grain de la voix
Copyright © 1981 by Editions du Seuil
All rights reserved
Published simultaneously in Canada by
Collins Publishers, Toronto
Printed in the United States of America
Designed by Constance Fogler
First edition, 1985

Library of Congress Cataloging in Publication Data
Barthes, Roland.
The grain of the voice.
Translation of: Le grain de la voix.
1. Semiotics—Addresses, essays, lectures.
2. Discourse analysis—Addresses, essays, lectures.
3. Barthes, Roland—Addresses, essays, lectures.
I. Title.
P99.B28713   1985   410   84-16821

This collection includes most of the interviews given in French by Roland Barthes. We have tried to account for all of them, but since we do not have a complete list of his interviews, it is possible that we have overlooked a few. We trust that journalists and the reading public will forgive any such omission.

The best possible preface would have been a description by Roland Barthes himself of what an interview is. We will never have such a description now, but we do have a few pages where Roland Barthes analyzes, with admirable clarity, the passage of the spoken word to the word transcribed: we thought it fitting to begin with these pages, where the stylet of writing interlaces with the grain of the voice.

Contents

From Speech to Writing / 3

Do Things Mean Something? / 8

On Film / 11

I Don't Believe in Influences / 25

Semiology and Cinema / 30

On Behalf of the "New Criticism," Roland Barthes
    Replies to Raymond Picard / 38

On *The Fashion System* and the Structural Analysis
    of Narratives / 43

The Fashion System / 56

Conversation on a Scientific Poem / 63

On *S/Z* and *Empire of Signs* / 68

L'Express Talks with Roland Barthes / 88

Roland Barthes on Criticism / 109

Digressions / 113

Interview: A Conversation with Roland Barthes / 128

The Fatality of Culture, the Limits
    of Counterculture / 150

Pleasure / Writing / Reading / 157

The Adjective Is the "Statement" of Desire / 172

An Almost Obsessive Relation to
    Writing Instruments / 177

The Phantoms of the Opera / 183

Roland Barthes versus Received Ideas / 188

What Would Become of a Society That Ceased
    to Reflect upon Itself? / 196

The Play of the Kaleidoscope / 198

Twenty Key Words for Roland Barthes / 205

Literature / Teaching / 233

The Surrealists Overlooked the Body / 243

The Crisis of Truth / 246

A Great Rhetorician of Erotic Figures / 252

Of What Use Is an Intellectual? / 258

A *Lover's Discourse* / 281

The Greatest Cryptographer of Contemporary
    Myths Talks about Love / 290

On the Subject of Violence / 306

A Few Words to Let in Doubt / 312

An Extremely Brutal Context / 319

Roland Barthes on Roland Barthes / 321

Dare to Be Lazy / 338

For a Chateaubriand of Paper / 346

From Taste to Ecstasy / 351

On Photography / 353

The Crisis of Desire / 361

Biography / 367

The Grain of the Voice

INTERVIEWS 1962–1980

La *Quinzaine littéraire*, March 1–15, 1974

From Speech to Writing

This text by Roland Barthes prefaces the first series of Dialogues *produced by Roger Pillaudin for France-Culture and published by the Presses Universitaires de Grenoble.*

We talk, a tape recording is made, diligent secretaries listen to our words to refine, transcribe, and punctuate them, producing a first draft that we can tidy up afresh before it goes on to publication, the book, eternity. Haven't we just gone through the "toilette of the dead"? We have embalmed our speech like a mummy, to preserve it forever. Because we really must last a bit longer than our voices; we must, through the comedy of writing, *inscribe ourselves* somewhere.

This inscription, what does it cost us? What do we lose? What do we win?

The trap of scription

First of all, roughly speaking, here is what falls into the trap of scription (this word, pedantic though it may be, is preferable to *writing*: writing is not necessarily the mode of existence of what is written). It is evident, in the first place, that we lose an innocence; not that speech is in itself fresh, natural, spontaneous, truthful, expressive of a kind of pure interiority; quite on the contrary, our speech (especially in public) is immediately theatrical, it borrows its turns (in the stylistic and ludic senses of the term) from a whole collection of cultural and oratorical codes:

speech is always tactical; but in passing to the written word, it is
the very innocence of this tactic, perceptible to one who knows
how to listen, as others know how to read, that we erase; innocence
is always *exposed*; in rewriting what we have said we protect ourselves, we keep an eye on ourselves, we censure and delete our
blunders, our self-sufficiencies (or our insufficiencies), our irres-
olutions, our errors, our complacencies, sometimes even our
breakdowns (why shouldn't we have the right, while talking, at
this or that point made by our partner, to *dry up?*), in short, all
the watered silk of our image-repertoire, the personal play of our
self; speech is dangerous because it is immediate and cannot be
taken back (without supplementing itself with an explicit reprise);
scription, however, has plenty of time; it can even take the time
to "turn the tongue seven times in the mouth," as we say in
French (never has proverbial counsel been more illusory); in
writing down what we have said, we lose (or we keep) everything
that separates hysteria from paranoia.

Another loss: the rigor of our transitions. Often, we "spin out"
our discourse at little cost. This "thread," this *flumen orationis*
which disgusted Flaubert, is the consistency of our speech, the
law it creates for itself: when we speak, when we "expose" our
thoughts as they are put into words, we consider it worthwhile
to express aloud the inflections of our search; because we are
wrestling with language out in the open, we make sure that our
discourse "takes," "consists," that each step of this discourse is
legitimated by the previous step; in a word, we want a straightforward delivery and we show off the signs of this filiation in due
form; hence all those *buts* and *therefores* in our public speech,
all those repetitions or explicit denials. It isn't that these little
words have great logical value; they are, if you like, *expletives* of
thought. Writing is often sparing of them, venturing into asyn-
deton—that cutting figure which would be unbearable to the
voice, as unbearable as a castration.

Which brings us to a last diminishment inflicted on speech
through its transcription: the loss of all those scraps of language—
of the type "Isn't that right?"—that the linguist would doubtless
place in the category of one of the great functions of language,
the *phatic* or interpellant function; when we speak, we want our

interlocutor to listen to us; we revive his attention with mean-
ingless interpellations (of the type "Hello, hello, can you hear
me?"); unassuming as they are, these words and expressions are
yet in some way discreetly dramatic: they are appeals, modula-
tions—should I say, thinking of birds: songs?—through which a
body seeks another body. It is this song—gauche, flat, ridiculous
when written down—which is extinguished in our writing.

It should be understood after these few observations that what
is lost in transcription is quite simply the body—at least this
exterior (contingent) body which, in a dialogue, flings toward
another body, just as fragile (or frantic) as itself, messages that
are intellectually empty, the only function of which is in a way
to *hook* the Other (even in the prostitutional sense of the term)
and to keep it in its state of partnership.

Transcribed, speech obviously changes its receiver, and thereby
even its subject, for there is no subject without an Other. The
body, although still present (no language without a body), ceases
to coincide with the person, or, to put it better yet, the personality.
The speaker's image-repertoire changes space: it is no longer a
question of demand, of appeal, of a play of contacts; the concern
is to set up, to represent an articulated discontinuity; i.e., in fact,
an argumentation. This new project (here we are voluntarily
increasing the oppositions) can easily be seen in the simple ac-
cessories which transcription adds (because it physically possesses
the means) to speech (after having removed all the "scoria" that
have been said): first of all, very often, true logical pivots; we are
concerned now not with those tiny liaisons speech uses to fill up
its silences (*but, therefore*) but with syntactical relations full of
real logical semantemes (of the type *although, in such a manner
that*); in other words, what transcription permits and exploits is
a thing repugnant to spoken language and classified by grammar
as *subordination*: the sentence becomes hierarchical; in it is developed, as in the staging of a classic drama, the difference of
roles and stage positions; in becoming social (since it passes to a
larger and less familiar public), the message recovers a structure
of order; "ideas," entities so difficult to delineate through inter-
locution, where they are constantly overwhelmed by the body,
are put here in the foreground, there in the background, yet

elsewhere in contrast; this new order—even if only subtly discernible—is served by two typographical artifices which may thereby be added to the advantages of writing: parentheses, which do not exist in speech and which permit the clear indication of the secondary or digressive nature of an idea, and punctuation, which, as we know, divides up meaning (and not form, sound).

Thus, in the written word a new image-repertoire appears, that of "thought." Wherever there is a concurrence of spoken and written words, to write means in a certain manner: *I think better*, more firmly; I think less for you, I think more for the "truth." Doubtless, the Other is always there, in the anonymous figure of the reader; consequently, the "thought" staged through the conditions of the script (as discreet, as apparently insignificant as they may be) remains dependent upon the self-image I wish to present to the public; it is not so much an inflexible mold of givens and arguments that concerns us as it is a tactical space of propositions—that is, all things considered, of *positions*. In the debate of ideas, very widespread today thanks to mass communication, each subject is led to situate, to mark, to position itself intellectually, which means: politically. That is doubtless the current function of the public "dialogue"; contrary to what happens in other gatherings (judicial or scientific, for example), persuasion and the demolition of an opinion are no longer what is truly at stake in these new protocols of exchange: the concern is rather to present to the public, then to the reader, a kind of theater of intellectual occupations, a staging of ideas (this reference to the theater does not in the least discredit the didactic or analytic interest, the sincerity or the objectivity of the views exchanged).

Such is, it seems to me, the social function of these *Dialogues*: taken together, they form a communication in the second degree, a "representation," the evident shifts of two image-repertoires: that of the body and that of thought.

Writing is not the written

Of course, a third practice of language remains possible, one necessarily absent from these *Dialogues*: *writing*, properly so called, the kind which produces texts. Writing is not speech, and this separation has received a theoretical consecration these past few years; but neither is writing the written, transcription; to write is not to transcribe. In writing, what is *too* present in speech (in a hysterical fashion) and *too* absent from transcription (in a castratory fashion), namely the body, returns, but along a path which is indirect, measured, musical, and, in a word, *right*, returning through pleasure, and not through the Imaginary (the image). It is, after all, this voyage of the body (of the subject) through language which our three practices (speech, the written, writing) modulate, each in its fashion: a difficult voyage, twisted, varied, to which the development of broadcasting—that is, of a speech at the same time original and transcribable, ephemeral and memorable—now brings a striking interest. I feel that the *Dialogues* transcribed here are of value not only for their mass of information, of analyses, of ideas and arguments which cover the vast range of modern intellectual and scientific reality; the *Dialogues* have also, as they will be read, the value of a differential experience of languages: speech, the written, and writing engage a separate subject each time, and the reader—the listener—must follow this divided subject, different depending on whether he speaks, transcribes, or formulates.

Le Figaro littéraire, October 13, 1962
From an interview conducted by Pierre Fisson

Do Things Mean Something?

Roland Barthes gives us his views on the present state of the French novel.

One is an essayist because one is a thinker. I, too, would like to write short stories, but I dread to think of the difficulties I would have in finding the words to express myself. In France, essayists have always had to do something else—that is their task. What has interested me passionately all my life is the way men make their world intelligible to themselves. It is, if you like, the adventure of the intelligible, the problem of meaning. Men give a meaning to their way of writing; with words, writing creates a meaning which the words do not have at the outset. That is what must be understood, that is what I try to express.

On the subject of the New Novel, there is one thing which must be made clear. One must realize that society has managed to integrate the writer. The writer is no longer a pariah, he no longer depends on a patron, he is no longer in the service of a well-defined class. The writer in our society is almost happy. These are simply findings, no conclusion can be drawn from them, but they must be considered if one is to understand. On the one hand, there are the happy writers; on the other hand, a complex and evolving society, full of contradictions.

What has been said about the New Novel? That it has taken

refuge far from reality; that, in seeking a certain technicality, it has abandoned its responsibilities.

When this line is taken, reference is made to the great models of literature—Balzac, Stendhal, etc. It must be noted that these novelists represented a clearly defined, well-structured society, and that their novels were therefore realist; these novels signified a reality and sometimes—a fact which is not often emphasized—a nostalgic reality.

Nowadays, political events, social unrest, the war in Algeria are not much in evidence in the New Novel. They say: The works are not committed [*engagées*]. That is true, but the writers as people and citizens are committed and they undertake this commitment with courage.

It has been said: The writer must commit his work. But this is just theory, since it meets defeat every day. You may wonder about this failure . . . But it's simply because writing is the art of asking questions, not of answering or resolving them.

Only writing can ask a question, and because writing has this power, it can afford to leave questions in abeyance. When the questions asked are genuine, they are disturbing. The New Novel is perfectly aware of its role.

Kafka knew that literature depends on the way the questions are asked. What do you think makes Balzac fascinating even today? His ability to describe life? Certainly something else. He asked, perhaps without even knowing it, the right questions about bourgeois society.

Society today is particularly difficult to understand. Those living within this society are almost unable to analyze it. Class problems have become unthinkable in the terms used fifty years ago. We are living in both a class society and a mass society. The big, immediate problems seem confused. Political culture itself seems to be at a standstill. These different factors influence literature and find expression there.

Imagine a mind like Brecht's confronting life today; that mind would find itself paralyzed by the diversity of life. The world is becoming too rich in stimuli.

So we wonder: What is the question asked by the New Novel?

It asks a crucial question, one that is new and astoundingly simple: Do things mean something?

Until now, literature had never cast doubt on the meaning of things. That is to say, in this case, the totality of our surroundings, events as well as objects. The role of literature is thus to ask that question, to ask it through the narrative, the elements of the novel, the character, or the object.

The cry goes up: But why the object? An effort must be made. Man has always endowed the object with meaning, but on the other hand the object has never been used as literary material. Objects didn't matter in novels. Take *Les Liaisons dangereuses*, the only important object is a harp, and it's important only because it's used to hide messages. The New Novel has therefore tried to see objects stripped of their usual significance. Robbe-Grillet has brought a new way of looking at the object. He has shown it without memories, without poetry. This is a matte description, nonrealistic. The object appears without the halo of meanings, and that is what gives birth to anxiety, which is a profound, and metaphysical, feeling.

This rather huge undertaking is technical on the one hand and philosophical on the other. Where will it end? I don't know. When a work is successful, it asks its question with ambiguity and, in that way, becomes poetic.

There are great differences between all these works, but perhaps they have one fault in common: there is a discordance between the possibility of the work and the form given to it. A poem holds you because it is short, an overlong poem loses its strength; the same thing happens to the New Novel.

What is extraordinary is the serenity, the assurance of all these novelists. But the reader can also ask questions; so he can ask: Why has eroticism disappeared from literature? He may wonder if there are true and false ways of being bored, and he can ask himself finally why writers don't want to do anything anymore but make movies.

Cahiers du cinéma, no. 147, September 1963
From an interview conducted by Michel Delahaye
and Jacques Rivette

On Film

We here begin a series of interviews with certain prominent figures of contemporary culture.

Film has become a part of our culture like all the others, and all the arts, all interests, must take the cinema into account, as it does them. It is this phenomenon of reciprocal information, at times obvious (these are not always the best cases), often diffuse, that we would like, among other things, to try to examine closely in these conversations.

The cinema—always with us, sometimes in the background, sometimes in the foreground—will thus be situated, we hope, within a larger perspective, one which the archivists or idolizers (who also have their role to play) sometimes make us forget.

Roland Barthes is the first of our honored guests.

How do you fit the cinema into your life? Do you consider it as a spectator, and as a spectator-critic?

We should begin perhaps with filmgoing habits, with the way in which the cinema enters our lives. I myself don't go to the movies very often, barely once a week. As to the choice of film, it is never, really, a completely free choice; I would prefer of course to go to the movies alone, because, to me, the cinema is a completely projective activity; but, owing to the social aspect of life, we usually go to the movies with one or two others, and at that point the choice becomes, like it or not, *encumbered*. If I were to choose in a purely spontaneous fashion, my choice would

have to have the nature of total improvisation, free of any kind
of cultural or crypto-cultural imperative, guided by the deepest
forces within myself. What causes a problem in the life of the
filmgoer is that there is a more or less diffuse ethics of the films
one must see—imperatives, necessarily cultural in origin, which
are rather strong when one belongs to a cultural milieu (even if
only because one must oppose them to be free). Sometimes this
has its good points, as with all snobbery. One is always a bit
involved in a dialogue with this sort of law of cinematographic
taste, which is probably especially strong since film culture is a
recent development. The cinema is no longer something primitive; now people see in it the characteristics of classicism, acade-
mism, and the avant-garde, and you find yourself placed again,
by the very evolution of that art, in the middle of a play of values.
And so, when I choose, the films that one *must* see conflict with
the idea of total unforeseeableness and availability which the
cinema still represents for me, and they conflict, more precisely,
with the films which—spontaneously—I would like to see, but
which are not the films selected by that sort of diffuse culture
coming into existence.

> *What do you think of the level of this culture, as yet very
> diffuse, as far as the cinema is concerned?*

This culture is diffuse because it is confused; by that I mean that
the cinema permits a kind of mutual exchange of values: the
intellectuals begin to defend films popular with the general public,
and the commercial cinema can absorb avant-garde films very
quickly. This *acculturation* is characteristic of our mass culture,
but it has a rhythm that varies according to genre: in the cinema
it seems very intense; in literature, the preserves are much more
closely guarded; I don't think it is possible to belong to contemporary literature, the kind being written now, without a certain
knowledge and even a certain technical knowledge, because the
being of literature has passed into its technique. To sum up, the
present cultural situation of the cinema is contradictory: it mobilizes techniques, which explains the need for a certain knowledge and also the feeling of frustration if this knowledge is lacking,

but the being, the existence of the cinema is not in its technique, while the contrary is true of literature: can you imagine a *littér-ature-vérité*, analogous to the *cinéma-vérité?* With language, this would be impossible, truth is impossible with language.

> *And yet we refer constantly to the idea of a "cinemato-graphic language," as if the existence and definition of this language were universally admitted, whether you take the word "language" in a purely rhetorical sense (for example, the stylistic conventions attributed to the dolly shot or the low-angle shot), or in a very general sense, as the relation between a signifier and a signified.*

For myself, it's probably because I have not succeeded in inte-grating the cinema within the sphere of language that I consume it in a purely projective manner, and not as an analyst.

> *Isn't it, if not impossible, at the very least difficult for the cinema to gain entrance to that sphere of language?*

We can try to be more precise about that difficulty. It seems, at present, that the model for all languages is speech, articulated language. Now, this articulated language is a code, it uses a system of signs which are not analogical (and which consequently can be, and are, discontinuous); the opposite holds true for the cin-ema, which presents itself at first sight as an analogical expression of reality (and, moreover, continuous); and we don't know how to tackle a continuous and analogical expression in order to in-troduce, to initiate an analysis along linguistic lines; for example, how do you divide (semantically), how do you vary the meaning of a film, of a film fragment? Thus, if a critic wanted to treat the cinema as a language, abandoning that metaphorical inflation of the term, he would first have to discern whether there are elements in the cinematic continuity which are not analogical, or which partake of a deformed, or transposed, or codified analogy, ele-ments systematized in such a way that they can be treated as fragments of language. Now those are problems of concrete re-search, which have not yet been approached and which could be dealt with initially through some sort of cinematic tests, after which we would see if it is possible to establish a semantics, even partial (doubtless partial), of film. It would be a question of isolating cinematic elements by applying structuralist methods, of seeing how these elements are understood, what signifieds they correspond to in such and such a case, and, by causing variations, seeing at what point the variation of the signifier entails a variation of the signified. Then we would have truly isolated linguistic units in film, and we could go on to construct their "classes," systems, declensions.

> *Doesn't this intersect certain experiments made on a more empirical plane at the end of the silent film era, mainly by the Soviets, experiments that were not very conclusive, except when these elements of language were taken up by someone like Eisenstein within the perspective of a poetics? However, when this research remained on the level of pure rhetoric, as with Pudovkin, it was soon called into question: everything happens in the cinema as if, as soon as a semiological relationship was posited, it was immediately contradicted.*

In any case, if one succeeded in establishing a kind of partial semantics on precise points (in other words, for precise signifieds), it would be very difficult to explain why the whole film is not constructed as a juxtaposition of discontinuous elements; we would then run into the second problem, the discontinuity of the signs— or the continuity of the expression.

> *But even if these linguistic units were discovered, would that take us any farther, since they were not made to be perceived as such? The impregnation of the spectator by the signified takes place at another level, in a different fashion than the impregnation of the reader.*

Our outlook on semantic phenomena is doubtless still quite narrow, and what we find the most difficult to understand, finally, are what could be called the great signifying units; we have the same difficulty in linguistics, since stylistics is not very far advanced (we have a psychological, but not yet a structural, stylistics). Cinematographic expression probably also belongs to that order of the great signifying units, corresponding to signifieds which are global, diffuse, latent, not in the same category as the isolated and discontinuous signifieds of the articulated language. This opposition between a microsemantics and a macrosemantics would constitute perhaps another way of considering the cinema as a language, by abandoning the plane of *denotation* (we've just seen that it is rather difficult to approach the first, literal units on that level) in order to move to the plane of *connotation*; i.e., to the plane of signifieds which are global, diffuse, and, in a way, secondary. We could begin here by taking inspiration from the rhetorical (and no longer literally linguistic) models isolated by Jakobson, endowed by him with a generality extensive throughout articulated language and which he himself applied, in passing, to films. I mean metaphor and metonymy. Metaphor is the prototype of all the signs which can be substituted one for another by reason of similarity; metonymy is the prototype of signs which signify through a contiguous relation, through contagion one might say; for example, the riffling leaves of a calendar, that is a metaphor; and we'd be tempted to say that in films, all montage, i.e., all signifying contiguity, is a metonymy, and since the cinema is montage, to say further that the cinema is a metonymic art (at least at present).

> But isn't montage at the same time an indefinable element? Because everything can be montage, from a "revolver" shot with six images to a huge tracking shot five minutes long showing three hundred people and thirty or so interlacing actions; besides, you can splice these shots one after the other—which wouldn't put them in the same shot for all that . . .

What would be interesting to do, I think, would be to see if a cinematographic process could be methodologically converted into signifying units and to see if the elaborating processes correspond to the reading units of the film; that is every critic's dream, to be able to define an art by its technique.

> *But the procedures are all ambiguous; for example, the standard rhetoric says that the overhead shot signifies crushing, oppression; well, you can see two hundred cases (at least) where that shot simply doesn't have that meaning.*

This ambiguity is normal and is not what complicates our problem. The signifiers are always ambiguous; the number of signifieds always exceeds the number of signifiers: otherwise, there would be neither literature nor art nor history nor anything of what makes the world go round. The strength of a signifier does not come from its clarity but from the fact that it is perceived as a signifier—I would say: whatever the resultant meaning may be, it is not things but the place of things which matters. The bond between the signifier and the signified is of much less importance than the organization of the signifiers among themselves; the overhead shot [*la plongée*] may have signified crushing, but we know that this rhetoric is outmoded precisely because we feel it is based on an analogical relation between "to plunge" [*plonger*] and "to crush," which seems naïve to us, above all today when a psychology of "denial" has taught us that there could be a valid relation between a content and the form which seems to be most "naturally" its contrary. In this awakening of meaning provoked by the overhead shot, what is important is the awakening, not the meaning.

> *Exactly—after an initial "analogical" period, isn't the cinema already emerging from this second period of the "anti-analogy" through a more supple, uncodified use of "figures of style"?*

I think that if the problems of symbolism (because analogy puts into question the symbolic cinema) are losing their clarity, their acuity, it's above all because between the two great linguistic paths indicated by Jakobson, metaphor and metonymy, the cinema seems, for the moment, to have chosen the metonymic path—or, if you prefer, the syntagmatic path, the syntagm being an extended, arranged fragment, actualized by signs; in short, a section of narrative. It's very striking that, in contrast to the literature of "nothing happens" (the prototype of which would be *Sentimental Education*), the cinema, even the kind which doesn't seem at the outset to be commercial, is a discourse in which the story, the anecdote, the plot (with its major consequence, *suspense*) are never absent; even "fantasy," which is the emphatic, caricatural category of the anecdotal, is not incompatible with very good cinema. At the movies, "something is happening," and this fact is naturally closely related to the metonymic, syntagmatic path I was just talking about. A "good story" is indeed, in structural terms, a successful series of syntagmatic *dispatchings*: given such and such a situation (sign), what can follow it? There is a certain number of possibilities, but these possibilities are finite in number (it is this finitude, this closure of the possible which founds structural analysis), and that is why the director's choice of the next "sign" is significant; meaning is in fact a liberty, but a liberty under surveillance (by the finite number of possibilities); every sign (each "moment" of the narrative, of the film) may be followed only by certain other signs, certain other moments; in discourse, in the syntagm, the operation which consists in prolonging a sign by another sign (according to a finite and sometimes very restricted number of possibilities) is called a *catalysis*; in speech, for example, the sign *dog* can be catalyzed only by a small number of other signs (barks, sleeps, eats, bites, runs, etc., but not: sews, flies, sweeps, etc.); the narrative, the cinematographic syntagm is also subject to rules of catalysis, which the director doubtless observes empirically, but which the critic and analyst should try to rediscover. Because, naturally, each dispatching, each catalysis has its role to play in the ultimate meaning of the work.

> *The attitude of the director, insofar as we are able to judge, is to have a more or less precise idea of this meaning beforehand, and to find it again more or less modified afterward. During the filmmaking, he is almost entirely caught up in work which is not preoccupied with its*

> *ultimate meaning; the director fabricates successive little cells guided by . . . By what? That is just what it would be interesting to determine.*

He can only be guided, more or less consciously, by his profound ideology, the attitude he takes toward the world; because the syntagm is just as responsible for meaning as is the sign itself, for which reason the cinema can become a metonymic, and not a symbolic, art without losing any of its responsibility, quite the contrary. I remember that Brecht suggested to us, at Théâtre Populaire, that we organize an exchange of letters between him and some young French playwrights; that would have taken the form of "playing" the production of an imaginary play, i.e., of a series of situations, like a chess game; one would have put forth a situation, another would have chosen the subsequent situation, and naturally (that was the point of the "game"), each move would have been discussed as a function of the work's ultimate meaning, that is, according to Brecht, of its ideological responsibility; but French playwrights, well, we didn't have any. In any case, you see that Brecht, a keen theoretician—and practitioner—of *meaning*, was strongly aware of the syntagmatic problem. All this seems to prove that there are possibilities of exchange between linguistics and film, providing you choose a linguistics of the syntagm rather than of the sign.

> *Perhaps the consideration of film as a language will never be fully realizable; but at the same time such a consideration is necessary, in order to avoid this danger of enjoying the cinema as an object which would have no meaning but would be purely an object of pleasure, of fascination, completely deprived of all roots and of all signification. Now, the cinema, whether we like it or not, always has a meaning; therefore, there is always an element of language involved . . .*

Of course, the work always has a meaning; but, if I may say so, the science of meaning, which is presently experiencing an extraordinary promotion (through a kind of prolific snobbism), teaches us paradoxically that meaning, so to speak, is not enclosed within the signified; the relation between signifier and signified (i.e., the sign) seems initially to be the very foundation of all "semiological" reflection; but later on you acquire a much broader viewpoint on "meaning," one much less centered on the signified (everything that we have said about the syntagm runs in this direction); we owe this broadening to structural linguistics, of course, but also to a man like Lévi-Strauss, who showed that meaning (or more exactly the signifier) was the highest category of the intelligible. In the end, it is the humanly *intelligible* which interests us. How does the cinema manifest or connect with the categories, functions, and structure of the intelligible elaborated by our history, our society? This is the question which might be answered by a "semiology" of film.

> *It is doubtless impossible to produce the "unintelligible."*

Absolutely. Everything has a meaning, even nonsense (which has at least the secondary meaning of being nonsense). Meaning is so fated for mankind that art (as liberty) seems to be used, especially today, not for *making* sense, but on the contrary for keeping it in *suspense*; for constructing meanings, but without filling them in *exactly*.

> *Perhaps we could take an example here: in the (theatrical) production of Brecht, there are elements of language which are not, initially, open to codification.*

With regard to this problem of meaning, the case of Brecht is rather complicated. On the one hand, he had, as I said, an acute awareness of the techniques of meaning (which was original, considering that Marxism is not very sensitive to the responsibilities of form); he was familiar with total responsibility for the slightest signifiers, such as the color of a costume or the position of a spotlight; and you know how fascinated he was by the theaters of the East, in which signification is very codified—it would be better to say: coded—and consequently not very analogical; finally, we have seen the meticulousness with which he worked, and with which he wanted others to work, on the semantic responsibility of "syntagms" (epic art, which he championed, is moreover a strongly syntagmatic art); and naturally, all this technique was thought of in terms of a political meaning. *In terms of*, but perhaps not *with a view to*; and it's here that we touch on the second aspect of Brechtian ambiguity; I wonder if this *committed* meaning of Brecht's oeuvre isn't, after all, in its way a *suspended* meaning, a meaning *withheld*; you remember that his dramatic theory includes a sort of functional division of the stage and the auditorium: the work must ask the questions (in terms obviously chosen by the author: this is a responsible art), it is left to the public to find the answers (what Brecht called the *issue*); meaning (in the positive sense of the term) moved from the stage to the audience; to sum up, there is in fact, in Brecht's theater, a meaning, and a very strong meaning, but it is always a question. This is perhaps what explains why this theater, although it is certainly a critical, polemic, committed theater, is not, however, a militant theater.

Can this approach be extended to the cinema?

It always seems very difficult and rather vain to carry over a technique (and meaning is one) from one art to another; not from a purism of genres, but because structure depends on the materials used; the spectatorial image is not made from the same material as the cinematographic image, it doesn't lend itself in the same fashion to editing, duration, perception; the theater seems to me a much "coarser," or let's say, if you like, a "rougher," art than the cinema (drama criticism also seems to me more coarse than film criticism), and it therefore seems closer to direct tasks of the polemic, subversive, challenging order (I leave aside the theater of agreement, conformism, and repletion).

> *You evoked, a few years ago, the possibility of determining the political signification of a film by examining, aside from its plot, the attitude which informs it as a film: the left-wing film being roughly characterized by*

> *lucidity, the right-wing film by an appeal to magic, ho-cus-pocus . . .*

What I wonder now is if there aren't arts which are by nature, by technique, more or less reactionary. I believe that of literature; I don't believe that a literature of the left is possible. A problematic literature, yes, that is, a literature of suspended meaning: an art which provokes answers but which doesn't give them. I think that, in the best of cases, that's what literature is. As for the cinema, I have the impression that it is, on this level, quite close to literature, and that it is, by its material and structure, much better prepared than the theater for a very particular responsibility of forms which I have called the technique of suspended meaning. I believe that the cinema finds it difficult to provide clear meanings and that, with things as they stand, it ought not to. The best films (to me) are those which best withhold meaning. To suspend meaning is an extremely difficult task requiring at the same time a very great technique and total intellectual loyalty. That means getting rid of all parasite meanings, which is extremely difficult.

> *Have you seen any films which have given you this impression?*

Yes, *The Exterminating Angel.* I don't believe that Buñuel's warning at the beginning: I, Buñuel, say to you that this film has no meaning—I absolutely do not believe that it is a coquettish affectation; I believe that it really is the definition of the film. And, within this perspective, the film is very beautiful: one can see how, at each moment, meaning is suspended, without ever being, of course, nonsense. It is not at all an absurd film; it's a film that is full of meaning; full of what Lacan calls "significance." It is full of significance, but it doesn't have *one* meaning, or a series of little meanings. And in that very way it's a film which disturbs profoundly, and which forces you to go beyond dogmatism, beyond doctrines. Normally, if the society of film consumers were less alienated, this film would, as they say vulgarly and correctly, "make you think." One could moreover show, but it would take time, how the meanings which "take" at each instant, despite ourselves, are caught up in an extremely dynamic and intelligent dispatching toward a subsequent meaning, which itself is never definite.

> *And the movement of the film is the very movement of this perpetual dispatching.*

There is also, in this film, an initial success which is responsible for its overall success: the story, the idea, the plot have a distinctness which gives an illusion of necessity. You get the impression that all Buñuel had to do was push the button. Up until now, I was not much of an admirer of Buñuel; but here Buñuel has been able to express his entire metaphor (because Buñuel has always been very metaphorical), his entire arsenal and personal reserve of symbols; everything has been swallowed up by that kind of syntagmatic distinctness, by the fact that the dispatching is made, at each instant, exactly as it should be.

> *Moreover, Buñuel has always admitted his metaphor with such frankness, has always known how to respect the importance of what comes before and what comes after it in such a way that it was already isolated, put in quotation marks, and therefore bypassed or destroyed.*

Unfortunately for the ordinary fans of Buñuel, he is defined above all by his metaphor, the "richness" of his symbols. But if modern film has a direction, it can be found in *The Exterminating Angel* . . .

> *Apropos of the "modern" cinema, have you seen L'Immortelle?*

Yes . . . My (abstract) relations with Robbe-Grillet complicate things for me a bit. I'm not pleased; I wouldn't have advised him to make movies . . . Well, there, in *L'Immortelle*, there you have metaphor . . . In fact, Robbe-Grillet doesn't kill meaning at all, he scrambles it; he thinks it's enough to mix up a meaning for it to die. It takes more than that to kill meaning.

> *And he gives more and more weight to a meaning that is more and more flat.*

Because he "varies" the meaning, he doesn't suspend it. Variation imposes a stronger and stronger meaning, on the order of an obsession: a reduced number of "varied" signifiers (varied in the musical sense) refers to the same signified (that is the definition of metaphor). On the contrary, in *The Exterminating Angel* (leaving aside the kind of derision initially aimed at repetition, in the scenes that are literally repeated), the scenes (the syntagmatic fragments) do not make up an immobile series (obsessional, metaphorical), but participate in the gradual transformation of a festal society into one of constraint—they form a duration that is irreversible.

> *What is more, Buñuel has taken chronology seriously; nonchronology is an easy trick: it's a false token of modernity.*

We come back to what I said in the beginning: the film is beautiful because there is a story; a story with a beginning, an end, suspense. These days, modernity too often appears as a way of evading the story, or evading psychology. A work's most immediate criterion of modernity is to avoid the "psychological," in the traditional sense of the term. But, at the same time, we can't get rid of that same psychology, that affectivity between human beings, that relational charm that is no longer addressed by works of art (here's the paradox) but by medicine and the social sciences: today psychology survives only in psychoanalysis, which, whatever intelligence and breadth of interest are involved, is practiced by doctors: "the soul" has become in itself a pathological phenomenon. There is a sort of resignation evinced by modern works when faced with the interhuman, the interpersonal relationship. The great movements of ideological emancipation—let's say, to speak frankly, Marxism—have passed over the private person; doubtless, things could not have been otherwise. Yet we know very well that in this there is still a gap—there's still something that doesn't work: as long as there are conjugal "scenes," there will be questions to put to the world.

> *The real subject of modern art is the possibility of happiness. Nowadays, everything happens in the cinema as if there were a general realization of the impossibility of happiness in the present, with a sort of recourse to the future. Perhaps the years to come will see attempts at a new kind of happiness.*

Exactly. No great ideology, no great utopia is responding to this need today. We've had a whole literature of science-fiction utopias, but the kind of micro-utopia that consists in imagining psychological or relational utopias simply doesn't exist. But if the structuralist law of the rotation of needs and forms applies here, we should soon arrive at a more existential art. In other words, the loud anti-psychological declarations of these last ten years (declarations in which I myself participated, of course) must be reversed and will become outmoded. Ambiguous though Antonioni's art may be, it is probably here that he touches us, seems important to us.

To sum up what we would like to see now: syntagmatic films, "psychological" films—films that have a story.

France-Observateur, April 16, 1964
From an interview conducted by Renaud Matignon

I Don't Believe
in Influences

For more than ten years now the criticism of Roland Barthes has fascinated, even enthralled the best young writers of today. Ever since Writing Degree Zero *appeared in 1953, Barthes has been reinventing a morality of exactingness and difficulty, applying to literature his passion for understanding and his thirst for truth, relentlessly tracking down man and history, subjecting them to the test of his insistent thoroughness. Some people find this difficult to put up with—no writer is safe anymore. And now we have his latest book,* Critical Essays: *can revenge be far off? Barthes is no longer the young author we must treat gently to safeguard the future, or a novice made harmless by awkwardness. He has become the man to overthrow, the irritating witness who must disappear if we are ever to return to the little games we used to play, the elegance and outbursts of feeling, the unself-consciousness, the grand style, the dainty turn of phrase.*

And yet Roland Barthes still defies us bravely. The essays he is publishing now are magazine pieces, prefaces, answers to questionnaires, or unpublished remarks: he writes of Brecht, Robbe-Grillet, Butor; but also of La Bruyère, Voltaire, even Tacitus; and theatrical costume and structuralism and criticism—Barthes's work seems quite varied, and sometimes quite contradictory. What is he driving at? Now it is his turn to answer our questions.

*Your book gathers together pieces on very diverse matters
and periods. Do these texts have anything in common?*

I explained in my preface why I didn't wish to give a retrospective
unity to texts written at different times: I do not feel the need to
arrange the uncertainties or contradictions of the past. So the
unity of this book can only be a question: *What is writing? How
does one write?* I have essayed different answers to this question,
in languages which may have varied in the course of ten years;
my book is, literally, a collection of *essays*, of different experiences
which nevertheless always address the same question.

*You have often challenged the old criticism that relied
on impressions and moods, that pronounced absolution
or condemnation. Do you think it is now possible to
define a real critical method to replace that approach?*

I don't think there is such a thing as literary criticism *in itself*;
there is no critical method independent of a more general philosophy; it's impossible to talk about literature without referring
to psychology, sociology, aesthetics, or morality: criticism is necessarily the parasite of a larger ideology. As far as I'm concerned,
I'm ready to acknowledge any criticism which declares the ideology on which it is inevitably based; but it follows that I feel
obligated to challenge any criticism lacking in such frankness.

What influence do you think your book might have?

The very form of these essays denies any "doctrinal" intention;
in my eyes they constitute a gathering of materials, a "repertory"
of critical themes intended for those interested in literature and
modernity; to me, the reader is a virtual creator, to whom I offer
an instrument for study, or rather (since it is not a work of schol-
arship), a collection of "references."
    Moreover, in general, I'm not sure what an "influence" is; to
my mind, what is transmitted is not "ideas" but "languages," i.e.,
forms which can be filled in different fashions; that's why the

notion of *circulation* seems to me more appropriate than *influence*; books are "currency" rather than "forces."

> *Your consideration of literature usually leads you to an extreme distrust of the writer in relation to himself, to his material, and to language most of all: this is essentially a negative attitude. Do you think you have in fact had a disturbing—or even an impoverishing—influence on certain of your contemporaries?*

I could ask for nothing better than to acknowledge a "negative" influence, because I don't think that in literature a "negative" attitude must be necessarily "impoverishing"; consideration of the limitations, defections, or impossibilities of writing is an essential element of literary creation, and for a hundred years now, from Mallarmé to Blanchot, great works have been created from this *absence*; even Proust's novel, which seems to us so "positive," so liberating, is born explicitly of a book impossible to write.

However, I repeat, negative or not, I don't believe in *influences*; it's possible that I have given—fleetingly, partially, and perhaps at the price of some misunderstandings—an intellectual, even an intellectualizing voice to certain creative preoccupations of certain contemporaries; but this has been nothing more than a coincidence of languages.

> *Paradoxically, such an attitude leads you, a critic who conceives of a work as the total commitment of the writer, to extol the least committed of works, those most abstract and shut in upon themselves—for example, Butor or Robbe-Grillet.*

Those writers have often told you that they do not in any way consider themselves estranged from or indifferent to society or the times. There are many connections between history and literature, starting with writing itself. We must try—and this may be one of the tasks of criticism—to perceive these multiple connections, not in order to reinforce literature's isolation, but, on the contrary, to understand how it is linked by a chain of con-

straints to human misfortune, which is always literature's real
object.

> *The most recent important literary movement which you*
> *have defended—the New Novel, as it is called—seems*
> *today to be at an impasse. Do you think that this impasse*
> *weakens your critical concepts, that it is also an impasse*
> *for your method?*

I have never defended the New Novel; I defended Robbe-Grillet,
I defended Butor, I love the writing of Ollier, Claude Simon,
and Nathalie Sarraute, and that is quite different. I have always
thought that the New Novel was a sociological phenomenon, not
"doctrinal" at all; of course, this sociology is not insignificant,
and it would be interesting someday to tell the story of the New
Novel; but from the point of view of creative research, the New
Novel's *impasse* is as artificial as its promotion. Neither Robbe-
Grillet nor Butor nor any of their companions is personally at an
"impasse," and that's what counts: if the New Novel is dead, then
long live its authors!

As for my "research," it always concerns what could be called
a sort of historical essence of literature; my research has thus no
other subject than works which exist, but the limits of this subject
are continually expanding. I reserve the right to defend and to
criticize tomorrow, in new terms, the work which is perhaps being
born today.

> *On what criterion do you rely to decide whether a book*
> *belongs in the ranks of real literature?*

As a matter of fact, I don't classify books in such a cut-and-dried
manner, according to some literary Good and Bad. Some works
more than others give me the feeling of exploring certain limits
of literature, in short, they seem *dangerous*, and it is of them,
obviously, that I want to speak—without always being able to, I
might add.

Having said that, I think that the distinction between "good"
and "bad" literature cannot be made according to simple and

definitive criteria: this is a separation in which we ourselves are always involved, it's one of those autonomies on which we cannot pass judgment; we should consider this distinction with that spirit of "vertigo" that Michel Foucault applied to Reason and Unreason; and this would be perhaps, after all, the essential subject of any theoretical book on literature.

Image et Son, July 1964
From an interview conducted by Philippe Pilard
and Michel Tardy

Semiology and Cinema

*Cinema seems somehow to resist semiological analysis.
What do you think are the reasons behind this difficulty?*

We should perhaps begin with the project of semiology. The term
and the project come from Saussure: he envisioned a general
science of signs in which linguistics would be only a department,
obviously quite an advanced department since it was, of course,
already established as a science. Beginning with this project, one
considers the gradual exploration of various sign systems other
than language, systems differing essentially in that their sign substance is no longer articulated sound; one can refer, for example,
to elementary systems where the signifiers are objects; ethnology
has fairly well covered this area (systems of communication through
knotted strings, stones, broken branches, etc.). When you reach
a society as complex as ours, however, especially a mass society,
this notion of the "object" or the "signifying material" becomes
rather problematical, for the simple reason that these objects are
used largely to exchange marginal information. Consequently, it
becomes apparent that communication through objects presents
a certain richness only if it is reinforced by language; objects must
be supported by a kind of discourse. For example, studying object
systems such as those of clothing or food, one quickly notices
that they are significant (that they signify) only because there are
people or publications speaking of clothing or food. This is true
to such an extent that we may well wonder if this semiology-to-
be isn't already doomed, in the sense that it has perhaps no proper

object in modern society, since each time a communication system is based on a substance other than language a moment inevitably appears when these substances are seconded by language. This is an essential aspect of our civilization, which is a civilization of words, despite the invasion of images. And we might also wonder if the semiological project won't be quickly endangered by various paralinguistics focusing on all forms of human discourse about objects that make them signify through speech. To return to the image, it is obviously a mysterious object. Does an image signify? We're working on this question, but for now we can only point out difficulties, impossibilities, sources of resistance. The major obstacle in considering the image as a signification system is its so-called analogical character, which distinguishes it from articulated language. The image's analogical aspect is linked to its continuous aspect, a continuity that, in the case of film, involves not only a spatial component but also reinforcement by a temporal continuity, the succession of images. Now, when linguists consider systems marginal to language, such as animal or gestural languages, they find that symbolic (i.e., analogical) systems are "poor" systems, because they support almost no combinative operations. *Analogy* makes it almost impossible to combine a restricted number of units in a rich and subtle manner. This is why linguists have until now refused to recognize as real language such symbolic systems as the "languages" of bees and of crows, or communication by gesture. The symbol—by that I mean an analogical relation between signifier and signified—would thus be beyond the reach of linguistics, or even of a rigorous semiology. But we should not give up on this too soon. Because in a film, and this is a working hypothesis, there is of course an analogical representation of reality, but, insofar as this discourse is received by a society, it contains elements that are not directly symbolic but are already interpreted, even "culturalized," conventionalized; and these elements can form secondary signification systems superimposed on analogical discourse—we might call them "rhetorical elements" or "elements of connotation." They would thus form an object of analysis for semiology.

The difficulty arises then in the demarcation of these two planes of denotation and connotation.

Obviously, film presents these two elements inextricably entwined. For example, I recently saw the film *That Man from Rio*. Well, this type of movie is crammed with cultural signs: when you see the Brazilian architect, you notice that he is in a way "covered" with signs telling us that he is a builder of fantastic designs, a whimsical adventurer, etc. His hair, his accent, his clothes, his house, and so forth—all function as signs. But these signs are experienced by us only in an anecdotal continuity captured by the camera. However, as soon as the language of analysis can conceptualize a certain number of appearances or phenomena provided by the film, we may presume they are signs.

Do you think that linguistic support is absolutely necessary to make them signify?

That's another problem because it assumes that the analyst, who creates that division into signs only through his own language, must have a complete theory of semiological analysis and must know at all times what his place is within the very systems he is obliged to describe. He uses a metalanguage, even if only to designate signifieds. If I want to designate what is signified by the hair, clothing, and gestures of the Brazilian architect, who is on the whole a concept of "Latin-American construction adventurism," I am obliged to use a very cultural, very "intellectual" language. That is a great problem for semiological analysis, but it's also proof of the research's validity. Because it can be maintained, in the social sciences, that only sciences which "think" their own language along with their object can be productive. The first historical example was given by Marxism, which is a vision of reality that *thinks* the person who *speaks* it. The second example would be psychoanalysis, since one cannot psychoanalyze without being aware of the psychoanalyst's place within the psychoanalytic system . . . One cannot deal semantically with an object like film using only a simple nomenclature of pure denotation, an innocent nomenclature.

> *Isn't there another problem insofar as film uses several*
> *signifying substances, such as—among others—linguistic*
> *and iconic substances? And isn't there a problem in the*
> *structural relation between these different messages? Isn't*
> *unity established only on the level of connotation?*

Those are questions to which we do not yet have the answers,
and we realize, moreover, that the choice of procedure is vitally
important. Should we try to reconstitute the two systems of dialogue and image separately, then establish a system compre-
hending these subsidiaries, or should we plunge in Gestaltist
fashion into the totality of messages to distinguish their formative
units? Such matters haven't been decided yet. Certain Americans,
Kenneth Pike in particular, have tackled the problem; Pike has
considered situations of daily life in which there is a mixture of
words and gestures, a case of complementary systems with different substances.

> *Don't you think that the analytic method could be in-*
> *dicated more specifically, since there are systems that use*
> *only one signifying substance (the radio, for example)?*
> *And some films hardly use the linguistic "channel" at*
> *all.*

True—not long ago I attended a private showing of *Future Eves*,
a short subject by Baratier about the construction of store man-
nequins, and there was no commentary. On the one hand, there
was a musical sound track, which is obviously very important;
and on the other, the very absence of commentary serves as the
signifier of something: it adds a certain ambiguity, a certain in-
humanity to the film . . . I think it would be better to work first
on the image alone, and to concentrate on the more obvious
cases of signification, the stereotypes. One could take several
commercial films and select the "connotators," then draw up
inventories of cultural-symbolic signs; perhaps at that point it
would become easier to see what the next step should be. A sort
of film rhetoric could then be established, a "rhetoric" almost in
the pejorative sense of the word, a stereotyped inflation of mes-

sages; only afterward could films deviating from this rhetorical
code be considered. I saw *That Man from Rio* and Bergman's
The Silence one right after the other; obviously, a rhetorical analysis of *The Silence* would be much more difficult than an analysis
of the other film. This is because Bergman's rhetoric, a collection
of stereotyped signs, is constantly opposed, twisted, destroyed—
often to the benefit of another, much more individual and subtle
rhetoric. We can therefore feel justified in believing that semiological analysis will one day lead us to an aesthetics . . .

> *You're proposing to begin with the "image alone." Does
> that mean using films conceived for a purely visual con-
> sumption, i.e., silent films (which introduces the prob-
> lem of a diachronic study), or contemporary films without
> their sound tracks?*

I think that in the early stages it's better to leave aside the diachronic aspect. A study could be made of perhaps ten commercial
films released within any period of two or three years—for example, a group of films starring Belmondo: his presence in a film,
for several years now, implies a certain homogeneity of the public
as readers of codes. Starting with unity of readership, one can
reasonably infer unity of code. It's the same for Gabin . . . One
never thinks of actors as a unifying element, and yet that's a very
good sociological factor of "homogenization" of the public and
thereby of the film's interpretation. There are of course other
unifying categories which come to mind, but they are much more
complex: the Western, for example, or "French" comedies of the
kind Gabin often plays, like *Monsieur*, where you see a typical
French social milieu . . .

> *In order to define the different semantic aspects within
> film, don't you think that a functional analysis of the
> type created by Vladimir Propp might be desirable? Such
> an analysis would perhaps permit us to discover, within
> films of different categories (Westerns, gangster movies,
> etc.), a series of equivalent functions.*

That raises another question. On the one hand, one can try to establish a rhetoric of film, i.e., an inventory of discontinuous signs, the connotators. That is what linguists call the paradigmatic plane: the reconstruction of lexicons. But another approach to the problem entails reconstituting the structure of narratives, what Souriau calls "diegesis." Apropos, here are Propp's work on Russian folktales and Lévi-Strauss's research on myth. And these two types of analysis, even though they belong to the same complex, are quite distinct. Functional analysis is perhaps more important, richer, and more pressing than rhetorical analysis. With the functional approach one understands more or less how a film is made, from the operational point of view: it's a kind of "dispatching," a distributional network of situations and actions where a given situation engenders a number of possibilities, only one of which is selected, and so on. That is what Propp studied in Russian folktales. There is thus a large structural network of narrative situations and actions, but since this network is sustained by characters, whom Propp calls *dramatis personae*, each character is defined by attributes, by a certain number of signs which are within the scope of semiology. In the case of *That Man from Rio*, for example, at a certain point the situation requires the appearance of individual X, who fills a certain position, and all this is still on the structural level; but once you define this individual as a Brazilian architect, a colorful con artist and adventurer, etc., you are introducing semiological elements. The individual's attributes are not his essence, he is first defined by his place in the narrative network. It is only afterward, so to speak, that the individual is grammatically "declined," that a paradigm is established. In the case of secondary characters, this is perhaps a bit complicated, but it's easy to see a possible typology of main characters. In the case of roles played by Belmondo, the paradigm varies very little, and it's at the level of the network that changes appear.

> Still following Propp's line, one could doubtless imagine that films could be evaluated separately in categories which aren't uniquely cinematographic, such as tales, comic strips, television shows, and so on.

Quite right. And that is why all this research is so promising. There's a lot of work to be done in these areas, especially in the structural analysis of narrative forms; because in analyzing films, radio serials, popular novels, comic strips, and even news items or royal chronicles, etc., perhaps we will find common structures. Our research would thus open onto an anthropological category of the human image-repertoire . . .

> *Nevertheless, film as a sociological product is after all very different from a folktale, in the sense that many films, on the level of production, are tailored expressly to the real or supposed needs of the public. As a result, aren't there operational precautions to be taken before even beginning this study?*

Your question is a basic one, and at the moment we have no answer. In fact, the question is to learn if an anthropology of the image-repertoire [*l'imaginaire*] is possible. If we were to find the same structures in a film and in ancient tales, we would strengthen the probability of the anthropological interpretation—otherwise, everything would be left to sociology. What is at stake is thus very important, and it really is a gamble, because we're still uncertain where we stand. That explains the tension between anthropology and sociology. We need to know if certain narrative forms are "native" to certain civilizations.

> *All these suggestions for research you've been mentioning are thus based on a kind of assumption . . .*

Of course. But that is unavoidable. It's a working hypothesis that owes its daring, so to speak, to the Saussurean distinction between language and speech, *langue* and *parole*. Code and messages are separated, and this distinction is quite liberating. The semiological or structuralist programs do not deny at all the necessity for sociological analysis: sociology then becomes the science linking "speech" and "messages" with their situation, their social context, individual and cultural elements, etc. It's obvious that there are, within distinct social groups, more or less stereotyped and codified "speech" habits. That is why such importance is being given nowadays to the ideas of "idiolect," of "writing" in literature—these are in a way "sub-codes," intermediary stages between language and speech. There are also sub-codes in film: there are movies for certain audiences, and their structures owe a great deal to one milieu or another. But there is perhaps beyond all this a great "language" of the human image-repertoire. That is what is at stake . . .

Le Figaro littéraire, October 14–20, 1965
From an interview conducted by Guy Le Clec'h

On Behalf of the "New Criticism," Roland Barthes Replies to Raymond Picard

Roland Barthes's On Racine *was roundly criticized by Raymond Picard, a Racine specialist. The debate then grew into a confrontation between partisans and adversaries of the "new criticism."*

I asked Roland Barthes if he would like to respond to Picard's comments. His composure during our talk betrayed a slight sting of irritation.

Allow me to thank your newspaper for giving me the opportunity to explain myself. I don't want to exaggerate matters, but I cannot ignore what Picard has said. This quarrel has assumed, on his part, a character of verbal excess which makes it difficult to return things to the level of ideas and methods.

> *Don't you find it curious that Racine should be at the center of all this?*

Picard is focusing his attack on me because I wrote about Racine, who is his property. It's his game preserve. Myself, I maintain that Racine belongs to everyone. He is the most scholarly of authors, the one in whom are reflected all the ideas people have about the French national genius. Racine is the point of convergence for a host of taboos which I think should be dispelled.

But now Picard's accusations reflect an obstinate, even an obsessional tone. His criticism is becoming "terrorist," a thing of words, of adjectives like "amazing," "incoherent"—this sort of business doesn't interest me at all.

> *But what do you think of his arguments against your interpretation of Racine?*

Picard maintains that I am using biographical criticism at the very moment when I reject it. But it is not the same thing to say, "Orestes is Racine at twenty-six," and to mention that Racine made a habit of a certain ingratitude, a widespread character trait which appears in known events of his life and makes possible such a statement as: "The importance of ingratitude in the life of Racine is well known." What could all people who are twenty-six years old have in common? That's a prime example of the kind of biographical criticism that establishes a systematic relation between the author's life and his work. New psychological theories challenge this kind of explication, which certain academics are still using.

> *And what do you think of the reproach concerning "solarity"?*

According to Picard, Racinian characters are associated with different "solarities." But depth psychology has taught us to accept certain substitutions as valid. Working from a symbology, I can manipulate certain rules which permit me to rediscover the common characteristics, the profound unity of apparently quite different symbols. Picard rejects this psychology. That is his right. Myself, I speak of Racine in the language of our times, using structural and psychoanalytical analysis, in the cultural sense of the word. Incidentally, Vatican II has just recognized psychoanalysis, and I don't see why criticism should lag behind the Church.

> *Did you really describe Bajazet as an inconsistent character?*

To bring to the stage an inconsistent character is doubtless very difficult. This doesn't imply at all that the creation of such a character is itself inconsistent. It is Bajazet's inconsistency which holds the tragedy together.

> *To sum up, does the opposition between your critical system and the university's boil down to a question of method?*

I have outlined this opposition with restraint and an appreciation of nuance. Picard asserts that academic criticism doesn't exist. He is wrong, because the university is an institution. It has its own language and value system, sanctioned by examinations. There is an academic way of talking about literature. After all, Picard himself, in his preface to the Pléiade edition of Racine's works, declares war on this academic criticism. When I picked up the refrain, I wasn't thinking of Picard but of certain academics who have written on Racine using the old biographical method. In any case, the university shouldn't be sacred. It can be criticized.

> *What is the new criticism looking for?*

Look, here is a quotation from Valéry, an author dear to Picard, which explains it very well: "Criticism, insofar as it is not merely opining according to its tastes and humor—i.e., talking about itself while dreaming that it speaks of a literary work—criticism, insofar as it would pass judgment, consists in comparing what the author meant to do with what he actually did. While the value of a work lies in a singular and inconstant relation between that work and a reader, the proper and intrinsic merit of the author is a relation between himself and his design: this merit is relative to the distance between them; it is measured by the difficulties encountered during creation."

Valéry here describes insightfully what might be called merit criticism, academic criticism which seeks to bind a work to its author's declared intentions. Value criticism, which the new criticism practices, develops with much more attention and finesse the relation between a "past" work and a present reader. It is again Valéry who declares: "The work endures insofar as it is capable of seeming completely different from what its author made."

I am the one, in fact, who believes Racine may still be read today, I am the real guardian of national values. Modern criticism, in fact, asks a vital question: Can modern man read the classics? My *Racine* is a meditation on infidelity, and it is thus in no way cut off from problems which concern us today.

So it is madness to claim that the new criticism doesn't love literature, because it lives only through its love of literature. This criticism reserves the right not only to caress the object of its love but to *invest* it.

> *Isn't the dialogue between classical author and modern reader encouraged by "academic criticism" also?*

Perhaps, but the meaning of a tragedy for a seventeenth-century spectator could be only an appetizer for today's audience. Besides, modern criticism has the merit of using the same language as the literature of our time. A modern novel has, more or less clearly, a Marxist or a psychoanalytical background. That language is familiar to modern criticism.

> *Then you don't think that your influence on students could be dangerous in any way?*

That I wouldn't know. But I don't like it when Picard declares war on students with whom I feel a certain solidarity because they seek to shake up a traditional vocabulary made of masses of platitudes. Now, and I say this plainly, between jargon and platitudes, I prefer jargon. To speak ironically about this need for license is easy but not very generous. It's shameful to judge someone on his vocabulary, even if his words are irritating. No vocabulary is innocent, everyone has mannerisms of language. That doesn't bother me. At a time when psychoanalysis and linguistics teach us to see in man something different from what the nineteenth century saw, it's not ridiculous to say that a fictional character has "semantic troubles."

Then you're in favor of a criticism that evolves with the times?

In any case, I'm for the historical fluidity of criticism. Society constantly invents a new language and at the same time a new criticism. The one that exists at this moment is fated to die one day, and that will be fine. But this quarrel reminds me of a comedy by Aristophanes. Socrates is up in the clouds while Aristophanes makes fun of him. If I had to choose, I'd still prefer the role of Socrates.

Les Lettres françaises, March 1967
From an interview conducted by Raymond Bellour

On The Fashion System *and the Structural Analysis of Narratives*

When, how, and why did you conceive this very special and unusual book, The Fashion System?

The project for this book came at a precise time in my life, following the lengthy afterword to *Mythologies*, when I had discovered—or thought I had discovered—the possibility of an immanent analysis of sign systems other than language. From that moment on, I wanted to reconstruct one of those systems step by step, to reconstitute a language both spoken by and unknown to everyone. And so I chose clothing. Writers like Balzac, Proust, and Michelet had already postulated the existence of a kind of language of apparel, but it remained to give a technical, not just a metaphorical, content to what are too loosely called "languages" (languages of film, photography, painting, etc.). From this point of view, clothing is one of those objects of communication—like food, gestures, behavior, conversation—which I have always profoundly enjoyed investigating because, on the one hand, they possess a daily existence and represent to me an opportunity for self-knowledge on the most immediate level (since I invest myself in my own life), and because, on the other hand, these objects possess an intellectual existence, offering themselves to systematic analysis by formal means.

*You evoke, in your foreword, a series of transformations
which brought your project to its final form. You also
write there: "This venture, it must be admitted, is already
dated." What do you mean by that, and what are the
stages that allowed you both to develop and to go beyond
the intuition of a method which you outlined at the end
of* Mythologies?

I began with a project which was, of course, resolutely semiological but which remained, in my mind, on a sociological ground.
Thus, I thought, in the first stage, that I would analyze the
language of actual clothing, the kind worn by everyone: I even
began my survey. But I quickly realized that one couldn't successfully complete this sort of sociological investigation without
working from a model (in the structural sense) against which to
measure the observations furnished by real society. I therefore
concentrated, in the second stage, on clothing as it is presented
in fashion magazines. And then a new uncertainty regarding my
method intervened (I remember a conversation with Lévi-Strauss
on this subject): I became convinced that one operation could
not effectively study combined systems, i.e., an object comprising
manufacturing techniques, images (in the form of photographs),
and written words all at the same time. The systems had to be
separated for analysis according to their individual substances,
their signifying materials.

*That is how you went from real fashion to written fashion,
or, more exactly, "described" fashion.*

Yes. This last choice, which was costly on the level of the work's
universality since the study was thus limited to an apparently
small territory, reinforced my profound conviction that semiology
is fundamentally dependent upon language, that there is language
in all languages. I would go so far as to say that fashion in its
complex form, which alone interests us, exists only through discourse on fashion, without which fashion can be reduced to a
very rudimentary syntax no richer than the highway code. There
aren't many miniskirts around; in real life, they're only another

fad, almost an eccentricity, but this rare phenomenon has rapidly
become the topic of general public discourse, and only thus does
it acquire real social and semiological consistency: what one says
shifts in some way instantaneously (I would almost say, *beforehand*) to what one wears and sees. I think that this methodical
restriction of my project corresponds roughly to semiology's evolution these past five years: sets of objects that are somewhat
complex do not signify outside language itself.

> *So, you're ultimately inverting the Saussurean proposi-
> tion when you affirm that it is not linguistics which is a
> part of semiology but semiology which is a part of lin-
> guistics. It is because it reflects this set of problems and
> marks their evolutionary stages, I suppose, that this book
> seems to you to constitute "already a certain history of
> semiology."*

Yes. *The Fashion System* corresponds to a "nascent" semiology.
For example, it still uses insistently a Saussurean plan and lexicon
(*sign, signifier, signified*). I know, from having participated myself
in this research, that for the last five years, while this book was
being written, Saussure's theories have been "completed" (indeed,
contested) by a new linguistics represented principally by Chomsky, but also by certain of Jakobson's and Benveniste's analyses;
this new linguistics is less taxonomic because it concerns itself
less with the classification and analysis of signs than with the rules
of speech production. I have been following this evolution, particularly on the question of the linguistic analysis of literature.
But if I maintain the Saussurean categories for "written" clothing
it's because they seem to me precisely proper for the definition
and analysis of objects reified and mythicized by mass culture.
On the level of literature, the signified is always overshadowed
by the play of signifiers, but where social objects are concerned,
ideological alienation is immediately back in force, in the very
existence of a full, identifiable, namable signified.

> *The full signified would thus be the signifier of aliena-
> tion?*

You could put it that way, at least if the image, even a utopian one, that remains after the end of alienation didn't in the last instance destroy the very antinomy of signified and signifier.

> *In the conclusion of your book, a kind of final invocation, you insist on the position of the author, the semiologist, before or rather in (as you clearly specify) the systematic universe which is the object of his inquiry. Then again, it seems that the very possibility of "reading" peculiar to a work of this order is linked to an architecture that tends to dissolve "the analyst within the system" and yet is also the surest sign of his presence.*

My book is an itinerary, a patient, almost meticulous voyage accomplished by an ingenuous man who tries to see how meaning is constructed, how men construct it—in this case, how fashionable clothing is made meaningful: thus, the book becomes a voyage of discovery, a topical itinerary of meaning. And yet this itinerary is presented not as a personal voyage but as a grammar, a description of levels of meaning, of units and their combinatory rules; in short, as a kind of syntax of description. The book will be justified if, being itself a composed object, it manages to evoke before the reader's eyes, in a kind of homologous fashion, a new object which is clothing in the written mode.

> *Was the absence of illustrations deliberate?*

My work applies essentially—beyond the subject of fashion—to *description*. I deliberately refused to rely on images and illustrations because I believe (and here I'm thinking as much of literature as of fashion) that description has no relation to seeing. It's always said that descriptions make one see; I think that they don't make one see anything at all; they are of a purely intelligible order and are thereby even heterogeneous to all imagery, which could only encumber and alter them.

> *You're taking a position contrary to that of Lévi-Strauss, who considers the iconographic document within the*

scope of his enterprise and gives it a relatively important part in the logical imagination of his books.

My object is, fully and entirely, writing. Writing cannot be made into the simple "translation" of the image or word, or even into an object among other objects of transmission, expression, or translation. Writing—I'm not saying speech—is a self-sufficient system, and that is perhaps why it stirs up endless questions.

Then the description of fashion seems to you closer to literature than to myth?

Fashion literature is bad literature, but it's still writing.

What do you think of that principle of surrealist aesthetics which called for the promotion of photography within literature in order to throttle precisely the use of description as such? To me it seems linked to the inclusion/ exclusion of myth in relation to literature—if you think, on the one hand, of the theoretical importance Breton gave to the object and mythological thought, and also of the importance Lévi-Strauss accorded to surrealism in awakening the modern passion for myth.

There are other ways to destroy description besides eliminating it. The revolutionary task of writing is not to supplant but to transgress. Now, to transgress is both to recognize and to reverse; the object to be destroyed must be presented and denied *at the same time*; writing is precisely what permits this logical contradiction. By devoting itself to a simple destruction of language (through the intrusion of images or the radical disarticulation of meaning), surrealism—whatever may have been the soundness of its intentions and the importance of its precursory role—remained on the side of unitary logic, which it opposed but did not transgress (in the sense just mentioned): the opposite is not the reverse. What is opposite destroys, the reverse challenges and denies. It seems to me that only "inverted" writing, presenting both straight language and its contestation (let's say, to save time, its *parody*), can be revolutionary. As for myth, writing doesn't exclude it—or respect it: writing, much more than imagery, can both present and challenge myth.

> *This analogical game that you establish implicitly be-*
> *tween fashion and literature finds a direct echo in the*
> *double orientation of your work, since you have recently*
> *published an important text, "Introduction to the Struc-*
> *tural Analysis of Narratives" (appearing in the special*
> *edition of* Communications *devoted to that topic), which*
> *seems to reply in a way to your* Critical Essays *the way*
> The Fashion System *replies to* Mythologies.

The Fashion System is an attempt to apply semiology to a precise object that is exhaustively analyzed. The text on the narrative conforms to a purely didactic, even propaedeutical intention; it is closely linked to the activity of a research group organized under the auspices of the École Pratique des Hautes Études and the Centre d'Études des Communications de Masse; my article is intended essentially to promote and assist research. Obviously, it's absolutely indispensable that my text be followed by concrete analyses to evaluate and correct my observations. *Communications 8*, in which my article appears, is given over largely to a structuralism of classification, or, if you prefer, of the spoken, of the utterance, of content. The various articles as a whole lack— because it wasn't within our present capabilities—a linguistics of writing: it's in that sense that my text neither studies nor really singles out contemporary literature, even if it does take a position on literature.

One could say that the structuralism proposed here is to some extent homogeneous with the standard, academic, popular works it challenges, because it doesn't really break with Aristotelian culture (Aristotle was the first to analyze the narrative); it is evidently possible for this structuralism to describe modern literature in terms of deviations (not normative, of course) in relation to a strong narrative model. But we can also imagine (and we will doubtless have to) quite another critical path: the creation of an analytical instrument in contact with modern works—let's say

from Mallarmé to Bataille—written after the great literary and
historical division of the last century, works embodying real revolutionary virtue; that instrument will measure, not structures,
but the *play* of structures and their inversion along "illogical"
paths; it will then be possible to apply this new instrument to
works of the past, thus giving birth to truly political criticism—
political because it will spring from the new absolute of modernity.
It seems to me that we are here to work toward this transition.

> *How do you envision the mastery of both the infinitude*
> *of narratives and the narrative's infinite detail?*

Since Saussure, that has been the very problem of linguistics:
how does one master the considerable number of words in their
infinite combinations? The first step is to divide the "details" (the
units) into formal classes which can then be manipulated: the
divisions *Seduction* or *Deceit*, for example, at least at the first
level, already eliminate the need to speak of all seductions and
every deceit, providing that the structure of these sequences is
determined, just as the division *Verb* makes it unnecessary to talk
about each and every verb. The next step is to find the formal
rules of structural transformation to understand how forms engender narratives (somewhat as Todorov did in the issue of *Com-*
munications devoted to *Les Liaisons dangereuses*). Because it always comes to this, in the end: to master is to systematize.

> *You were speaking of encouraging work on specific texts.*
> *Have you thought about attempting an analysis of this*
> *sort yourself?*

Before the infinity of narratives in the world, the choice must be
arbitrary. I always hope to return to the "militant" literature that
is being written today, literature that wants to examine the works
of the past from a certain "ex-centric" point of view, and I have
been looking for a "double" work which presents itself in such a
literally narrative manner that it ends up challenging the narrative
model itself, as if it enclosed the narrative within quotation marks
(and, as we know, quotations must be accurate); this work would

be apparently naïve and actually quite devious, like the narrative of a battle made jointly and in a single voice by Stendhal's Fabrice and General Clausewitz. I believe I have found such a work in Kleist's *The Marquise of O*, which I hope to analyze one day.

> *Such a project might permit you to renew that interest in the relation of forms and history which furnished the basis for your first literary essays, in particular* Writing Degree Zero.

That relation is important to me and I have never lost sight of it, even if I thought to put it aside for a while to exorcise that superego of history which terrorized—and paralyzed—French intellectuals until the appearance of structuralism. Now we're beginning to glimpse a kind of reward for structuralism's patient silence before history. Thanks to several of Bakhtin's analyses, for example (which Julia Kristeva introduced at my seminar, as the works of that Soviet author are not available in French), we glimpse the possibility of analyzing literature as a dialogue with other writings, other *écritures*—a dialogue of writings within a writing. The writing of a clearly defined body of work (Dostoevsky, Sade, Hugo) contains within what seems to be a line of words a complexity of repetitions, parodies, echoes of other writings, so that in talking about literature one may now speak, not of inter-subjectivity, but of intertextuality, as Julia Kristeva has shown by studying Lautréamont in this way. If literature is a dialogue between writings, it is evidently the entire space of history which returns to literary language—returning, however, in an entirely new fashion, one unsuspected by our historians, sociologists, or theoreticians of literary production.

> *Don't you think that you risk, with this internal play of writings, what Sartre would call a new kind of formalism, one that will again swallow up history?*

It's remarkable how often one hears it stubbornly repeated that formalism is congenitally antipathetic to history. I myself have always tried to state the historical responsibility of forms. Thanks to linguistics and translinguistics, we will perhaps finally avoid the impasse to which sociology and history always lead us: the improper reduction of history to the history of referents. There is a history of forms, structures, writings, which has its own particular time—or rather, *times*: it's precisely this plurality which seems threatening to some people.

> *This "particular time" of literature seems to suggest the idea of a long detour through a formal space, wending its way back to conclude almost where Maurice Blanchot both begins and ends.*

Blanchot belongs to the incomparable, the inimitable, and the inapplicable. He is *in* writing, he is in that transgression of knowledge which constitutes literature.

> *And yet, though he obviously transgresses knowledge, Blanchot offers us a kind of wisdom. But in fact it's a "science of literature" that we're invoking here. How do you conceive of this relation between literature and science?*

To me, the position of science is problematical, and my opinion on this differs from that of other structuralists. This is doubtless because my object is literature; I think that it's no more possible, in considering a work, to go back to the old subjective and impressionistic positions than it is to leap in the other direction into a positivism of literary science. Confronted by this double impossibility, I try to specify certain scientific projects, to "try them out" more or less, but I never conclude them with a typically scientific pronouncement, because literary science may in no case and in no way have the last word on literature. Therefore, the fundamental problem, in my eyes, is not a theory of literary science but the language of literary science.

> *Do you really think that that is a problem peculiar to the "science of literature" or to the other structural disciplines as well? And do you have on this point, in a more general*

fashion, the sense of an impact on the various social sciences today?

As for structuralism, in the larger sense of the word, I think that the moment of separation is approaching (supposing that the time of unity ever existed). There has been a vast exchange of ideas and terms at the level of disciplines and discourses (linguistics, ethnology, psychoanalysis, criticism), and what seems to have been acquired from different directions is the radical challenge to the subject as *full* subject (it would be better to say "filled up"): man is no longer the center of all structures. But I think the divergence will come in fact from science's new status, which, in my opinion, cannot be dissociated from the status of scientific language itself: the differences that divide and will continue to divide Lacan and Lévi-Strauss, for example, can be read from now on in their way of writing; i.e., in their ideological and methodological relation to writing.

I suppose that such a concern is not unaffected by your personal relation with this scientific language, these metalanguages you often talk about.

I speak less of them these days. When I write, it seems to me that I'm trying to establish a kind of game with science, a certain masked parody. I think more and more that the critic's profound intention is the destruction of metalanguage, an intention which obeys an imperative of truth: writing could not be, in the last instance, "objective," because objectivity is only one image-repertoire among others. Scientific metalanguage is a form of language's alienation; it must therefore be transgressed (which doesn't mean destroyed). As far as critical metalanguage is concerned, it can't be "gotten around" except by instituting a kind of isomorphism between the language of literature and language about literature. The science of literature is literature itself.

You say that your text on the narrative takes a stand on literature without singling out contemporary literature; actually, it grants modern literature an essential privilege,

> *that of being a "language of the very conditions of language," which "holds before discourse the mirror of its own structure." And you add: "Today, to write is not to recount." In fact, you violently devalue the narrative, or, rather, narration within the narrative.*

Is contemporary literature really losing interest in the narrative? If it seems that way to us, it's doubtless because we still think of the narrative as a strong model, forgetting that poetic discourse, for example, is also a narrative, even if we don't call it one: we don't see that what must be destroyed is not the narrative but the logic of the strong model. Also, we must not forget that contemporary literature's tasks are many, long, and complicated; there is perhaps a kind of "plan," a historical program in literature over the last hundred years: until now, this literature has tackled above all the problem of the writer, the subject of the utterance, because that's where there is incredibly strong and manifestly ideological resistance: the authority of the "author's" psychological subject is still very powerful. The new narrative's time will doubtless come soon, it's already on its way, prefigured by Mallarmé's views on poetry-fiction, the infinitely digressive structures of the Proustian novel, Bataille's narratives, Sollers's research.

> *But the Oedipus complex, which you invoke at the end of your text as the time and place of the narrative's invention for the child, is the narrative par excellence as a series of actions where synchrony and diachrony are in absolute equilibrium, and that is what today's literature can no longer—or not yet—say.*

The Oedipus complex is a narrative, but this narrative is never made known except through the subject's discourse, where it is presented not as a unitary, monological narrative (even if it is a monologue) but as a form broken into fragments, repetitions, infinite metonymies. In its current effort, contemporary literature is at the level of that same expression of an *apparently* obscured narrative, one which has no other place (no other referent), however, than its own utterance.

It would seem that science's discourse—I'm thinking of Freud, of Lévi-Strauss—finds itself alone in ensuring, without qualms and in its own characteristic way, a kind of real narration, as if keeping itself close to myth as such represented the surest chance of bridging the chasm which defined for Hermann Broch the tragedy of our modern world: the gulf between mythological and scientific rationality.

Instead of arranging a contrived conclusion to our discussion, I would like to ask you several questions, rather treacherously strung together, which seem to arise from everything we have said.

Doesn't it seem to you:

—that the great break in some modern narratives originates in the impossibility of eliminating as well as of establishing meaning: insofar as, on the one hand, such a narrative cannot attain Mallarmé's "nothing" which you invoked precisely as the absolute structure of language, cannot attain that strong, absolutely synchronic "hypermodel" that only Blanchot has identified and embodied by establishing the myth of literature as the impossible Livre à venir; insofar as, on the other hand, thus engaged in the diachronic dimension of a fragmented language, the modern narrative has proven incapable of mastering this fragmentation through the synchrony which only a new, strong narrative model can provide, in the implicit or "devious" mode, as you put it;

—that certain intellectual discourses, inversely, constitute a strong model of this type, in a form which is explicitly meant to grasp the hidden balance between the logical and the chronological in objects which these discourses, in the name of the highest truth, attempt to represent analytically through an analogical model;

—that it is not by chance that you yourself, seeking to undertake a project of this order in literature, have been led to choose your object not from French literature, not from our rhetorical, psychological, sociological literature, but from the German, a literature that has

> *never had as strong and univocal an interest in the subject*
> *of the utterance because it has always kept itself close to*
> *the thought of myth, in a kind of structural a priori of*
> *the idea and its narrative interpretation which, through*
> *two centuries of literature, science, and philosophy, has*
> *sought to mythically balance the representation of natural*
> *life as the universal of culture.*

It's true that French literature has always debated much more with man, the central subject, than with myth; it's also true that its very language has been formed in the rhetorical, classical, and Jesuitical mold. To be true to itself today, it must therefore *escape* these conditions, and its very past opens up original paths of escape. We must use precisely that absence of mythic space which typifies our literature. Myth is not linked exclusively to a strong model, orderly narratives, and significant (i.e., signifying) narration. Even more, in France, where myth is incurably petit-bourgeois (until things change), we must both desire and criticize myth, we must overturn language; it seems to me that nothing revolutionary can be done, in this society, without that inflection of parody I mentioned, an inflection sorely lacking in surrealism; nothing can be done without *duplicity*, nothing can be written except within a play of structures and writings. Bourgeois society, or consumer society, or technological society will always salvage myth for its own use. There is only one thing a writer has the power to wrest from this society: its language; but before this language can be destroyed, it must be "stolen"; it seems to me that this "theft" defines new paths of transgression taken by both intellectual and literary discourse in their relation of constant intercommunication.

France-Forum, June 5, 1967
From an interview conducted by Cécile Delanghe

The Fashion System

Roland Barthes, you have just published The Fashion
System—*a title which is somewhat deceptive, if not provocative. One expects to read incisive commentary, along
the lines of* Mythologies, *or else a sociological analysis.
It's nothing of the kind. Your book is in fact a scientific
work, very austere, containing many pages which re-
minded me (to my annoyance, I admit) of the algebra
textbooks and grammatical analyses of my childhood!*

I will say right away that the title of my book is not a provocation,
my intention being not so much to offer a new point of view on
fashion as it is to constitute a work of research. This work is,
moreover, part of a general movement in current research which
has been called "structuralism." This movement of thought
and analysis attempts to discover, by extremely precise methods,
the structure of social objects, cultural images, stereotypes—in
archaic societies as well as in our modern technological societies.

For my part, I have focused on the phenomena of our society
that are (and here I must use a rather vague term) sets of utilitarian
objects: food, houses, streets, fashion . . .

*In short, you could have constructed a "housing system"
or a "nutrition system" just as you constructed one for
fashion?*

Though we have always known that these "objects" have very
different and precise functions, now we are convinced that they
are also methods of communication, instruments of meaning. It
was Saussure who first postulated the existence of a general science
of signs; he thought that linguistics would be only a part of that
science. This postulate has regained currency through the development of linguistics, the science of human language; linguistics is very well established now and serves as a model for
structuralism. Linguistic concepts and descriptive rules are applied to collections of objects outside articulated language; we
analyze these collections just as we do a language when we want
to discover its grammar.

> Regarding fashion, you have voluntarily limited your
> analysis to articles on women's clothing from fashion
> magazines; i.e., to the written description of fashion.
> Now, I speak here for the thousands of fashion-magazine
> readers when I say that nothing is more expressive, more
> convincing to women than the image; if there is a text
> or caption, it's nothing more than an invitation to admire
> a picture. My proof is that no woman buys a dress without
> trying it on; in other words, without going beyond purely
> verbal persuasion.

I do not deny the extraordinary richness of clothing which is
actually worn. If I limited myself to its written description, it's
for methodological and sociological reasons. Reasons of method:
in fact, fashion does put several systems of expression into play—
material, photography, language; and it was impossible for me to
analyze rigorously a very heterogeneous subject matter, I could
not do work of any precision while passing casually from pictures
to written descriptions, and then to observations which I might
make of actual clothing. Given that the semiological approach
consists in dividing an object into elements to be distributed
among formal general classes, it was in my interest to select the
purest, most homogeneous subject matter possible. My choice
was also justified by the fact that today fashion magazines have
a truly enormous circulation; they are part of mass culture. All

statistics bear that out. Consequently, clothing described in fashion magazines (which might seem to you less real, less interesting than clothes worn in real life) acquires new dimensions as a projection of a collective image-repertoire. It is a medium for images, stereotypes, a great wealth of elements that are not real, it's true, but utopian in nature. In this way, written clothing is akin to movies, comic strips, or popular novels. Finally, there is a stereotyped image of femininity that hides behind the phraseology of fashion magazines.

> *Surprisingly, you do not use abstraction and purely formal analysis in describing this image. Why this infraction, if I may call it that, of your chosen project?*

I did this much more to show where such a description could fit into the system than for a description which is itself, to my mind, superfluous. Because everyone who has ever read a fashion magazine is familiar with the typical image of a woman projected by these publications. It's essentially a contradictory image, it must be admitted, since this woman must be *everything* at once in order to represent the greatest possible number of women readers. Although she is a busy executive secretary, she relaxes during the day and has ample time for every holiday. She goes off to the country every weekend and travels constantly to Capri, the Canary Islands, Tahiti, and yet every trip takes her to the South of France. She loves absolutely everything, from Pascal to the latest jazz. She never engages in adultery or affairs; she travels only with her husband; she never has any financial worries. In short, she is both what the woman reader is and what she dreams of being. On that point, fashion is like all that old-fashioned literature for young ladies—it's the language of a mother who "protects" her daughter from all contact with evil.

> *Do you really think that the reader perceives all these signals sent to her? It's quite possible that her imagination finds things to feed on there, but fashion magazines, like other periodicals, are also businesses, and they cannot overlook the fact that women, with a few exceptions,*

aren't as daringly stylish as the magazines would have them be. A clothing company sent a questionnaire to hundreds of young women; they haven't completely analyzed the results yet, but they already have a fair idea of the general response: the women's hems are within a few inches of the knee; when it's cold, they don't wear those "adorable little" inexpensive fur coats but simple woolen coats; for dancing, a dress instead of "evening pajamas," etc. It's almost as if they weren't speaking the same language.

A fashion-magazine reader is almost in a conversational situation; while two people talk, they understand each other very well, but at the same time they don't analyze their words grammatically. In the same way, the fashion-magazine reader isn't conscious of the mechanisms which produce these signs, but they reach her. These signs are extremely varied, by the way; of course, everyone knows we exchange rather elementary information through the clothes we wear, information not only about our social or professional situation, about our age class, as the ethnographers say, but also about this or that social usage, ceremony, or occupation: "A dress for the evening, for shopping, for spring, for the student, for the carefree young woman . . ." Moreover, fashion tries to make the garments it describes correspond to what we want to express about ourselves, the complex role we want to play in society; for example, the adolescent who follows punctiliously the current "military fashion" for young people thereby communicates to everyone around him that he wants to be recognized as belonging to a certain group, with its own values and mentality.

You say that we can read in a garment both the general meanings you described as elementary and the meanings claimed by the individual. This last aspect of the question must have posed a technical problem for you. Since your intention was to make an inventory of the semiological units in fashion articles, it seems difficult, in my layman's opinion, to establish the analysis on the level of the individual.

That is the illusion we all have regarding individuals, and of course we need this belief, this illusion, in order to live. But in fact, after one has considered many facts with scientific detachment, one realizes that every individual can be classified. Psychological tests are divised for that very purpose. One realizes also that people can attribute any meaning to any form; there is no stable relation between form and content. For example, take short skirts: nowadays they're said to be erotic, but fifty years ago the same thing was said about long skirts. Today the shortness of the skirt is rationalized by an erotic factor.

> *And yet it's often said that current fashion is the sign of a women's revolution, or rather, women's evolution. A short tunic over Amazonian legs—this is more than just another silhouette, it's almost another woman. It's an entire femininity made up of shadows and mysteries which is vanishing. The classic clothing accessories, certain furs, jewelry, certain types of leather, these are out of style. Another thing that seems to mark the end of an epoch: the standard to which everyone quite readily refers now is no longer wealth but youth. The short skirt wasn't imposed on street fashion, it was born there, in London.*

I don't think that this particular fashion corresponds to any sociological phenomenon. I do think that all the reasons we have for explaining or justifying a garment are pseudo-reasons. The transformation of an order of signs into one of reasons is defined, moreover, as rationalization; in other words, one rationalizes after the fact something produced for completely different motives, for formal motives. In his work on the psychoanalysis of clothing, Flügel gave several examples of this social conversion of symbol into reason: the long, pointed shoe is not understood by the society which adopts it as a phallic symbol, its usage is attributed rather to simple hygienic motives. Let's take an example less dependent on psychoanalytical symbolism: in about 1830, the starching of cravats was justified by advantages of comfort and hygiene. One even sees, in these two examples, the beginning of a perhaps deliberate tendency to make a sign's rationale the very opposite of its physical character: discomfort reverses into "comfort." What must be emphasized here is that even if clothing is in fact always organized as a general sign system, the system's meanings are not stable; they evolve and disappear at the mercy of history.

> *Then, if you had written your book fifty years ago, your analysis would still have been the same?*

Absolutely. I did not describe a particular fashion; I was very careful to make a formal inventory that stands apart, thereby, from the content of fashion. Fashion is a combinative with an infinite reserve of elements and transformational rules. The set of fashion features is drawn, each year, from a reserve of characteristics that has its own constraints and rules just as grammar does. And if fashion seems unpredictable to us, it's because we're judging from the viewpoint of human memory. But if you enlarge the scale of observation, if you consider not just a few years but a span of forty or fifty years, you notice phenomena of a great regularity. An American ethnologist, A. L. Kroeber, proved this irrefutably: the rhythm of fashion change is not only regular (the amplitude is about a half century, complete oscillation takes a century) but tends to alternate forms according to a rational order; for example, the breadth of the skirt and that of the waistline are always in an inverse relation; when one is narrow, the other is wide. In short, on a time scale of adequate duration, fashion is an orderly phenomenon, and this order comes from within fashion itself.

> *Here I simply must interrupt; because it really seems these days that fashion has gone crazy, from metallic dresses to astronaut fashion, a craziness that's unique. Everything is possible, fashion extravagances have gotten to such a point that you almost want to shut your eyes so you won't have to see any of it. Returning again to the example of the miniskirt—I don't see any other period except prehistory where hems were so short.*

All that is relative, and in a sense the miniskirt example corroborates this kind of predictability of important fashion changes. Because you have to consider not the skirt's dimensions in themselves but only its relative dimensions. And the current phenomenon, that skirts have today reached the shortest length possible, could have been easily foreseen in relation to another standard of length, which is itself relative and which was reached around 1900. In other words, the miniskirt naturally seems very short to us, but the analyst pays attention only to this: it is not "very short" but "the shortest possible" with relation to the entire cycle. Of course, history is still a force that guards its liberty and keeps a few surprises in store, but, on the average, if the rhythm of fashion continues to be regular, skirts should start slowly lengthening from now on, through seasonal variations. Let's say that, by 2020 or 2025, skirts should be very long again.

> *That destroys a vision of fashion that has been shared for a long time by many poets and thinkers, a vision which makes fashion the favorite playground of free creativity, caprice, and frivolity. One of the merits of your book is to demystify this vision, but it's still somewhat saddening to lose it . . .*

But I certainly don't deny couturiers the creative liberty and inventiveness they bring to their work. It's just that when you put fashion in its historical dimension, you see only a profound regularity.

Sept Jours, July 8, 1967
From an interview conducted by Laurent Colombourg

Conversation on a Scientific Poem

What research and absorbing interests provided the background for your analyses of fashion?

Everything that I have written so far can be characterized by a certain diversity of subjects, since I have spoken about literature as well as about publicity or the myths of daily life, but my work also reflects a unity of subject, because what has preoccupied me ever since my first essay, *Writing Degree Zero,* is the problem of signification in cultural objects—with immense emphasis of course on one particular cultural object: literature. It's true that in the beginning I conducted my research on meaning with a certain linguistic background, but I had not realized until the afterword to *Mythologies* that the study of secondary meanings could be the object of a science itself derived from linguistics, or, in any case, the object of a truly methodical analysis.

At that point, I believed I had determined that it was possible systematically to study these problems of meaning in cultural objects according to a definite method. And all this was in the light of the science of meaning as it already exists—linguistics. It was then that I undertook what was to be a systematic exploration of some cultural objects from the viewpoint of meaning, of sense; and I began with clothing.

As for the position of this kind of research within the modern social sciences, you're aware that concurrently with this personal project (conceived when linguistics was not yet the prestigious model it has since become for many researchers) there was a considerable development of interest in linguistics, an expansion of the linguistic method's field of application, thanks to the independent and joint efforts of certain intellectuals—in the forefront of whom, of course, was Claude Lévi-Strauss. *The Fashion System* should therefore be understood in the context of this linguistic renewal of the social sciences and humanities.

> *At the beginning of your book, the reader finds several fundamental affirmations regarding language: "Human language is not only the model of meaning but also its foundation," or: "True reason desires us to pass from the institutive word to the reality it institutes"; or the description of language as "the fatal relay of every signifying order." Don't these propositions, which are of considerable import and less than self-evident, call for some kind of commentary?*

First of all, here is an explanation related to the history of the book itself: at first I had envisioned a study of the actual clothing worn by women, and I intended to apply to this clothing, which is a perfectly real object, a method of analysis that would reveal how clothing signifies. Because we know that clothing serves not only to protect and adorn us but also to exchange information, and there is thus apparently a vestimentary language which, in principle, ought to lend itself to linguistic analysis even though the signifying material is not articulated language. And then, bit by bit, encountering certain real difficulties having to do with the very technique of meaning, I realized that the language of actual clothing does indeed exist, but in an extremely summary and impoverished form. Its contents are minimal and its signifiers, despite the evident diversity of vestimentary forms, are poor. The code of actual clothing exists, but in the end it is neither richer nor more interesting than the highway code.

The impoverishment and scantiness of this real code contrast with what we know in other respects about the wealth of collective representations, the great proliferation of meanings within society, and also the real importance of clothing in the world. It is this distance between a very poor code and a very rich cultural world that induced me to turn my proposition around and suppose that a garment truly signified only insofar as it was seconded by human language. We "speak" our clothing in many ways, not only as an object of conversation but above all as an object of publicity, of commentary, of promotion. Articulated language constantly invests a garment, and furthermore there is neither thought nor inwardness without language: to consider clothing is already to put language into clothing. This is why it's impossible to consider a cultural object outside of the articulated, spoken, and written language which surrounds it. Thus, linguistics no longer seems to be a part of the general science of meaning: on the contrary, linguistics *is* the general science of meaning, which can then be subdivided into particular semiotics according to the objects encountered by human language.

> *In your book you distinguish between style, which is personal, and writing, which is collective, and you analyze fashion writing. But then, who is speaking in those anonymous fashion-magazine articles? Could we say that it is society which "speaks" fashion writing?*

We can say that it is the whole of society which speaks the forms of vestimentary language, and that it is only a small group which speaks its contents. Fashion's vestimentary language derives from a general code of terms and relations produced by society—which, because of its formality, has an almost universal character. It is the whole of society that elaborates the language, the *langue* of fashion. But, of course, if you use language to express particular contents, then you restrict the transmission of the message, and we can say that in fact it is only a part of society, for example, fashion designers or fashion editors, which speaks this general fashion language and fills it with specific contents. But I did not study such contents, I remained on the level of an entirely formal analysis. I studied fashion language in the proper sense of the word "language" [*langue*], as an abstract system—exactly as one would study, in a language, the noun, adjective, verb, article, subordinate clause, etc., without paying any attention to individual sentences. I did not study this or that fashion, but Fashion, as a purely formal system of relations.

> *What would you say to the reader who might think, when confronted with these structural and formalist analyses, that something has been missing in your work since the more committed and moralist writings of* Mythologies?

First of all, that nothing is ever completely lost: a life's work is fundamentally continuous, and in order to realize a certain wholeness of that work, we know that it is sometimes necessary to exchange this totality for successive moments which often seem to contradict each other, or to become lost and abandoned. At that time in my life, I needed to carry out—with a sort of radical purity—a project which would be systematic, and systematically formalist. Because, you see, I was getting too enamored of the facile ramifications of ideas, those windfall opportunities of content. But my project is moving along, and now I'll go on to something else.

Second, I would like to say that a critique of the world is, of course, much less direct in a formal work than in a work like *Mythologies*. But one can criticize the world, and the ideological alienation of our daily life, on many levels: *The Fashion System* also contains an ethical affirmation regarding life, the same affirmation as in *Mythologies*, which is that there is an evil, a social and ideological disorder, ingrained in sign systems which do not frankly proclaim themselves as sign systems. Instead of recognizing that culture is an unmotivated system of meanings, bourgeois society always presents its signs as justified by nature or reason. In this sense *Mythologies* and *The Fashion System* present the same argument and demonstration—concerning, it's true, objects which seem less important than political events or social problems, which have a greater claim to collective emotion.

> *Exactly, one can't help feeling that there is a disproportion between the object of this book (fashion-magazine articles) and the method of presentation. Must semiology*

> be condemned, through its desire for thoroughness, to
> objects that are modest, insignificant, or futile?

Of course not! On a practical level, I wished to make a methodological demonstration. Therefore, the object mattered little;
the lighter and more frivolous the object, the easier it was to
encompass, and the easier it was to put forward the method for
which the object was only the pretext. Second, at a more profound
level, I would say that *The Fashion System* can also be understood
as a poetic project: the creation of an intellectual object from
nothing, or almost nothing. Slowly, before the very eyes of the
reader, an intellectual object takes shape in all its complexity. So
that one could say (that would be the ideal, if the book is a success):
In the beginning, there is nothing, the fashionable garment doesn't
exist, it's a thing of great frivolity and no importance . . . but
finally a new object comes into existence, created by analysis.
That is what I meant by a properly poetic project, one which
fabricates an object. There are examples or famous precedents of
a "philosophy of nothingness," of the interest there is in working
on "nothing." Not only because themes of the emptiness or de-
centeredness of structures are important in current thought, but
also because someone like Mallarmé did exactly what I would
have liked to redo regarding fashion. *La Dernière Mode* [*The
Latest Fashion*], the magazine that he wrote and edited, was
fundamentally a kind of impassioned variation, in his manner,
on the theme of emptiness, of nothingness, of what Mallarmé
calls *le bibelot* [the trinket].
   If one believes that there has always been a passion for signification, if there really is an anthropological importance to meaning—and that is not a futile object—well, that passion for meaning
is exemplified in objects very close to nothing. There should be
a critical movement that both deflates seemingly important objects
and shows how people make sense from nothing. It's somewhat
within this perspective that I situated my investigation, if not my
results . . .

Les Lettres françaises, May 20, 1970
From an interview conducted by Raymond Bellour

On S/Z and
Empire of Signs

"The text, in its mass, is comparable to a sky both flat and profound, smooth, without borders or guidemarks, and just as the soothsayer traces an imaginary rectangle in the sky with the end of his wand to examine, according to certain principles, the flight of birds, the commentator traces zones of reading through the text, in order to observe the migration of meanings, the outcropping of codes, the passage of quotations."

That S/Z, in its turn, should be the very text it describes, comparable to a sky (Blanchot says, for Joubert as for Mallarmé, that the sky embodies the very idea of the Book, of the overflowing of all books toward one another), suggests that intellectual discourse, more surely than the narrative or poem, today performs the role—when needed—of the great works of parody and transgression that punctuate the history of Western discourse with their critical violence.

I would like to suggest here something outside the conventions of the interview: that Roland Barthes's two latest books, S/Z and Empire of Signs, *bring the marvelous touch of inspiration renewed by writing and thought to a body of work open, since the publication seventeen years ago of* Writing Degree Zero, *to all the paradoxes of a passion for literature reflected in the exacting demands of a science of signs. S/Z, because the commentary repeats the text with both rigor and abandon, a double excess that opens to analysis a field of shifting infinity, borne along by the bliss of a mind at play.* Empire of Signs, *because it renews, in the minor mode of the documentary, the tradition which, from Swift to Sade to Fourier, lets us listen to the delirium and nostalgia of unreasonable reason: a utopian discourse expressing itself here in musing petition for a codified voluptuousness of the sign, for an ideal consummation of all social intercourse, as well as for a transformation of the narcissism bound to the ambiguous depths of the subject, of the Name as sign and symbol of desire, and finally of the book as the realm of the Name.*

The work of Roland Barthes, as if to pay homage to the truth of Utopia, sustains this extreme contradiction in the conjunction of S/Z and Empire of Signs: *a brilliant and precise relation between the narcissism of the writer and the narcissism of the text.*

> *The title S/Z symbolizes, rather wittily, the reading you have worked out for* Sarrasine, *a little-known novella by Balzac. What does the experiment of S/Z represent to you?*

I should say, in the first place, that the year I began work on *Sarrasine*—the seminar I gave at the École Pratique des Hautes Études and the book that followed it—was perhaps the happiest and busiest of my working life. I had the exalting impression that I was tackling something really new, in the exact sense of the word: something which had never been done before. I had wanted for a long time to devote myself to a microanalysis, a patient and gradual analysis, in order to further structural analysis of the narrative. This analysis could not be exhaustive, of course, because it's impossible to catalogue every scrap of meaning in a perpetual analysis, like some sort of perpetual calendar. I was profoundly happy to find myself perfectly at ease entering a kind of textual and critical substance different from the usual experience of commentary, even when this criticism is quite original. The experience of S/Z represents for me, before anything else, the blissful pleasure of work, and of writing.

> *I suppose that this pleasure comes from the decisive fact that you were able, for the first time, to breach the es-*

*sentially deceptive barrier that always remains between
the work and its commentary, and to leave the text, as
it were, without reserves, at least in your reading. But
why* Sarrasine? *In an interview three years ago, you spoke
to me of undertaking such a project with Kleist's* The
Marquise of O.

My choice was in some ways a chance one, though it is difficult,
when the chosen text involves castration, to pretend to ignore the
working of unconscious determination. However, I did need a
text written originally in French to ensure its accessibility to my
reading, to increase my grasp of the connotations, particularly on
the stylistic level. I am currently doing a similar study of a short
story written in English by Edgar Allan Poe but translated into
French by Baudelaire. While in Baltimore I had begun studying
the first three pages of Flaubert's *Un Coeur simple* using the same
method, but I let it drop because it seemed to me a bit dry, lacking
in the kind of symbolic extravagance I later found in Balzac.

*In any case, I think the arbitrariness of the choice can
only be in proportion to the violence of its motivation.*

Absolutely, and there's no reason to feel uncomfortable
about it.

*It does seem, however, and your examples show this,
that the choice could fall only on a classical text.*

Actually, I'm not sure that a step-by-step commentary of a modern
text is possible, for several reasons of a structural nature. First,
the litigious commentary (what I call the step-by-step method)
implies a constraining order of reading, from beginning to end,
in short, a certain irreversibility of the tutor text; now, only a
classical text is irreversible. Second, the modern text, which aims
at a certain destruction of meaning, does not possess associated
meanings, connotations. Of course, it is possible to talk about
modern texts, making them "explode": Derrida, Pleynet, Julia

Kristeva have done that with Artaud, Lautréamont, Sollers; but
only the classical text can be read, skimmed, browsed, if I may
say so. The method determines the choice of text; that's one of
the aspects of critical pluralism.

> *How do you justify the division of the text into units,
> since, by adopting here the set purpose of a strictly suc-
> cessive analysis, you practically explode the fundamental
> question you yourself put to structural analysis in polem-
> ical terms, in* Poétique No. 1: *Where does one begin?*

My gradual analysis follows the novella, dividing up the signifier,
which is the material text, and following along with it as the
analysis unfolds. Each reading unit—or lexia—corresponds ap-
proximately to a sentence, sometimes a little more, or a little less.
The division into units can remain arbitrary, purely empirical,
and without theoretical implications, if the signifier does not pose
a problem in itself. With Balzac, we are in a literature of the
signified, which has a meaning, or meanings, and thus permits
the division of the signifier according to the signifieds. This division has the essential function of defining units through which
pass a reasonable number of meanings: one, two, three, four
meanings. Because if you dealt with the text paragraph by paragraph, you would lose articulations which would then have to be
reintroduced in the heart of these larger units, risking an overload
of meaning each time.

> *In this regard, one thing is striking in the construction
> of the book: that, having thus divided the analysis into
> a series of very short segments (from 1 to 561) in order
> to record all the meanings at their very apparition, you
> were able to preserve those theoretical interventions (from
> I to XCIII) which form the richest, most thoughtful part
> of your book and which always seem to spring from the
> textual commentary itself, thus inscribing the critical op-
> eration within a novelistic structure which repeats the
> structure of its object.*

On that point I gave in to a sort of impulse, which explains the euphoria I felt in writing this text. It was a response to a lassitude, almost a distaste, in any case an intolerance, which I still feel—perhaps on a purely personal and temporary level—toward the dissertation and its forms of exposition. It no longer gives me any pleasure to write a text that must adapt itself to a more or less rhetorical or syllogistic model of expression. There are texts of this nature that are extraordinarily beautiful, and necessary, even today. I myself will quite probably have to return to this format someday, but at the moment I can only try to undo, destroy, disperse the dissertational discourse, to the advantage of a discontinuous discourse.

> *It seems to me that Lévi-Strauss already found it necessary to do the same thing with his* Mythologiques, *as did Clémence Ramnoux with her commentary on the fragments of Heraclitus, in rather different approaches, appropriate to their different objects.*

In fact, it is the same movement, and to those names one could easily add Lacan, Derrida, Julia Kristeva, and Sollers, in his theoretical notes. With some of them, such as Lévi-Strauss, a new composition of discourse is involved, an effort to go beyond the monody of the dissertation toward a polyphonic composition; with others, like Lacan, there's a lifting of the secular censure which obliges every "intellectual" text to soften the shock and abruptness of its formulations: there was no French Nietzsche to dare to dis-course from brilliance to brilliance, from abyss to abyss. In fact, I plan to undertake in the near future an analysis of the intellectual text, of the writing of science (as I did for the narrative with *Sarrasine*).

Let me add this: I might have anticipated, in thus breaking up the text, that this discontinuous work would cost me the possibility of grasping larger structures, the ones represented in an intelligent outline of a book. But I was never hampered by this fragmentation, and I found that the structuration of the text functioned admirably even when rhetorical models were abandoned, suitable as they were. One of the discoveries of my analysis is that I was able to "speak" the text, without ever feeling the need to outline it. Thus, there is really no other structure to this work than my reading, the advance of a reading as structuration. In a word, I radically abandoned so-called critical discourse to enter a discourse of reading, a writing-reading [*une écriture-lecture*].

> *Which you sum up in this declaration: "What is important is not to reveal a structure but (as much as possible) to produce a structuration."*

I'm not the only one to distinguish between structure and structuration. That opposition is inscribed in the historical process of literary semiology. In fact, one must go beyond the statics of the first semiology, which tried precisely to discover structures, structure-products, object-spaces in a text, in order to discover what Julia Kristeva calls a productivity—i.e., a working of the text, a junction, a coupling into the shifting infinity of language. An exact evaluation of a text's degree of closure should be made. The classical text is closed, but only partially, and I wanted to find out, through a method appropriate to this hypothesis, how the text connects—even in a limited or alienated fashion—with the infinite productivity of language.

However, I'm afraid that this operation may be perceived simply as a necessary mode of contemporary discourse and that the public, in fact, may co-opt this movement, recuperating it under the reassuring alibi of the usual *explication de texte*.

> *It's that infinite productivity you're referring to, I suppose, in the polemical formula "everything signifies," implying a paradoxical exactingness which often leads to redundancies between the text-analysis and your commentary.*

It's a formula meant to deflect a kind of aporia, of impossibility: that is—if everything does not signify, then there would be some insignificance in a text. What would be the nature of this insignificance? Natural? Futile? These are not very scientific notions, if I may say so, and that seems to me to pose a very grave theoretical problem, perhaps an insoluble one.

However, there may be moments in the text, perhaps fewer than you seem to think, where the literalness of the statement— the denotation—is enough in a way to exhaust its meaning. It should be noted that even at this level there is at least one connotative meaning, which is: *Read me literally.* The strength of the denotation dispenses in that case with a secondary semantic hook-up. To say "everything signifies" is to indicate that if a sentence seems to lack meaning on the interpretative level, it signifies on the level of language itself. "Everything signifies" thus returns to that simple but essential idea that the text is entirely penetrated and enveloped by meaning, that it is completely immersed in a kind of infinite intermeaning [*intersens*] that stretches between language and the world.

> *Could you define precisely—to permit a better evaluation of what these statements mean regarding interpretation and analysis—the five codes which you feel govern the production of meaning in* Sarrasine?

I did in fact distinguish five main semantic fields or codes. Admittedly, I don't know if this selection has any theoretical stability; similar experiments would have to be done on other texts to find out.

1. *The code of narrative actions* (or proairetic code, a term borrowed from Aristotelian rhetoric), which ensures that we read the novella as a story, a succession of actions.

2. *The semantic code* gathers together signifieds which are more or less psychological, atmospheric, pertaining to character. It's the world of connotations in the current sense of the term. For example, when a character's portrait is meant to transmit the message "He is irritable," but without ever pronouncing the word "irritability," then irritability becomes the signified of the portrait.

3. *The cultural codes*, broadly understood; i.e., the set of references and the general knowledge of a period which support the discourse. For example, psychological, sociological, medical knowledge, etc. These codes are often very strong, particularly in Balzac.

4. *The hermeneutic code* covers the setting into place of an

enigma and the discovery of the truth it conceals. In a general fashion, this code governs all intrigues modeled on the detective novel.

5. *The symbolic field.* As we know, its logic differs radically from the logic of reasoning or of experience. It is defined, like the logic of dreams, by elements of intemporality, substitution, and reversibility.

> *It seems that you wanted to show the interplay of these different codes without establishing a real hierarchy among them, but that the symbolic code enjoys a prevalence expressed as much in the title—S/Z, a monogram of castration—as in the stylistic fascination of the interpretation. You yourself admit to "a certain pleasure in describing it, and the appearance of privilege granted to the symbolic system."*

I did, in fact, try to suspend the working of hierarchy, or at least to keep it fluctuating among the different instances guiding the textual reading. But this hierarchy reestablishes itself as if on its own, if only by structural differentiation, first of all, insofar as the classical text itself hierarchizes these codes. The hermeneutic and proairetic codes seem to dominate the others because they support the "thread" of the story; their essentially irreversible logic is governed by a logico-temporal code which determines the classical narrative as readerly. In contrast, the other codes are reversible and imply a different logic: they are formed by particles of meaning sprinkled all through the text. Thus, we accede little by little to an order of pure signifier, a signifier which still remains quite alienated on the level of cultural codes and psychological signifieds but which, in the symbolic field, carries to the highest degree that reversibility of terms, that nonlogic, or that other logic bearing the energy and power to explode the text which distinguish modern literature.

Moreover, although I tried to maintain an equal balance among the codes to point out the semantic plurality of the text, there is nevertheless a noticeable prevalence of the symbolic field, for two reasons:

1. The content of a novella recounting the entanglement of its hero with a castrato is dependent, in its very literality, on a symbolism which seizes center stage: how could the contingent condition of the castrato fail to evoke continually castration itself, a symbolic theme if ever there was one?

2. I think that the symbolic or parapsychoanalytic reading is irresistibly seductive to us today, strengthened by an obvious persuasive power. Here it's the human body itself which provides the symbol.

> *I wonder if this prevalence doesn't show that the symbolic code would be, in fact, the one which organizes all the other codes, justifying them insofar as it is concealed by them. The penultimate section of S/Z, where you describe synthetically "the three entrances" to the symbolic field—entitled "antithesis," "gold," and "body," i.e., language, economy, and sexuality—forms in fact a movement away from commentary and toward the outline of an interpretation. Without in any way prejudging an articulation among these entrances (which puts into play the theoretical interrelation of psychoanalysis, Marxism, and language theory, of infrastructure and superstructure), couldn't this symbolic code be considered not as an object but as a matrix of production, as the structure supporting and motivating the structuration of the text as a dynamic whole?*

What you say is true if the symbolic field is defined as the encompassment of all substitutions effected by the text; that is what I did in the course of my analysis by putting into one field the symbol (in the larger sense) and the avatars of antithesis, gold, and the body, and by setting this field in opposition to the other codes, which are more directly cultural and thus apparently more superficial. Understood in this global sense, the symbolic certainly prevails over the minor codes and effects the structuration of the text, as you correctly put it. Gold, meaning, and sex: it is the interplay of these three particular symbolisms which assures the dynamic of the text.

But within this vast symbolic field, in the aforementioned larger sense, there is a tendency to designate as more properly symbolic things which derive from the body, from sex, from castration, from psychoanalysis; that's what I did myself, thus restricting the meaning of the word "symbol" in the final interpretation you mentioned. I said that the complete symbolic field of the text could be entered in three ways: through the rhetorical or poetic entrance (antithesis), the economic entrance (gold), and the symbolic entrance, symbolic here in a partial and precise sense of the term (the body, the psychoanalytic reading). What is important to me is to insist on the equality of these three entrances: none of them prevails over or controls the others. The third entrance (psychoanalytic symbolism) may seem larger and more important than the others, for reasons I mentioned, but I feel that the equality of the entrances must be maintained, because it is this principle that allows us to recognize the pluralism of meaning and the constant hold on the text of a different history: Marx, Freud, and even Aristotle can all speak of this text, and rightfully so—let's put it this way: they may speak with arguments that are within the text. There are more or less narrow doors in the text, but no *main entrance*, an image rather more worldly than structural.

I should like to insist on one point regarding this symbolic code, understood in its restricted sense. You use—to remain on the symptomatic level of the terminology— an explicitly Freudian and Lacanian vocabulary, for example when you describe the gesture of the narrator's friend when she touches the castrato as an acting out, or "conversion hysteria," and when you add: "Her gesture of touching is indeed the irruption of the signifier into reality across the barrier of the symbol: it is a psychotic act." But you also write: "What is here called 'the symbolic' does not depend on psychoanalytic knowledge." Your entire analysis continually reveals this double game

> *of attraction and retreat regarding a psychoanalytic inter-*
> *pretation.*

In *On Racine* I had already used psychoanalytic language as a
kind of koine, a cultural vulgate. I should like to mention that
although I generally do not much like the word "essay" when it's
applied to critical work (when the essay then appears to be a falsely
prudent way of being scientific), I can accept the word if it is
understood as "to essay a language on an object, a text": one tries
out a language as one tries on a garment; the better it fits, i.e.,
the farther it goes, the happier one is. My recourse to psychoanalytic language, as to all other idiolects, is ludic in nature, citatory—and I'm convinced that everyone does this, in more or
less good faith. One never owns a language. A language can only
be borrowed, it "passes around," like an illness or currency. In
S/Z you could see that, in spite of all deontology, I did not "list
my sources" (except for Jean Reboul's article, which brought the
Balzac novella to my attention); if I neglected to mention my
creditors (Lacan, Julia Kristeva, Sollers, Derrida, Deleuze, Serres,
among others)—and I know they have understood this—it's to
emphasize that in my eyes it's the entire text, through and through,
which is citatory. I indicated this in my presentation when I
recalled the roles of *compilator* and *auctor* in the Middle Ages.

That said, and so as not to evade your question in the very
terms that framed it—which are terms of the "truth" of a language—it is possible that my "ludic" attitude toward psychoanalysis glosses over or implicates the impossibility of determining, at this time, the ideological commitment of psychoanalysis:
is it still, on the whole, a psychology of the Subject and the
Other, or has it already acceded to the infinite permutations of
a subject-less language? That is doubtless what is being debated
(or will be) between Lacan and *Tel Quel*. I am presently wavering
between these two positions, and I do so "honestly," insofar as I
am as yet unable to foresee all the consequences of either opinion;
therefore, a somewhat ludic position and a play of reflections in
my work tend at least to minimize the risk of dogmatism, of
monologism, the risk of returning to a unique signified.

I don't see why a more specifically psychoanalytical inter-pretation, speaking by virtue of a certain truth in the formation of meaning (and of nonmeaning), should nec-essarily constitute monologism and proscribe plurality in the decoding of the text.

I wonder if, by that beautiful and necessary flattening of the text which you theorize in affirming that the no-vella's worth depends on the fact that "the latent moves straightaway onto the level of the manifest," you don't end up missing something in the text that would bring into play, in the text itself, a certain relation between the manifest and latent contents. I was struck, in your anal-ysis, by the short shrift you gave to certain aspects of the Lanty family, the relatives and heirs of the castrato hidden in their mansion in the guise of an enigmatic old man. Balzac emphasizes in particular the double resemblance of Marianina and Filippo with their mother, Madame de Lanty, the castrato's niece, who appears as a model of the Balzacian woman: wife, mother, and the very object of desire. It seems that this network of narcissistic relations articulated on a lineage introduces into the text an incestuous and Oedipal reference (underlined by the words: "This mysterious family had all the attraction of a poem by Lord Byron," which functions as a symbolic index as well as a literary reference). It could be important in defining (with relation to the central form of castration) the system of desire, the symbolic matrix which supports and determines the very production of the text.

This silence regarding the Oedipus complex, which structures the desire of the subject as both writer and reader, seems symptomatically revealed through the way you have tried to remove the author (the subject of the utterance, in this case Balzac) as the traceable origin of the narrative, manifested in the text by his signature and all that it entails as well as by the duplication incarnate in the narrator. You suggest this disappearance when you say you want to recognize in writing "the substance of a

> connection, *not a filiation,"* to abolish all reference to
> an origin, to the Father (as formulated in Freud, or
> Lacan, and just recently in Guy Rosolato's Essays on the
> Symbolic). *I don't see why the two descriptions would
> be in opposition or mutually exclusive: doesn't it infringe
> on the plurality of codes, in the symbolic field itself, to
> set them in opposition to each other?*

Your question-objection shows how good a reader of Lévi-Strauss
you are, because he himself, in a personal letter you could not
possibly have known about, communicated to me a brilliant and
convincing demonstration of incest in *Sarrasine*. And yet Lévi-
Strauss's demonstration is . . . Lévi-Straussian, not Freudian.
Are we even sure that Lacan's latest work gives as decisive a role
to the Oedipus complex as you seem to think?

As for the author, if I have radically withdrawn Balzac from
my commentary—for which reason, I add in passing, it is an
error to see in my work a "reading of Balzac": it's a reading
. . . of reading—it's because I thought it was important to show
that one could "get to the bottom" of a text without laying it at
someone's doorstep; besides, even if one did determine the prove-
nance of a text, it would just be one critical code among many.
I had even begun coding, in my work, all the possible references
to Balzac's life and works as units of the scholarly and university
code, a cultural code if there ever was one; would the literary
historians and psychologists have been more satisfied with that
than with my silence? What I resist is the idea of the author as
the locus of property, heritage, filiation, Law. However, if one
day this authorial determination can be put into proper perspective
within a multitext, a fabric of connections, then the author could
be reinstated—as a paper being present in his text by virtue of
inscription (I cited Proust and Genet on this subject). I would
even say that I look forward to this development; I should like
one day to write a bio-graphy.

> *This formal desire to escape the grip of determination is
> strongly reflected in the commentary's very language. In
> fact, it begins with that recourse to quotation you men-*

> *tioned, a perpetual movement of concepts, as if a concept*
> *could never be introduced without being immediately*
> *undone, a mirage in the shimmering advance of the text.*

If what you say is true, it's because I am *within* the writing, which
is my desire. What is fundamentally unacceptable to me is scientism; i.e., that scientific discourse which considers itself as science
but refuses to consider itself as discourse. There is only one way
to make the work into a dialectic: through a readiness to write,
to enter into the movement of writing, as exactingly as possible.
The wavering of a concept is not something to be rectified by a
consensus of competent readers; it is maintained by the author's
system, his idiolect—it's enough that concepts be adjusted among
themselves within the discourse in such a way that the other text
(the tutor text, whatever object it may be which occasions one's
own writing) is contacted obliquely, not examined head-on.

> *In those conditions, do you think that kind of analysis*
> *can be valuable as a methodological model permitting*
> *further applications?*

I don't think—and I don't hope—that my work has value as a
scientific model applicable to other texts; in that case it would be
deformations of the method which would produce results. My
commentary may have a certain future on a more modest level,
a didactic rather than a methodological level. It could, for example, provisionally furnish the teaching of literature—I say provisionally, because nothing says we must continue to "teach literature"—not with a model but with a possibility of liberating
the *explication de texte*, of making it enter the space of reading;
teaching could be opened up to the domain of the symbol.

> *What is the objective possibility of this happening, con-*
> *sidering that a thirty-page novella generated a commen-*
> *tary two hundred and twenty pages long?*

That is a problem I'd like to tackle: how does one pass from a
tutor text of thirty pages to a novel of ordinary length?

*Don't you think that this extension in itself risks provok-
ing a return to codifications of the sweeping, synthetic
type?*

Yes, the risk is that the novel will be outlined in large sections
to avoid fastidious recapitulations. Because on many pages the
codes, the signs, are repeated—as in any language; you can see
this in *Sarrasine*: the redundancy would quickly become boring.
To my eyes, this is not so much a theoretical problem as it is a
compositional one. How should this type of analysis be developed?

In any case, novel or novella, if these analyses are to be continued, texts must be found which are neither one-dimensional
nor excessively unusual, and which thereby allow interpretation
of their resistance to the plural of writing. In *Sarrasine* I certainly
found a text extraordinarily suited to my project.

*Which you put into theory as follows: "There is no other
proof of a reading than the quality and endurance of its
systematics, its functioning." Doesn't that suggest that
the operation of commentary aims to permit a kind of
rehierarchization of literary values insofar as the commentary constitutes in itself a literary experience, or, in
your words, a discourse of reading, a writing-reading?*

Yes, and that's nothing to be afraid of. *Mutatis mutandis*, the
Middle Ages lived solely on rereading ancient texts, in Greek or
Latin. Perhaps literature will now be precisely that: an object
made of commentaries, a tutor of other languages, period. Who
knows?

*To illustrate your views from a different angle, I would
like to talk to you now about a book published at the
same time as S/Z—Empire of Signs, where you deal in
an even more polemical and personal fashion with the
delicate question of the status of meaning.*

In that book I chose to speak of Japan, of my Japan, a system of
signs I call Japan.

> *I feel that your love for Japan harbors another, much more fundamental love: a love of reserve in regard to meaning.*

I thought I read, in many aspects of Japanese life, a certain regime of meaning which to me seems almost ideal. In my work, I have written constantly on signs, meaning, signification, in quite varied domains; it's only natural that I myself should have a kind of ethic of sign and meaning, which informed my work.

> *How would you define this ethic?*

In two words, which create more problems than they solve, an ethic of the *empty sign.* Japan offers the example of a civilization where the articulation of signs is extremely delicate, sophisticated, where nothing is left to the nonsign; but this semantic level, expressed in the extraordinary finesse with which the signifier is treated, in a way means nothing, says nothing: it doesn't refer to any signified, especially not to any ultimate signified, and thus for me it expresses the utopia of a world both strictly semantic and strictly atheistic. As many of us do, I profoundly reject our civilization, *ad nauseam.* This book expresses the absolute revindication of a complete alterity which has become necessary to me and which alone can provoke the fissuration of the symbolic order, of our symbolic order.

> *How do you explain this apparently contradictory phenomenon which permits you to recognize this ideal and liberating image of a harmony of meaning and non-meaning in a society where economic reality and ideological values form a system quite as repressive as that of our own societies?*

Japan is in the very special position of a feudal society that transformed itself, in less than a century, through extraordinary economic expansionism. The ethical presence of feudalism maintains in this intensely "technicized"—and not really Americanized—society a set of values, an art of living, which is probably rather fragile in the light of history, and which must be linked to the fundamental absence of monotheism. Thus, a system that is almost entirely immersed in the signifier thrives on the perpetual retreat of the signified: that is what I tried to show on the essential level of daily life (food, housing, makeup, the system of street addresses, etc.). This fashioning of the signifier, of the symbolic, reflects—despite its inscription in a capitalistic type of exploitative regime—a certain success in civilization and thus a partial but indisputable superiority over our Western societies, where the liberation of the signifier has been hampered for more than two thousand years by the development of monotheism and its hypostases ("Science," "Man," "Reason").

Thus, I've put into practice the requirement addressed in a different fashion by the commentary on *Sarrasine*: to test a certain pluralism of levels, to imagine a kind of disconnected dialectic, floating among different determinations. I was thus able—insofar as a demand for historical pluralism is dawning on the very level of Marxist theory itself—to situate myself, during a brief essay, on a par with a surface: i.e., absolutely flush with a certain thin layer of life, which must obviously be classified among what are traditionally called the superstructures (but, as you know, I'm not comfortable with the image of *above* and *below*).

Finally, I must say that this essay occupied a moment in my life when I felt the necessity of entering completely into the signifier, i.e., of disconnecting myself from the ideological instance as signified, as the risk of the return of the signified, of theology, of monologism, of law. This book is in a way an entrance, not into the novel, but into the novelistic: i.e., the signifier and the retreat of the signified, however valuable its political implications might be.

> *There is a striking illustration of this separation in your evocation of the Japanese students, the Zengakuren, a text made even more significant by its placement near the end of the book: "Finally, in a superb audacity of the sign, it is sometimes accepted that the slogans chanted by the combatants should announce, not the Cause, the Subject of the action (what one is fighting for or against)—*

> *this would be once more to make language the expression*
> *of a reason, the assurance of a good cause—but only that*
> *action itself ('The Zengakuren are going to fight'), which*
> *is thus no longer covered, excused by language—an ex-*
> *ternal divinity superior to the combat, like a Marseillaise*
> *in her Phrygian bonnet, but duplicated by a pure vocal*
> *exercise which simply adds to the volume of the violence*
> *one more gesture, one muscle more."*
>
> *Doesn't this dissociation denote a kind of break with*
> *the central preoccupation you formerly expressed as the*
> *political commitment of form, the critical relation of*
> *form and history, the theoretical opening onto the pos-*
> *sibility of a praxis?*

If I've changed on this point, it's an alteration, not a denial. I could no longer be content with relating forms to ideological contents as I did in *Mythologies*. Not that I think that this is worthless, but nowadays this kind of relation is second-nature: today everyone can denounce a form's petit-bourgeois character. The struggle must be taken further now, it is not signs that must be cracked wide open—signifiers on one side, signifieds on the other—but the very idea of the sign: an operation that might be called a semioclasm. It is Western discourse as such, in its foundations and elementary forms, that we must now try to break apart.

> *In this sense you're rejecting any determinative influence*
> *on research by concrete political commitment.*

To remain on the direct level of this relation is to be condemned to repetition and stereotypes; it isn't even knowledge, just the repetition of knowledge, a catechism. One can't invent, shift things around. Invention, I think, must take place beyond all this. In the West, in our culture, our languages, we must wage a deadly serious and historic battle with the signified. That is the question dominating this interview, which could be entitled "The Destruction of the West," within a nihilistic perspective in an almost Nietzschean sense of the term—nihilism as an essential and inevitable phase of the struggle toward "a new way of feeling, a new way of thinking."

> *Here we seem to touch on a limit characteristic of the relation between writing and politics, and between writing and science.*
>
> *When you refuse all determination, you suggest as a contradictory requirement of intellectual discourse a truth formulated by Mallarmé under the ambiguous term of "literature": writing itself, as the signifier of desire, forms the closed field of its own liberation; it logically includes the political term, without which nothing can be conceived, but includes it as a utopia, and its action, to remain unfragmented, must be exercised as "restrained action," in a purely problematic relation with history, "with a view to later or never."*
>
> *And thus you shut yourself up within the Empire of Signs, that "cabinet of signs" which you rightly call the "Mallarméan habitat." You are the fetishist of the text, refusing any wisdom, even from Marx or Freud, which might cut the "braid" of the text—as Sollers tends to do, exercising a kind of ideological pressure on your book by his example.*
>
> *On the cover of S/Z you invoke "the (collective) edification of a theory which liberates the signifier"; do you think the word "theory" corresponds to this movement? Doesn't it rather imply that—inevitably—the discourse which liberates knowledge, more than any other discourse, sustains itself only by the castrating gesture, which inscribes fetishism, for example, within the field of knowledge?*

I do not think that *to await* is *to shut oneself up*. It should be noted that, in our culture, closure is always presented as shameful; we still practice a romantic mythology, an alpine mythology of vastness, openness, totality, stirring inspiration. But counterclosure is not necessarily an opening, it's more likely to be freedom from the tyranny of the center. That is precisely what I felt I'd learned in Japan: a dwelling, such as the Japanese house, is tolerable, even delightful, if it can be emptied-out, un-furnished, de-centered, dis-oriented, dis-originated. This emptiness, which I just described as "nihilism" (referring to Nietzsche), is both necessary and transitory; in my eyes it's the current postulation of ideological combat in our society: it's too late to keep the text as fetish, in the manner of the classics and romantics; it is *already too late* to cut this fetish-text with the knife of castrating knowledge, as do the scientists, the positivists, and sometimes the Marxists; it is *still too early* to cut (off) the cutting, to strike out knowledge, without making it seem, with regard to what is called political reality, like a second castration, a castration of castration. This is our situation, we have to live amid the unlivable. As Brecht used to say, and he could hardly be suspected of flagging revolutionary confidence: *That's the way the world goes, and it's not going well.*

L'Express, May 31, 1970

L'Express *Talks with*
Roland Barthes

Roland Barthes is little known to the general public, but his reputation has been considerable among intellectuals at home and abroad since the publication of his first book, Writing Degree Zero. *The founder, in France, of semiology, or the science of signs, he has just published a lengthy and particularly arduous essay,* S/Z, *and a somewhat more accessible book on Japan,* Empire of Signs.

> *Why did you devote an entire book to the analysis of* Sarrasine, *a novella by Balzac?*

Because *Sarrasine* is a limit-text within which Balzac goes very far indeed, even involving parts of himself he did not understand very well and for which he did not assume responsibility either morally or intellectually, even though they had an effect on his writing.

And also because I wanted to trace a kind of formal grid of *reading*, a survey of possible readings of this text. What I did was like a film in slow motion. I created a slow-motion image of *Sarrasine*, like a film director who de-composes a sequence, showing it at a slower speed.

> *Why did you speak of a limit-text?*

The narrator of the novella, who is not Balzac, declares: "Perhaps, after all, I am inventing this story." And he says this within the story. It's this kind of remark, this kind of unusual "perhaps," that leads me to speak of a limit-text.

I tried to show that this novella belongs to a superior category, one in which a narrative puts *itself* into play, becoming a party to the narrative representation *as* a narrative. One of the possible résumés of the novella is that the narrator is in love with a young woman he meets at a ball, Madame de Rochefide, that he knows a secret she would like to discover, and that he wants to spend the night with this young woman. A tacit contract is established: a good story in exchange for a night of love. Give and take.

As in The Thousand and One Nights.

Yes, and in that story also the narrative is an object of exchange. Why do we tell stories? For amusement or distraction? For "instruction," as they said in the seventeenth century? Does a story reflect or express an ideology, in the Marxist sense of the word? Today all these justifications seem out of date to me. Every narration thinks of itself as a kind of merchandise. In *The Thousand and One Nights*, a narrative is traded for one more day of life—in *Sarrasine*, for a night of love.

It's the same with Sade. In his novels, there is an almost obsessional alternation between orgiastic scenes and metaphysical considerations, which most people studiously avoid. The reader of *Philosophy in the Boudoir*, for example, if he reads the narrative from beginning to end, really buys an orgy for the price of a philosophical dissertation, or vice versa.

What is the place of this novella within Balzac's work?

Balzac died in 1850, and *Sarrasine* was written in 1830, relatively early in his career. He listed it among the *Scenes of Parisian Life*.

Since a narrative is an object of barter, would you tell us the story of Sarrasine?

With pleasure. The first part takes place in a Parisian salon during the Restoration, and the explicit theme of the novella is a condemnation of bourgeois society. Balzac, whose views were monarchistic, criticizes wealth acquired through speculation, the gold of the *nouveaux riches*, and he places it within the symbolic field of gold without origins, gold undignified by a landed past such as the aristocracy could claim.

In the second section, *Sarrasine* becomes the narrative of castration. Zambinella, the character at the heart of the enigma, is a castrato. His name means "little leg" or "little doll," and even, in my opinion, "little phallus." And the bastard gold of the *nouveaux riches*, that almost alchemical gold sprung from a void, corresponds precisely to Zambinella, who is a nothing, insofar as he is a fake woman, a castrato.

I don't think it's farfetched to establish a close relation between the emptiness of the castrato and the emptiness of the Parisian new money.

> *Doubtless, but Sarrasine, who gives his name to the novella, is a sculptor, and we learn in the course of the narrative that he has been assassinated for having loved Zambinella, whom he believed to be a woman. Your interpretation risks not corresponding to that of the average reader, who simply reads Balzac and "gets along."*

But I assure you, I "get along" quite well when I read Balzac. In any case, there are always at least two levels of reading. The reader you mention is the naïve reader, who reads Balzac just like that, spontaneously, and who enjoys reading the story, finds it interesting, and reads on to the end, to learn how things turn out.

This kind of reader consumes the anecdotal story line in its temporal unfolding, page after page, month after month, year after year. Indeed, he reads the text according to a millenary logic, since this logic, for the Western world, goes back to the *Iliad* and the *Odyssey*, and continues more or less up through Hemingway.

And then there is the reader attentive to the symbolic, who

reads more profoundly and reaches the symbolic richness of the narrative.

Do these two readers coexist in you?

Of course, and they coexist in everyone, they must. But, given that the second level of reading is subconscious, the naïve reader must, by definition, remain unaware of it.

The symbolic order which coexists with the second level of reading does not possess—as Freud clearly showed—the same temporal logic as the first reading; it's an order in which "before" and "after" do not exist, no more than they do in dreams. Its time is reversible, it is a symbolic configuration of forces, complexes, images. For the naïve reader, on the contrary, time is essentially irreversible.

The symbolic reader is someone who analyzes the text, discerning its signifying structure—which allows him to account for the approach of the naïve reader, to understand how he "gets along."

In other words, what you're defining, with your second reader, is criticism.

Yes, but only if this reader begins to write, comes to grips with the writing. And also on the condition that this criticism not be a thing of moods and impressions, which happens too often.

How would you define criticism?

For me, it's a decoding of texts, and here I'm thinking above all of the "new criticism," as it's usually called. Because the old criticism, after all, did not decipher texts, it didn't even raise the question of interpretation.

All "new criticism" can be situated in relation to that horizon. Decoding of the Marxist type, decipherment of the psychoanalytic type, the thematic type, the existential type—different styles and different ideological grounds, but the aim is always the same: the attempt to grasp a true meaning of the text in order to discover its structure, its secret, its essence.

> *As a comparison, where would you put George Painter's* Proust? *Is it old criticism?*

It isn't criticism, it's a biography. Beautifully done.

> *And what do you think of the Lanson–Truffaut series, which has introduced literature to generations of French high school students?*

Now that raises the question of the teaching of literature, which is a bit different.

I have always been struck by the fact that the authors of literary-history manuals come in pairs: Lanson–Truffaut, Castex–Surer, Lagarde and Michard, like comedy teams. Their choice is obviously biased. They're writing literary history; i.e., they make literature into a closed and culturally defined object, which would have its own internal history, where values are maintained almost like fetishes, implanted in our institutions.

What we should do for these students is give the very idea of literature a good shaking up, we should ask ourselves what literature *is*—for example, are texts by madmen literature? Or newspaper articles? And so forth.

> *This decipherment you ascribe to criticism, what does it do?*

It destroys. Understand me, I don't know if anything else is possible in the present state of things. But destruction in the larger sense of the word, as one speaks, for example, of negative theology.

> *There's a term in cybernetics: to perturb.*

Exactly. To perturb, to subvert. And to answer your question, I think that criticism can participate in a kind of collective gesture, a collective action, taken up by others beside myself, for whom a good slogan would be those extraordinarily simple and infinitely subversive words of Nietzsche: "A new way of feeling, a new way of thinking."

> *We started off with Zambinella, the "little phallus," and here we are about to remake society. Don't you think that you somewhat exaggerate the role of symbolic activity?*

No, I don't think so, because I can only agree with Lacan: it is not man who constitutes the symbolic, but the symbolic which constitutes man. When man enters this world, he enters a symbolic order which is already in place.

And he cannot be "man" if he does not enter the symbolic order.

> *You mean that from birth he is part of an upbringing, an education, a social class, institutions that are already established.*

Not completely. An institution is always established on the cultural level; it involves codes, protocols, a language. The symbolic is much more archaic, much more elementary.

Lacan tells us that the child is already entering the symbolic order when it discovers its own image in the mirror at the age of six months. This is the mirror stage, the moment when, for the first time, the child grasps the image of its entire body. As you know, man is an animal born too soon: biologically, a baby is always premature. There follows, for a certain number of months, a state of motor and verbal incapacity, a state of biological insufficiency and incompleteness. Well, it is this state defining what is properly human on the biological plane for which the small child finds symbolic compensation in seeing its own image reflected in a mirror!

What had been experienced as fragmented suddenly appears before the child as the image of the other. At that moment begins the adventure of intersubjectivity, of the imaginary construction of the self.

What about ancient societies that didn't have mirrors?

For Lacan, the demonstration obviously has a transitional value. The mirror is more like an allegory. What is important is the moment when the child perceives its body in a unified image. But the importance of the symbolic order is corroborated everywhere, and not only by the theoretical reflections of a psychoanalyst.

Psychosomatic medicine, for example, has been able to establish that specifically psychosomatic ailments such as asthma, or stomach ulcers, always originate in a disruption of symbolization. Psychosomatic patients do not symbolize enough. The ideal cure would be to inject them with the symbolic factor, thus making them neurotic.

Cure by neurosis. The medicine you propose seems strange, to say the least.

No, not at all. By the way, it's the psychosomaticians who propose this method, not I.

A neurotic is someone in whom a blockage has resulted from various censorships which annihilate all his symbols. His silence is a silence of censorship. The psychosomatic patient is in the opposite position. He does not symbolize his body, which remains matte, without echo. His silence is a silence of emptiness. His cure progresses to the extent that the symbolic function is successfully reestablished in him, for it is precisely that function which is hypertrophied in cases of neurosis.

You began writing about the importance of the symbolic almost fifteen years ago, in Mythologies.

Yes, in part. Those pieces were the result of some very strong feelings. I was annoyed, at the time, by a certain tone in the press, in the publicity of what is called mass communications. Irritated and intrigued at the same time.

What I didn't agree with was the presentation of an event in terms of a kind of implicit natural psychology. As if what was said about the event were obvious, as if the event and its meaning coincided naturally.

> *Why? Don't they coincide?*

No, and I'll give you an example. I remember that one of my first *Mythologies* dealt with "the writer on vacation": the better to sanctify this figure, we were shown that this person who is so different from everyone else goes on vacation just like an ordinary worker. It's exactly the same conjuring trick as the one which presents royalty in a "human" light, posing with the family, at home. Here discourse is faked, because it says they are like everyone else—in order to say, in reality, that they are not.

The banality of these people affirms and confirms their singularity. That is one of the mechanisms I tried to bring to light. I wanted not only to reestablish the process by which society elaborates meaning, but also to show how society tries, in fact, to impose this meaning in the guise of naturalness.

> *You also took on detergents, tourist guidebooks, plastic toys, and the star athletes of the Tour de France.*

Yes, I think I wrote about fifty "mythologies" in all. But one of the themes that has held my interest for a long time is fashion. There is a fundamental difference between actual fashion and its description in fashion magazines.

Everyone understands that clothing has meaning, and that it's important, because it's connected with eroticism, social life, all sorts of things. However, fashion itself doesn't exist without a system of transmission—images, photos, drawings, written texts, or even dresses worn in the street. And fashion is very difficult to get a grip on once you start trying to reconstruct the grammar of a substance which turns out to be poorly understood.

Then fashion doesn't exist, except as a system of meaning.

Exactly, but at the same time it's a rather impoverished system of meaning, which is to say that the many differentiations in clothing correspond to only a small list of differentiations in situations.

But the fashion system is very meaningful for women.

It is rich in meaning only on the level of the fashion magazine, which distinguishes between five in the afternoon, eight in the evening, eleven o'clock, and noon, cocktail time, an evening at the theater, etc. In reality, there is no five in the afternoon. From a sociological and statistical point of view, not long ago, in our country, there were only two outfits, working clothes and Sunday dress.

And today?

Nowadays, in our societies, things have become quite complicated, because mass culture mixes up ideologies, superstructures. Mass culture offers for consumption, to classes without the economic means to consume them, products which are often consumed only as images.

I don't want to belabor the obvious, but the subtle wealth of the semantic world of fashion as it appears in fashion magazines is completely unreal.

Can we do without mythologies?

No, of course not. No more than we can do without symbolic functions.

The only language that doesn't develop secondary meanings is mathematics, because this language is entirely formalized. An algebraic equation contains no associated meaning. Except if it is written on a blackboard, photographed, and published in an article on Einstein. At that point, a secondary meaning or connotation has developed, and the equation means: "I am a scientist, I am a mathematician."

> *Is it possible to imagine a pure, nonconnotative language outside of mathematics?*

No, I think that is a utopia. According to a certain Marxist conception, myths are imaginary and naïve productions linked to the phase in which humanity is not yet able to resolve the contradictions of reality. For that reason, humanity has "resolved" them by elaborating stories in which these contradictions are surmounted in imagination. And the Marxist reasoning is that when we have scientifically resolved these contradictions through socialism, the myths will disappear.

The problem is serious and I don't want to speak lightly about it. Marxism might very well anticipate that a socialist society will revise the map of language in some unheard-of, unimaginable way. But I think that, even then, one last contradiction, in the larger sense, will remain: the insurmountability of death. As long as there is death, there will be myth.

> *In that case, why do you reproach our society for its mythologies?*

Because, even though we are inevitably surrounded by signs, we do not accept these signs *as* signs. What I don't like about the West is that it creates signs and denies them at the same time.

> *Why is this?*

Doubtless for historical reasons, which have to do largely with the development of the bourgeoisie. It is obvious that the bourgeoisie has elaborated a universalist ideology guaranteed by God, or by nature, or last of all by science, and all these alibis function as disguises, as masks covering up signs.

> *Your entire undertaking, on its various levels—sociological, critical, literary—is thus one of demystification.*

Not really demystification, because what right have I to speak in the name of truth? But to batter away tirelessly at the "naturalness" of the sign—definitely yes!

You know, this struggle is an old story, and some of the forms it has taken may seem a bit archaic now, but in the eighteenth century people like Voltaire were already fighting away, trying to "relativize" contemporary French beliefs by comparing them to those of the Chinese, Persians, Hurons, and so forth. The great danger, for us in the West, once we have ceased to recognize the arbitrariness of signs, is conformity, that door open to moralizing constraints, moral laws, majority rule.

> *Is that why, in the West, you prefer the East, and Japan in particular?*

Yes, what interests me in Japan is an old problem of an almost ethical nature, my relationship with signs. Because I read Japan as a text.

> *What do you mean?*

Well, the inscriptions, the gestures of daily life, the tiny rituals of the city, the addresses, the food, their theater, which elaborates signs and parades them as signs, while our theater is based, above all, on expressiveness—everything Japanese seems to me to be the fortuitous markings of a text. In Japan, I am constantly reading signs.

> *But these signs are not written ones, properly speaking.*

They are not written in books but traced on the silk of life. And what fascinates me over there is that the sign systems, with their extraordinary virtuosity, their subtlety, their strength and elegance, are, in the end, empty. They are empty because they do not refer to an ultimate signified, as our signs do, hypostatized in the name of God, science, reason, law, and so forth.

What you mean by "empty signs" is not easy to understand.

I'll give you a simple example, and you'll see my point easily. A dictionary is composed of signifiers; i.e., words printed in bold type, each one of them furnished with a definition serving as its signified. Now these signifieds, these dictionary definitions, are themselves made up of other words, and so on forever. A dictionary is a perfectly paradoxical object, both structured and indefinite, which makes it a marvelous example, because it is an infinite structure vertiginously off-center, since the alphabetical order of its arrangement has no center.

In other words, what you like about Japan is that you can read it in any order, as a dictionary is read.

Yes, but in the West there comes a point when the dictionary, or, if you prefer, the inventory of everything in the world, comes to a halt with God, who is the keystone of the arch, since God can only be a signified, never a signifier: how could God ever mean anything besides himself? While in Japan, as I read things, there is no supreme signified to anchor the chain of signs, there is no keystone, which permits signs to flourish with great subtlety and freedom.

All civilizations in which monotheism plays a role are necessarily under the constraint of monism; they stop the play of signs at some definite point. And that is the structural constraint of our civilization. So you understand why I give such importance to everything that tends to break away from Western monocentrism, everything that opens onto a possible image of the plural.

It would be interesting to go more deeply into one of those Japanese sign systems you find so seductive.

Nothing is easier. Over there, they surround you constantly. In any case, perhaps one of the most explicit systems concerns food.

But first, how does a sign system function? Since Saussure, the classic model has been a chess game: there are pieces moved from

square to square on a chessboard, and rules governing this movement; i.e., there are things which are allowed and others which
are forbidden. Transposed to a system like alimentation, that
means we must begin by discerning the distinguishing features,
the pieces of the game.

In Japanese food, these elements are of different sorts. There
is "the raw," *la crudité*, a quite frequent quality which applies to
a thousand varieties of foods; there is "the sliced," generally into
very small pieces; color is another element. A plate of Japanese
food is a picture. And as you see, right away I've put myself on
a very formal level. I didn't say "rice means this, fish means that."
So you can see how the system works, how the different elements
fit together.

> *We have those same elements, the raw, the cooked, the*
> *sliced, and so on.*

Of course, but the parts of our meal aren't combined in the same
manner. The Western menu is very rigidly composed and ordered
in sequence.

Take restaurants: invariably they serve hors d'oeuvres, entrées,
roasts, cheeses, and desserts in an inexorable order. It's the logico-
temporal order of the classical narrative, and it's inflexible, as
irreversible as it is in the *Iliad* and the *Odyssey*, in *Les Liaisons*
dangereuses or the latest popular novel.

> *While, in Japan, a meal is like a novel by Robbe-Grillet.*

Better than that. In Japanese restaurants, the customer is given
chopsticks and served a tray on which the food is arranged. Chopsticks are marvelous eating utensils, they aren't pincers, or spears
like our forks. You lift up a mouthful of rice, a mouthful of
pickled vegetables, then more rice, then you take a swallow of
soup, etc. Each person composes his alimentary discourse in a
manner that is always absolutely free and reversible.

And that favors conversation to an extraordinary degree. The
Japanese do not have, as we do, subjects associated with each
part of the meal: consider the business lunch, as we correctly call

it, where the essential discussion takes place over dessert and coffee. The course of the conversation follows the irreversible order of the meal.

> *From the point of view of civilization, what do you de-*
> *duce from the fact that Japanese cuisine is at the antipodes*
> *from ours?*

Naturally, we mustn't deduce that, in relation to monotheism or monocentrism, Japanese food is polytheistic! But, step by step, all these sign systems form themselves into a vast mental structure.

There is a Japanese dish, sukiyaki, that seems quite significant to me. It's a kind of ragout that is in constant preparation. There is a large casserole on the table, where raw meats and vegetables are cooked as the meal progresses. An assistant replenishes both the boiling pot and the conversation, if I may put it that way. But, to be honest, I don't know Japanese, and it's through the language that one accedes most directly to the Japanese mentality.

> *Because language is the vehicle for ideas.*

Let's say that it's above all because a sign system which doesn't include articulated language at some points is unimaginable.

Saussure, the principal founder of modern linguistics, thought that linguistics was part of a larger science, the science of signs—an important part, doubtless, but just a part, the pioneering achievements of which would be followed by the development of other sectors into the larger discipline of semiology.

Today, however, I've come to the conclusion that even when sign systems other than articulated language are considered, such as food, or fashion, which we discussed earlier, it becomes apparent that these systems also are absolutely permeated by language.

> *What is semiology?*

In the canonical sense, the study of signs, of meanings.

What do you consider to be the fundamental importance of linguistics?

It has become almost banal to say so, but linguistics, on the operational level, has given us well-defined concepts of indisputable value, at least in the current phase of research in the social sciences and humanities. And it has given me efficient means for decoding literary texts or any other sign system. Moreover, linguistic research over the past fifteen years has led to the discovery of what are called decentered structures.

And what are they?

Let me return to the example of the dictionary. Linguistics teaches us that there are formations of sounds and meanings which are organized among themselves and consequently possess structural characteristics, but no pivotal center can be discerned at the heart of the structure.

The enemies of structuralism grumble that the notion of structure has always existed, and they wonder what all the fuss is about. Of course, structuralism, in one sense, is very old: the world is a structure, objects and civilizations are structures, we've known that for a long time. Still, what is entirely new is the perception of this decentration. And this is very hard to accept in a culture of the classical type, like ours.

Why is that?

Because our language, like our menu, is very rigid, very centered, to the extent to which it was codified in the seventeenth century by a small social class.

What was called until the grammarian Rivarol "the genius of the French language" masked the profound conviction that French was the best language in the world, just because we put the subject before the verb, and the verb before the complement. The classical writers were convinced that such was the natural and logical order of the mind. On that belief was founded French linguistic nationalism.

Nobody believes that anymore.

No, of course not, and at some universities the syllabus now includes contrasting languages, like Chinese or Japanese, to force future linguists to realize that there are languages which break completely with our Indo-European ones.

In the sixteenth century, Montaigne was still saying "that am I," and not "I am that," which was perfectly correct, since the subject is constituted by everything which happens to it and by everything it does. Because the subject is never itself until the end, as a product.

> *Could you be more precise about this phenomenon of the decentration of language, which you feel is so important?*

Willingly. If I say "I entered the building," my quite ordinary sentence is structured, in the sense that it obeys the rules of construction of French grammar. The form of the first-person subject, the verb, the complement of place—these are so many constraints. There are pieces and rules as in a chess game. And yet, at the same time, that structured sentence is not closed off. The proof that it isn't lies in the fact that it can be added to indefinitely.

The sentence can become, for example: "I who hate climbing stairs, I entered, while it was raining outside, the building at 25, rue de Berri." Intellectually, it's really a marvelous thing, the idea that a sentence is never saturable, that it is catalyzable, to use the accepted term, by successive fillings according to a theoretically infinite process: the center is infinitely displaceable.

I don't remember which linguist made this very beautiful and disturbing reflection: "Each one of us speaks but a single sentence, which only death can bring to a close." That sends a kind of poetic shiver through all knowledge.

> *Language would thus be a combinative, related to the idea of play.*

A combinative, yes, but only if the taboo around this word is broken, because it contains something a bit pejorative in relation to a certain humanist ideal. On the other hand, I wholeheartedly support the notion of play.

I like this word for two reasons. Because it evokes a properly ludic activity, and also the play of an apparatus, a machine, that tiny extra movement possible in the fitting together of its various elements.

Language is a blissful enjoyment of fabrication and function. It is related to a psychoanalysis of pleasure, and at the same time a dynamics of function among its elements, which is both restrictive and supple. Language could also be called a stereophony.

A stereophony?

Yes, by that I mean that it is a space, it puts thoughts and feelings into place according to different volumes and distances. Obviously, if I say: "Come in and close the door," that's not a very stereophonic sentence. But a literary text is truly stereographic.

Like Sarrasine.

Of course. Each sentence of Balzac's always has its own volume, its fortress of meaning. Take any passage from his novella . . .

Perhaps simply its title: Sarrasine.

Yes, fine. Here we have what seems to be an insignificant title, a word, a sound: Sarrasine. If we unfold the numerous meanings there, if we penetrate the fortress, the book immediately opens onto a question: What is Sarrasine? Is it a common noun, a proper noun? And if it's a proper noun, is it a man's name or a woman's? We don't discover the answers to these questions right away.

There is thus a first meaning. The initial question is quite voluminous in itself, since it extends with runners, like a strawberry plant. The question will blossom, but its stem remains unsupported through the whole first part of the novella, until much later, when it is replanted in logico-temporal ground, when we learn that Sarrasine is in fact a sculptor.

> *There is also something violently sexual in* Sarrasine. *It wouldn't be surprising, for example, if the novella recounted the rape of a woman by someone named Sarrasin.*

True. In French, the ending in a silent *e* usually indicates the feminine. So, before learning that Sarrasine is a man, we feminize this man in an obscure way. Not without reason, since the sexuality unveiled in the course of the narrative is quite problematical. And there would obviously be other possible meanings.

> *You have established what has become a classic distinction between the notions of writer* [écrivant] *and author* [écrivain]. *What is the point of this distinction?*

The writer is someone who thinks that language is a pure instrument of thought, who sees only a tool in language. For the author, on the contrary, language is a dialectical space where things are made and unmade, where the author's own subjectivity is immersed and dissolved.

> *Is the critic a writer or an author?*

It depends.

> *Well, are you an author or a writer?*

I would like to be an author. All value judgments aside, I mean that with regard to my project itself, not the result of what I do. Because the writing of an author is not an author's style.

Let's take things at the level of workmanship. A sociologist who writes an article is a writer when he refuses to use certain rhetorical figures. Antitheses, for example. If you read texts by sociologists, demographers, historians, you'll see that they're polished flat.

They don't put two antithetical words within the same sentence, like Victor Hugo. Neither do they use metaphors, or if they do slip one in, they treat it as something unclear which detracts from the truth.

An author, on the other hand, works in the *volume* of language we were just discussing, and is willing to renounce the guarantees of transparent, instrumental writing.

> *You say that being an author isn't a question of style, but neither is it the cultivation of obscurity.*

No, obviously, but the risk of obscurity is still involved. To me, one of the chief criteria of success for someone who, as they say in linguistics, performs the text, i.e., writes it, makes it, is the introduction into the same sentence of two or more codes, introduced in such a way that the reader can't decide in a given situation who is right and who is wrong, who or what is worth more than something else, etc.

For example, in *Sarrasine*, in the first part of the novella, the narrator, who knows the secret of the story he's telling, i.e., that this Zambinella loved by the sculptor Sarrasine is only a castrato, refuses to divulge his secret. To the young woman who asks him who the old man is (in fact, he is the now aged castrato), the narrator replies: "It's a . . ." The three suspension points, for someone who knows the end of the novella, cover up the word "castrato."

> *In other words, to write comes down to knowing how to handle suspense.*

No, not simply that, because there are scads of vulgar works containing lots of suspense, particularly in popular literature, which plays on that sort of thing.

If, in *Sarrasine*, Balzac puts in these three suspension points instead of the word "castrato," it's for two contending reasons. The first belongs to the symbolic order: there is a taboo on the word "castrato." The second belongs to the operative order: if, at that point, the author had written the word "castrato," that would have been the end of it, the whole narrative would have come to a halt. Thus, there are two instances here, one symbolic, one operative. The successful narrator is the one who knows how to mix the two so that we cannot decide which one is the real reason. An author's writing is essentially tied to a criterion of indeterminacy.

Aren't your two criteria restrictive?

Absolutely not. There can be another explanation, other codes can be involved, the historical code, for example, although that would be impossible in this particular case. Anyhow, an author's work must have plurality and indeterminacy of codes, which doesn't happen with a writer.

One last question. Why is the book entitled, enigmatically, S/Z?

I chose the title for its several possible meanings, and to this extent it also represents one of the aims of the book, which is to show the possibilities of a pluralistic criticism authorizing the interpretation of several meanings in a classical text. As for the oblique bar opposing S and Z, it's a sign from linguistics indicating alternation between two terms of a paradigm. Strictly speaking, it should be read S *versus* Z.

Yes, but why the opposition of those two letters?

Because I wanted to give a monogram emblematizing the entire novella, S being the initial of the sculptor Sarrasine, Z the initial of Zambinella, the transvestite castrato. In the book, I explain how these two letters can be considered in a symbolic way, since, in a very Balzacian spirit, a bit esoterically, we must take into account the evil spells of the letter Z, which is the letter of deviation, the deviant letter.

To have written Sarrasine with an *s* rather than a *z* within the body of the name, when French onomastic rules would in general dictate the writing of Sarrazin with a *z*, is the very model of a

Freudian slip, a tiny event of no seeming importance which, in reality, is profoundly significant. And then, in Balzac, there is the letter *z*.

And in Barthes, the letter s.

Yes, I'm used to having that *s* at the end of my name disappear into thin air. Now, you know very well that fiddling with a proper noun is a serious thing: it's interfering with property (which doesn't bother me), but also with integrity—to which no one is indifferent, I suppose, especially when he has just read a story of castration!

Roland Barthes, October 1962

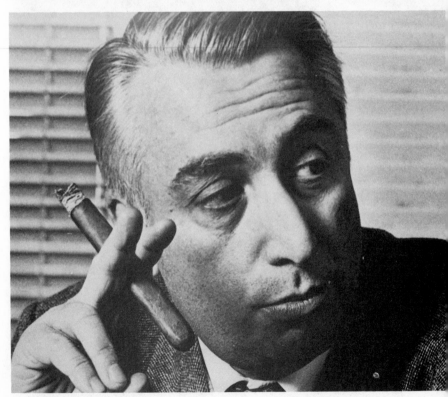

With Jean-Louis Ferrier, Michele Cotta, and Frédéric de Towarnicki
at *L'Express*, 1970

Signing books, 1971

(*top*) Interview, 1975
(*bottom*) With Jacques Henric, 1977

La Gazette de Lausanne, **February 6, 1971**
From an interview conducted by Edgar Tripet

Roland Barthes
on Criticism

Roland Barthes, your criticism aspires to the rigor of a scientific method. By that I mean that it approaches its object, the text, without any ideological criterion—aesthetic, ethical, or political—to reveal the laws governing the text. Doesn't this method have its own ideology, since it seeks to discover a meaning or meanings in the text?

Your question is one that is often asked, and I see springing up all around me arguments challenging such and such a text for ideological reasons. But this is futile! Ideology permeates all of society, even language; it has no extraterritorial privilege granting judgment from some point outside itself. That is why one must always define the position from which one speaks; or silence discourse and oneself, as certain leftists do.

Given this state of things, if there is a discourse that encompasses the discourse of ideology, it is indeed semiology, which, being a science of signs, can advance only by the criticism of signs, and therefore of its own language. This explains the mobility of this science, the rapidity of its evolution, the wearing out of its theoretical language, which barely has the time to establish itself before it is used up.

A student maliciously suggested to me as a project a critique of the ideology of semiology. I told her to go ahead with it. Why not? But the only valid work on this topic must be done from within semiology itself, a semiological critique of semiology. Otherwise, it would just be repeating over and over that semiology is ideology, but without proving that it is—on its own grounds.

> *Criticism of one ideology by another can lead simply to talking in circles—let's go on to semiology itself, particularly the manner in which a science of signs offers an approach to a literary text—a text made to be read, what you call a "readerly" text.*

First, let's make sure we agree on what a readerly text is. Some history is useful here—cultural history, and the history of language instruction in France. Up until Flaubert's time, rhetoric was taught, the art of writing. Since then, reading and writing have been separated, and it is democratization that has caused the loss of the art of writing while at the same time offering for the reader's consumption cultural objects produced by the bourgeoisie. Composition has survived, of course, but as an exercise subject to professorial taste for correction, while the *explication de texte* has assumed the major role. Learning to read, to read well, has its positive side, but also a negative one, since the gap has been widened between the small number of people who write and the large number who read without transforming what they're reading into writing. What separates the usual textual analysis from structural analysis is that the latter, by seeking out all the codes governing a text and its transformations, permits the rewriting of texts.

> *The rewriting of the same text . . . Like translation machines translating everything into the style of Dickens, because the code for that kind of style has been discovered. But since pastiche isn't really literature, in order to attain a new text, isn't it necessary to reintroduce the subjective factor?*

You know, the subjective has also been well defined these days. Between one text and another, there are only differences of desire, not of vocation—or else a vocation is a phantasm that becomes

real: at twelve years of age you dream of becoming an orchestra
conductor, and you become one.

> *Might one suppose—and you have hinted at this in the
> past—that a structural analysis of ever-increasing subtlety
> would eventually discover a foundation text, a model
> from which all literary texts would derive?*

On that subject, I've changed position completely. I did indeed
think at first that it would be possible to determine one or more
models from the study of texts, to work toward these models by
induction in order then to go back to the works themselves by
deduction. Greimas and Todorov, for example, continue to pursue such research directed toward a scientific model. But Nietzsche's
writings and what he says about the indifference of science have
been very important to me. Both Lacan and Derrida have confirmed my belief in this necessary paradox: each text is unique
in its difference, however saturated it may be with cultural and
symbolic codes, repetitions, and stereotypes.

> *Then your paradox falls back into another paradox which
> structuralism thought it had brought under some control:
> the subject, and its subjectivity.*

No . . . and yes! There is an unfortunate (or fortunate!) confusion
in French in this single word "subject," for which English has
two words: *subject* and *topic.*

> *That is a paradox that would carry us too far afield. In
> S/Z, you divide literary texts into two categories: readerly
> texts, which lend themselves to reading, i.e., more or
> less all of literature until now; and writerly texts, which
> each reader is called upon to rewrite . . .*

. . . texts that yield writing. But that literature doesn't exist yet,
or just barely. They are texts yet to come. There has been a break,
in this century and the last, and of course it is always the same
names that come up: Lautréamont, Artaud, sometimes Bataille,

whose texts seem readerly but which are often on the brink of illegibility through the workings of a polyvalent logic.

> *But then who will read anymore? Who will read what, and how?*

In my opinion, one should read anything at all. I enjoy reading, and I don't go as far as certain members of the *Tel Quel* group who condemn all literature. I think one should read in desirous anticipation of what a text will be; one should read texts of the past in a nihilistic perspective, almost as if they were in a state of becoming.

> *That makes me think of those musical scores where each instrument interprets more or less as it pleases the signs, the marks that have replaced notes on the staves.*

Yes. At a concert where the listener is invited to participate in the orchestra's space, to join in the music-making. But I distrust spontaneity, which is directly dependent on habits and stereotypes. At present, for a creator, there is still only the ruse of getting around the code in order to subvert it; to reveal it and destroy it at the same time.

> *That is the story of the serpent that bites its own tail. To free myself from one code, I employ the ruse of another, which, in turn, will reveal its limiting or repressive aspects as a code thanks to the vantage point of the following code, and so on, ad infinitum . . .*

And yet there is no other alternative. You know, limitation, order, barbarism are always possible. Lenin said: "Socialism or barbarism." One can also say socialism *and* barbarism when one sees a culture of stereotypes hardening within mass culture itself. So we must press on . . . and see what happens.

Promesse, no. 29, Spring 1971
From an interview conducted by Guy Scarpetta

Digressions

> This *outside* (the Orient) passes in fact
> through our *inside,* but of course it
> does so by way of a history and a logic
> which make of its passage the history
> and logic of a blindness.
>
> PHILIPPE SOLLERS

*We'll begin, if you will, with the necessity to question
the Orient—to question our misunderstanding of the Orient, our blindness to the Orient—which doubtless comes
down to questioning the ideological gesture that permits
this misunderstanding—the imperialism and Christianity
of our point of view on the Orient; perhaps more than
a simple "geographical" continent, a text is opening up
before us, and we have only a presentiment of what is
at stake.*

*Empire of Signs opens a definite breach in this con-
trolled misunderstanding: the Japan you "read" there is
nothing more than a "reserve of features," you tell us—
or: "the very fissure of the symbolic" (a breach or fissure
to be understood from now on in the light of Artaud's
writings on Balinese theater, Brecht's on Chinese theater,
and Eisenstein's on kabuki—as an opening onto a repressed outside, as a cultural immersion, or, as you put
it, "a revolution in the propriety of symbolic systems")*

—a breach or fissure that we expect you to enlarge,
or to irritate—an urgent surgical stroke, endlessly renewed.

A gesture that intervenes, also, in "the lassitude, almost
a distaste, in any case an intolerance [. . .] regarding the
dissertation and its forms of exposition"—an intolerance
you emphasize by the necessity "to undo, destroy, disperse the dissertational discourse to the advantage of a
discontinuous discourse." And so we will ask of you neither "interview" nor articles (rhetorical modes of the
development and overload of the signified)—but instead a kind of counterpoint to a few "bookmarks," in
Rottenberg's expression, marks inserted in your book
—which we hope will permit another textual series to
unfold, as if musically, in this "between" where the
symbolic is breached: writing that is, here, like a
carved wound.

Point number 1. The reading of a contradiction, which
should perhaps be accentuated rather than "smoothed
out": this Japan presented immediately as an empire of
signs, and in the very weave of the text as an "unheard-
of symbolic system, entirely detached from our own," is
finally read as WRITING, the unfolding of a multiple practice which exceeds the very space of the sign (in its fundamental hierarchy: signifier, signified, referent)—the
Space, if you like, of a hinge, where meaning ebbs and
flows, offers and refuses itself, in infinite interrogation
(every signified already positioned as a signifier)—the
precise interweaving of "codes" and the disappearance of
the hierarchy which founds the concept of "code." This
is marked in the text: "A brightness so vivid, so subtle
that the sign vanishes before any particular signified has
had the time to 'take' "/"Empire of signs? Yes, if it is
understood that the signs are empty, and the ritual is
without a god."

Now comes the question of what is played out in your
text, let's say, between Saussure and Derrida, the end of
all "formalistic" (positivistic, mechanistic) possibilities of

> *any* reading *of the Orient: a zone which the dominant
> ideology tries* in vain *to control, the site of an irreme-
> diable* collapse.

1. FORMALISM

We should not be too quick to jettison the word "formalism,"
because its enemies are our own: scientists, causationists, spiri-
tualists, functionalists, "spontaneists"; attacks against formalism
are always made in the name of content, the subject, the Cause
(an ironically ambiguous word, referring as it does to a faith and
a determinism, as if they were the same thing); i.e., in the name
of the signified, in the name of the Name. We don't need to
keep our distance from formalism, merely to take our ease (comfort, on the order of desire, is more subversive than distance, on
the order of censure). The formalism I have in mind does not
consist in "forgetting," "neglecting," "reducing" content ("man"),
but only in *not stopping* at the threshold of content (let's keep
the word, provisionally); content is *precisely* what interests formalism, because its endless task is each time to push content back
(until the notion of origin ceases to be pertinent), to displace it
according to a play of successive forms. Isn't this what has been
happening to physics itself, which, since Newton, has been endlessly moving matter back, not for the benefit of the "spirit," but
on behalf of the aleatory (remember Verne quoting Poe: "Hap-
penstance must be the matter of unceasing and rigorous calculation"). It is not matter which is materialist, but the retraction,
the lifting of safety catches; what is formalistic is not "form" but
the relative, dilatory *time* of contents, the precariousness of references.

To wean ourselves from all the philosophies (or theologies) of
the signified, i.e., of the Fixed Point, since we who are "literary"
do not have access to that sovereign formalism, mathematics, we
must use as many metaphors as possible, because metaphor is a
means of access to the signifier; in default of algorithms, metaphor
will expel the signified, especially if it can be "dis-originated."
(By "non-originated metaphor" I mean a chain of substitutions
without an obvious first, or founding, term. Sometimes language

itself produces comparisons which are, if not non-originated, at least reversed: tinder [*l'amadou*] is a substance which burns easily; it derives its name, in Provençal, from the ardent lover [*l'amoureux*]—it's the "sentimental" that here allows us to name the "material.")

Today I propose this metaphor: the stage of the world (the world as stage) is occupied by a play of "decors" (texts); if you raise one backdrop, another appears behind it, and so on. To refine the image, contrast one theater with another. In Pirandello's *Six Characters*, the play takes place on the "bare" stage of the theater: no settings, only the walls, pullies, and ropes of the backstage area; the character (the subject) is formed little by little from a "reality" which is (*a*) reduced, (*b*) internal, (*c*) causal; there is machinery, the subject is a puppet; therefore, despite its modernism (acting without scenery, on a bare stage), this theater remains spiritualistic: it opposes the "reality" of causes, of underlying depths, to the "illusion" of flats, paint, scenic effects. The Marx Brothers' *A Night at the Opera* shows us this same situation (in a burlesque manner, of course: an additional token of truthfulness). In the dazzling finale, the old witch of *Il Trovatore*, a parody in herself, sings merrily away, her back turned to a complete merry-go-round of backdrops: each flat comes down only to be promptly hoisted away and replaced by another; the unwitting old woman is successively framed by different "contexts" (all strange and irrelevant: decors from every opera in the repertoire pop out of storage and pass fleetingly in review), unaware of the permutation behind her: each line of her aria becomes a misinterpretation. This charivari is bursting with symbols: the absence of background replaced by the changing plural of decors, the coding of contexts (from the operatic repertoire) and their mockery, delirious polysemy, and finally the illusion of the subject, singing its image-repertoire for as long as the other (the spectator) is watching, believing itself to be speaking before the background of a unique world (decor)—a complete *mise en scène* of the plural which derides and dissociates the subject.

Point number 2. The thought, radically new (but opened as a possibility by Marx and Freud), of the absence of center: *a city whose center is empty, dwellings without a "focus"—marked, in the very writing of the text, by the ideogram* 無 , *MU, emptiness.*

Or this: "The shock of meaning, torn, extenuated to the point of irreplaceable emptiness without the object's ever ceasing to be significant, desirable. Writing is after all, in its way, a satori: satori (the Zen occurrence) is a more or less powerful (in no way ceremonious) seism which shakes consciousness, the subject: it creates an emptiness of language. And it is also an emptiness of language which constitutes writing."

There is nothing more difficult to "admit," for a Western mind, than this emptiness (which everything within us longs to fill up, through that obsession with the phallus, the father, the "master-word"). There is violence in this confrontation—and the imperious need to avoid any unconscious recuperation that would make this emptiness itself a center, in a mystical reduction through which Western religion would regain, as if by law, its rights. How can this oblique and "repressive" return of the signified be avoided? How can this emptiness be written without being "expressed"? These are key questions in that practice of annulment which, since Mallarmé (who refracted it within the compromised term of "nothingness"), has been the constant, silent, and menacing other side of all our words.

2. EMPTINESS

The idea of decentering is certainly much more important than that of *emptiness*, which is ambiguous: certain religious experiences can quite easily accommodate an *empty center* (I suggested that ambiguity apropos of Tokyo, where the center of the city is occupied by the emperor's palace). Here again we must continually renew our metaphors. To begin with, what is abhorrent in *fullness* is not only the image of an ultimate substance, an indissoluble compactness; it is also and above all (at least to my mind) a *bad form*: subjectively, fullness is remembrance (the past, the Father), while its neurotic form is repetition, and its social form is stereotype (flourishing in so-called mass culture, in this endoxal civilization of ours). In contrast, *emptiness* should no longer be conceived (imagined) in the form of an absence (of body, of things, feelings, words, etc.: *nothing*)—here we are the victims of ancient physics; we have a somewhat chemical idea of emptiness. Emptiness is closer to the new, the return of the new (which is the contrary of repetition). I recently read in a scientific encyclopedia (which marks the extent of my limited knowledge on this point) the exposition of a theory in physics (the most recent, I believe) which gave me some idea of this emptiness (I'm becoming a believer in the metaphorical value of science); it is Chew and Mandelstram's theory (1961), called the "bootstrap" theory (after the expression "to pull oneself up by one's own bootstraps"); I quote: *"The particles existent in the universe would not be engendered from other, more elementary particles* (thus abolishing the ancestral specter of filiation, of determination), *but would represent the sum total of strong interactions at any given moment* (the world as an always provisional system of differences). *In other words, the set of particles would engender itself (self-consistence)."* The emptiness we are speaking of could be summed up as the self-consistence of the world.

> *Point number 3. The symptom (in the sense of giving oneself up, as Sollers says, to a cultural anamnesis) noted here by your reading of haiku. Turning around the impressionist or even* surrealist *interpretation of haiku (consider Breton's use of haiku in his* idealist *defense of the image—cf.* "signe ascendant" *in* La clé des champs), *you clearly indicate that* "what is aimed at is the foundation of the sign, which is classification"—underlining *at the same time the highly overdetermined character, here, of all* interpretation, *whereas* "this meaning does not become internalized, does not spread or wander into the infinity of metaphors, the spheres of the symbol"— *or again:* "Nothing has been gained, the word-stone has been cast for nothing: no waves, no ripples of meaning"— *just what Basho points out:*

> How admirable is he
> Who does not think: "Life is fleeting"
> When startled by lightning!

The problem is to find out if this absence of a paradig-matic instance cuts us off necessarily from the space of the sign—a question to be articulated on the very inser-tion of haiku into our culture, and particularly into our poetic discourse (where the sign comes into play and becomes worn out—precisely in the active multiplicity, the signifying depths of poetic discourse—and not in the "adequation of the signifier and the signified").

3. READABLE

With meaning abolished, everything remains to be done, since language goes on (the phrase "everything remains to be done" obviously sends us back to work). To my mind (perhaps I haven't emphasized this enough), the haiku's worth lies, paradoxically enough, in the fact that it is *readable*. What cuts us off most effectively from the sign—at least in this *full* world—is not the *contrary* of the sign, the nonsign, nonmeaning (the *unreadable*, in the current sense), because this nonmeaning is immediately recuperated by meaning (as the meaning of nonmeaning); it is useless to subvert language by destroying its syntax, for example: that is a paltry subversion, in fact, and one which is moreover far from innocent, since, as someone said, "small subversions make large conformisms." Meaning cannot be attacked head-on, by the simple assertion of its contrary; you must cheat, steal, refine—parody, if you must, but, better yet, counterfeit. The haiku, through an entire technique, even a code of metrics, has discovered how to evaporate the signified, leaving only a thin veil of signifier; and it's at that moment, it seems, through one last twist, that the haiku dons the mask of the readable, copying, while it somehow deprives them of all *reference*, the attributes of the "good" (literary) message: clarity, simplicity, elegance, finesse. The work of writing we have in mind today consists neither in improving communication nor in destroying it, but of *filigreeing* it; that is more or less what classical texts have done (parsimoniously), which makes them, whatever else they are, writing: a new stage has begun, however, initiated here and there in the nineteenth century, in which it is not meaning which is made (liberally) plural within a single code (the one of "writing well") but the entirety of language itself (as a "fluctuating hierarchy" of codes, of logics) which is stirred up; this must still be done within the appearance of communication, because the social and historical conditions for a liberation of language (in relation to signifieds, to the *property* and *propriety* of discourse) have not yet appeared anywhere. Thus, the present importance of the theoretical (guiding) concepts of paragram, plagiarism, intertextuality, false readability.

> *Point number 4. What is readable in the three preceding points is of course the question of the* materialist anchorage *of the* writing *designated by the word "Japan"— an anchorage that can be determined from the articulations of a complex way of life (relatively autonomous serial elements regulated, in their stratification, by relations of dominance and determination: in this case, "cuisine" as well as "theater," "wrestling" as well as "poetry," "manners" as well as "topology"), but also from* language—*brutally confronting us with everything that is ideological and unconscious in the way we live our relation to language (a language which, as we know, is not a superstructure—and which is also a "paternal language," as you put it; i.e., dominated by the instance of the Name). Here it is a question of language, not only as a "decentering" in relation to the obsession to communicate, thus leaving room for a generalized writing of traces and gestures, but also as a problematical site in the dialectically arranged "scope" of recognized intellectual activities.*

4. LANGUAGE

"Language is not a superstructure," you said. Two clarifications
are in order here. First of all, the proposition is unclear as long
as the notion of "superstructure" has not been clearly defined,
and it is presently undergoing a complete modification (at least
I hope so). And furthermore, if one thinks of history on the grand
scale, it is certainly possible to include language, all languages,
within a structural totality: there is a "structure" of Indo-European
languages (as opposed to Oriental languages, for example) that is
related to the institutions of that area of civilization (everyone
knows that the important break passes *between* India and China,
between the Indo-European and Asiatic languages, between
Buddhism and Taoism or Zen; Zen is apparently Buddhist, but
it does not belong to Buddhism; I'm talking about a division in
the history of languages, not in the history of religions).

In any case, even if language is not a superstructure, the relation
to language is political. This is perhaps not readily apparent in a
culturally and historically "compressed" nation such as France,
where language is not a political theme; still, if you simply raised
the question (by whatever means: the elaboration of a committed
sociolinguistics, or just a special edition of a magazine), you would
doubtless be astounded by the extent of its import (the French
are merely *asleep* in relation to their language, they have been
chloroformed by centuries of classical authority); in countries that
are less well-off, however, language is a burning issue; in the
formerly colonized Arab countries, language is a state issue of
great political weight. I'm not at all sure that we are currently
able to resolve such a problem. There is no political theory of
language, a methodology that would expose language's processes
of *appropriation* and permit study of the "propriety" of enunciative
means, something like the *Capital* of linguistics (for my part, I
think that such a theory will evolve little by little from the current
stammerings of semiology, and will prove in part to be the historical meaning of these explorations). This (political) theory should
decide in particular *where language ends*—and *if* it ends anywhere. In certain countries still encumbered by a former colonial
language (French), there currently prevails the *reactionary* idea

that one can separate language from "literature," that one can teach French (as a foreign language) and repudiate French literature (as "bourgeois"); unfortunately, language has no threshold, it cannot be stopped; one can at most close off and isolate grammar (and thus teach it canonically), but not vocabulary, still less the associative, connotative life of a language. A foreigner learning French quickly finds himself (or at least he ought to, if language instruction does its job) confronted by the same ideological problems that face a Frenchman in his own language. Literature is never anything but the deepening and extension of language, and on that score it is the largest of ideological fields, where the structural problem I mentioned a little while ago is debated (I say all this drawing on my experiences in Morocco).

Language is infinite, and we must draw appropriate conclusions. Language begins before language; that is what I wanted to say apropos of Japan, by my enthusiasm over the way I communicated over there, outside a spoken language incomprehensible to me, but in the rustle, the emotive breath of that unknown language. To live in a country where one doesn't know the language, and to live audaciously, outside tourist tracks, is the most dangerous of adventures (in the naïve sense that word can have in children's books). Such an adventure is more perilous (for the "subject") than braving the jungle, because one must *exceed* language, holding oneself within its supplementary margin, in its depthless infinity. If I had to imagine a new Robinson Crusoe, I would not place him on a desert island but in a city of twelve million people where he could decipher neither speech nor writing: that, I think, would be the modern form of Defoe's tale.

> *Point number 5. You write: "In the land I call Japan, sexuality is in sex, not elsewhere"; but you also write: "Over there, the body exists, unfolds, acts, gives itself, without hysteria, without narcissism, but according to a purely erotic project"; or this: "the great syntagm of bodies." It's as if we were confronted, upon abandoning* corporeal expression *(i.e., mind/body dualism) and any space limited to fetishism or transference, by permutations, and work (the transvestite, for example, does not*

> *"imitate" woman, but* plays *her). And what of—the*
> *question is perhaps ridiculous—the delicacy of this sexual*
> *play (which breaks away from the heated and redoubled*
> *violence a similar gesture implies in the West, for ex-*
> *ample, in the texts of Sade or Guyotat)?*

5. SEXUALITY

The delicacy of sexual play is a very important idea, and one that
is entirely unknown, it seems to me, in the West (a major incentive to interest). The reason for this is simple. In the West,
sexuality lends itself only to a language of transgression, and that
but poorly; but to make of sexuality a field of transgression is still
to keep it imprisoned in a binary logic, a paradigm, a meaning.
To think of sexuality as a dark continent is still to submit it to
meaning (black/white). The alienation of sexuality is consubstan-
tially linked to the alienation of meaning, by meaning. What is
difficult is not to liberate sexuality according to a more or less
libertarian plan but to disengage it from meaning, including
transgression as meaning. Look at the Arab countries again. There
certain rules of the "right" sexuality are easily transgressed by the
rather casual practice of homosexuality (on condition that homosexuality never be *named*: but that is another problem, the
immense problem of the verbalization of the sexual, forbidden
in civilizations of "shame," while that same verbalization is cher-
ished—confessions, pornographic representations—in civilizations of "guilt"); but this transgression remains implacably subject
to a regime of strict meaning: homosexuality, a transgressive practice, immediately reproduces in itself (by a kind of defensive
clogging-up, a reflex of fright) the purest paradigm imaginable:
active/passive, possessor/possessed, buggerer/buggeree, *tapeur/tapé*
(these *"pied-noir"* words, of mixed French-Algerian ancestry, are
suited to the occasion: once again, the ideological value of language). Now, the paradigm is meaning; and so, in these countries,
any practice that goes beyond the alternative structure, confusing
or simply delaying it (what some people there refer to disdainfully
as *making love*), is at the same time *interdicted and unintelligible*.
Sexual "delicacy" is in contrast to the rough character of these

practices, not on the level of transgression, but on the level of meaning; this delicacy can be defined as a *confusion of meaning*, with these paths of expression: either protocols of "politeness," or sensual techniques, or a new conception of erotic "time." All this can be said in another way: the sexual interdiction is completely lifted, not to the advantage of a mythical "liberty" (a concept only good enough to satisfy the timid phantasms of so-called mass society), but to the advantage of empty codes, which exonerates sexuality from the falsehood of spontaneity. Sade saw that very clearly: the practices he enumerates are governed by a strict combinative; they remain marked, however, by a properly Western mythical element: a kind of erethism, of fear, what you quite correctly called a *heated* sexuality—and sex is still sanctified when it is the object, not of hedonism, but of *enthusiasm* (animation, possession by a god).

Point number 6. A key point: the precise identification of writing as mise en scène, *through the puppetry of bunraku: work written in the volume of representation, and overflowing it; a reflection given in its method, affirming its production: it is perhaps here that the formation of a* network *of stratified, juxtaposed signifying activities is identified with the greatest precision—without ever yielding to a frozen "unity," a hierarchy of codes. Between the dolls of wood and cloth, and the handlers who make them move, between the bodies of wood or flesh and the* lateral *voice, obliquely off-track, a new space is clearly drawn, the theater of a writing, an unceasing textuality: "a spectacle complete but divided" / "the interplay of a combinative which opens out into the entire space of the theater"—where, under the sway of "citation," "the interweaving of codes, references, discrete assertions," we accede to* another *scene, a place thoroughly repressed by our Western theater so haunted, even in its fragmentary contestations, by interiorization or imitation. You write: "Work is substituted for inwardness"; and again: "The inside no longer commands the outside"—an observation which can only send us*

> *back to the dialectical logic inaugurated by Marx, de-*
> *scribed by Althusser: "The current distinctions between*
> *outside and inside disappear, as does the intimate bond*
> *of phenomena which is opposed to their visible disorder:*
> *we are faced with another image, with an almost new*
> *concept, definitively freed from the empiricist antinomies*
> *of phenomenal subjectivity and essential interiority, we*
> *are faced with an objective system regulated, in its most*
> *concrete determinations, by the laws of its assemblage*
> *and machinery." This point of contact with Marxist dis-*
> *course permits us to question this scene anew: does the*
> *signifier, as you put it, merely "turn itself inside out, like*
> *a glove"? Or are we already within that "system" where*
> *what permits the very concept of "signifier" is exceeded,*
> *where the word "signifier" has meaning only through*
> *being linked up to the words "work" or "transformation"?*

6. SIGNIFIER

The signifier: we must be determined to keep taking advantage of this word for a long time yet (we should note once and for all that it's not a question of defining the term but of using it; i.e., "metaphorizing" it, using it in opposition—mainly to the signified, which we believed in the early days of semiology to be its correlate, but which we now understand more fully as its adversary). Our present task is twofold. On the one hand, we must somehow conceive (by which I mean an operation more metaphorical than analytical) how *the depth and lightness of the signifier* may be expressed contradictorily together (remember that *lightness* may be understood in a Nietzschean sense); because although the signifier is not "profound," does not develop along a scenario of inwardness and secrecy, yet we must somehow immerse ourselves in the signifier, plunging far away from the signified into the matter of the text. How can one flee into lightness? How can one spread out without increasing in volume? To what substance can the signifier be compared? Certainly not to water, not even to the oceans, because they have boundaries; perhaps to the sky, to what is precisely *unthinkable* in cosmic space. On the other hand, this same metaphorical exploration should be made for the word "work" (which is, in fact, much more than *signified*, the true correlate of *signifier*). "Work" is also a *numen*-word (capable of strengthening a discourse), which I analyze as follows: associated with the problem of the text, it is to be understood in the sense described by Julia Kristeva, as *pre-sense work* [*travail pré-sens*]—work outside meaning, exchange, calculation, work within expenditure and play. I think we need to move in that direction. We should ward off certain connotations in advance: completely eliminate the idea of work as trouble, punishment, distress, and perhaps give up (at least to begin with, to be thorough) the metonymy that stands proletarian surety for all work, which obviously permits the "work" of the signifier to slip into the socialist camp (where it receives a mixed welcome, moreover); this metonymy should be considered more patiently, more dialectically. In short, the important question of "work" has fallen into a crevice, a blank space in our culture; I would say, elliptically, that this blank is exactly the same as the one which has up until now annulled the relation of Marx and Nietzsche: a most reluctant and resistant relation, which ought therefore to be examined. Who will take care of this?

> *Point number 7. This point of contact with dialectical materialism permits me perhaps (and "to bring things to a close") to ask about the* position *of the signifying activities that you are studying within a general and differentiated* social application *(i.e., outside the idealist myth of a unified history, "monistic" or logocentric). This question seems particularly important with regard to our reflections on the Orient, if we want to avoid those* two complicitous attitudes *(living their opposition on the basis of the same repression) which are the myth of a savage Orient, barbarous and backward, and cultural fetishism of the classic type, misunderstanding determination* in the last instance *by economics (a point all the more important, here, in that we are confronted by an economy of the* advanced capitalistic *kind). This question is indeed urgent, if it allows us to determine how the*

> *principal contradiction of our time (imperialism/social-*
> *ism) is specifically inscribed within the symbolic in-*
> *stance—and precisely in the East, because it is there, a*
> *bit to the south of Japan, that this contradiction is being*
> *played out in the most* decisive *fashion, where the con-*
> *frontation of signs has given way to the clash of* weapons.

7. WEAPONS

You oppose *signs* to *weapons* in a striking but still substitutive fashion, and you cannot do otherwise, because weapons and signs are the same thing: every combat is a semantic one, every meaning is warlike—the signified is the sinews of war, war is the very structure of meaning. We are at present engaged in a war, not of meaning (a war to abolish meaning), but of meanings: signifieds confront each other, furnished with all possible weapons (military, economic, ideological, even neurotic). At present there is not a single institution from which the signified has been banished (today one can seek to dissolve the signified only by cheating with institutions, in areas that are unstable, fleetingly occupied, un-inhabitable, contradictory to the point of sometimes seeming re-actionary). For my part, the paradigm which I try to take as an example, beyond any preferential political position, is not *im-perialism/socialism*, but *imperialism/something else*. I must accept the fact that this collapse just when the paradigm should conclude decisively, this opposition made lopsided by the curtailment, sup-plement, or diversion of the *neuter*, this gaping utopia—is the only place where I can take my stand at present. Imperialism is *fullness*; on the other side there is the *rest*, unsigned: a text without a title.

Signs of the Times, 1971
From an interview conducted by Stephen Heath

Interview: A Conversation with Roland Barthes

> *You have spoken of a certain distance that now separates you from your earlier work, and you have also said that a writer "must consider his past texts as if they were the work of another, which he takes up, cites, or deforms as he would do with a multitude of other signs." It also seems that you have always been quite conscious of occupying a relative place in the history of semiology (at the very moment of its publication, you acknowledged that* The Fashion System *was already a history of semiology). Would you tell us what your current preoccupations are, and in what way they continue or diverge from your earlier work?*

I am preoccupied—or rather occupied, because no painful concern is involved—by the idea that a history of semiology already exists, even though semiology in the strict, Occidental sense is only about ten years old; this history is marked by a very rapid acceleration; one could even say that it is history at breakneck speed. There has been such turbulence in semiology that it could be described as a ten-year spate of proposals, counterproposals, divisions, differences of opinion—differences of style between French semiologists, and also, more and more, ideological differences. Even on the scale of these past ten years, a history of semiology is possible, even necessary; as it happens, I have been linked to the birth of semiology through my first semiological text (the afterword to *Mythologies*, written in 1956); I myself am thus, on the partial and circumscribed level of my own work, a part of the history of semiology. I'm currently considering collecting my semiological texts into a book that, if published, could be presented precisely as a *history*; it could even be called *A Short History of Semiology*. So it's normal to find divisions, contradictions, jolts, progressions, perhaps even regressions in the course of my semiological works—they form a complete movement. The semiology of my current interests is, thus, no longer the semiology I saw, imagined, and practiced ten or fifteen years ago. As far as literary semiotics is concerned, there is a very definite break, between the *Introduction to the Structural Analysis of Narratives* and *S/Z*—in fact, these two texts correspond to two semiologies. The reasons for this mutation (because it is a mutation rather than an evolution) should be sought in recent French history—why not?—and then also in intertextuality, that intertextual space formed by the texts that surround and accompany me, proceed me, follow me, communicate with me. You know the ones I mean, I needn't name them, it would just be the same names of the familiar group.

Having said that, it's rather hard to be specific about where I am today, semiologically, because you never really know where you are until you write it out, but when it's published, you've already moved on. In an effort not to duck the question, I could say, however, that the present problem consists in disengaging semiology from the repetition to which it has already fallen prey. We must produce something *new* in semiology, not merely to be original, but because it is necessary to consider the theoretical problem of repetition. I would say, more specifically (and in this I differ perhaps from colleagues who are close to me in other ways), that my concern is not to show the relationships between semiology and ideology or anti-ideology, in short between semiology and the political, but rather to pursue a general and systematic enterprise, polyvalent, multidimensional, the fissuration of the symbolic and its discourse in the West. In that sense,

of course, the text that most closely represents my current preoccupation is my latest one, my book on Japan, even though it is
not a theoretical work.

And what of my work tomorrow? If I try to interrogate my
desire—which is the proper standard for work—I know that the
signifier is where I want to work: I want to work *in* the signifier,
I want to *write* (I acknowledge the vaguely regressive impurity of
the word, I don't deny whatever old-fashioned, let's say, stylistic
traces still cling to the concept, to the activity of writing). In other
words, what would truly please me would be to write within what
I have called "the novelistic without the novel," the novelistic without its characters: a writing of life, which could perhaps
rejoin a certain moment of my own life, when I was writing
the *Mythologies*, for example. They would be new "mythologies," less directly committed to ideological denunciation, but
thereby, for me, less involved in the signified: these texts
would be more ambiguous, more advanced and immersed in
the signifier.

> *You speak of the rapid pace of the history of semiology;
> has this headlong development ended in the recuperation
> or even the stereotyping of semiology itself?*

The impression of "recuperation" depends on one's degree of
ideological sensitivity: the greater one's sensitivity, the clearer it
is that semiology is being recuperated insofar as it is becoming a
success, because success requires a complicity of institutions.
Semiology is currently quite fashionable, but it is also, in fact,
being taught: the teaching of semiology is taking shape, and is in
demand. Once an institution becomes involved, one can say that
there is recuperation. And elements arose very quickly within
semiology which lent themselves to this recuperation. I'm not
making any petty criticism here, that is not my intention, but I
would say that any semiology that takes "scientific" objectivity as
its intention or security is a semiology containing the seeds of
institutional success: this is to be expected in a society that honors
"scientificity."

> *In your* Elements of Semiology, *in your commentary of Chapter IV of the second part of Saussure's* Course in General Linguistics *(where he insists on language as the domain of articulations, and meaning as an order that is, however, essentially division—to use your own words), you postulated ("utopically") the absorption of semiology into a new science, "arthrology, the science of apportionment." More recently, within the context of a discussion on the relationship between linguistics and literature, you noted several contestatory themes in the confrontation of the linguistic model by a semiology of discourse, and you suggested the possibility of the supersedure of linguistics (insofar as it is historically linked to speech), referring for support to the work of Jacques Derrida. Do you see a relationship between Derrida's work and the realization of that science you called arthrology? Where would you situate Derrida's work in what you have referred to as "the anecdotal history of semiology"?*

I don't think Derrida would ever acknowledge having wished to found a science, or even ever having thought about it; besides, neither have I. In fact, as far as I'm concerned, the reference to literary science, or arthrology, or semiology, has always been quite ambiguous, very devious, and I would almost say that it is often *faked*. Moreover, in *Critique et Vérité*, I did speak of a science of literature, but it was in general overlooked—to my dismay, because I formulated my sentence so that this would be seen by those who pay attention to ambiguities and ellipses—that in speaking of a science of literature I had put in parentheses: "if it exists one day"; which meant that I did not in fact believe that discourse on literature could ever become "scientific." The appeal to science can no longer be conceived either according to a psychological model (respect for certain values of "objectivity") nor according to a positivistic, alethic model (as a search for truth). I think that the only acceptable scientific model is that of Marxist science as delineated by Althusser's studies of Marx; the "epistemological break" he sets forth apropos of Marx shows us *the* science of today, and disengages science from ideology. It's obviously in such a fashion that we should be able to refer to science, but I'm not at all sure that semiology has reached that point at present, except perhaps in the work of Julia Kristeva.

As for that science of apportionment, division, discontinuity, what I referred to somewhat ironically as "arthrology," I should like to say that, for me, these notions of discontinuity and combinativity remain alive and important. At every moment of my life, wherever I go, even walking in the street, when I think, react, I constantly find myself on the side of thought that grapples with what is discontinuous and combinatory. Today, for example, I was reading a text by Brecht, admirable, as always, a text on Chinese painting, in which he says that Chinese painting puts things next to each other, side by side with each other. That's a very simple way of putting it, but very beautiful, and quite true, and what I want, after all, is precisely to feel the juxtaposition of things, the "next to."

Isn't that what you attempted in Empire of Signs?

Exactly. It seems rather simple, not very revolutionary, and yet if you think of the way in which the human sciences think, conceptualize, formalize, verbalize—it becomes clear that they are absolutely not acclimated to thinking about discontinuity: they are still dominated by the superego of continuity, a superego of evolution, history, filiation, etc. Every advance in thinking about what is discontinuous thus remains essentially heretical, revolutionary in the proper and necessary sense.

> *I would just like to add here that if I mentioned what you called "arthrology" in relation to Derrida's work, it was precisely because your postulation was offered "utopically," because the science Derrida calls grammatology is a science that creates itself negatively, as it were, questioning and undoing metaphysical discourses without ever becoming formalized into a science. In this context, it would seem—and here I return to what you just said about the present importance to you of your text on*

> *Japan—that what you do in* Empire of Signs *is displace yourself into these networks of signifiers culled from Japan in order to deconstruct, if I may say so, the Occidental signified holding you back. It is this experience of writing as deconstruction, as decentering, that I was trying to read next to the difficult discourse of Derridean grammatology, a discourse that might also be defined as utopian in that it aims at a beyond (of metaphysics) which is never realized except in the negative image of destruction.*

That's precisely it. In addition to everything I owe to Derrida, and which others owe him too, there is something that brings us together, if I may say so: the feeling of participating (of wanting to participate) in a period of history Nietzsche calls "nihilism."

> *In an essay on the possibilities of a structural poetics, Todorov described the object of such a poetics as the interrogation of the "properties of the particular discourse that is literature. Each work is thus considered only as the manifestation of a much more general abstract structure, of which the work is only one of the possible realizations." It seems that there is an emphasis there that is in part inspired by you—I'm thinking in particular of your research on the structural analysis of the narrative and, in fact, Todorov does note that what he means by the term* poetics *coincides rather closely with what you have called, in* Critique et Vérité, *"the science of literature."*
>
> *More recently, you have proposed to study instead "the reproduction of the production of a text" (what you would call, I believe, its structuration), also declaring in particular that "each text is its own model," and, in the first chapter of S/Z, you clearly keep a certain distance from any scientific poetics. Do you see this modification as an inevitable development of structural poetics, or as a more radical change, and where would you situate your analysis of* Sarrasine *within this context? What kind of*

modifications have been forced upon the structuralist
approach by its confrontation with the literary text as an
object of study?

Here we come back to that rapid evolution of semiology I was just talking about: there was a break which I situate, as you do, between *Introduction to the Structural Analysis of Narratives* and *S/Z*. On the former, when I hypothesized the existence of a general structure, from which one would then derive analyses of contingent texts, when I suggested the possible benefit of reconstituting a kind of grammar, a logic, of the narrative (and at that time I believed in this grammar, I don't deny it), it was really to underline once more what I had said in *Critique et Vérité*: the superego imposed on students and researchers by the traditional conception of literature, particularly by academic criticism and literary history, is a superego intended to be "scientific"; the new French criticism has been accused of being unscientific and has been tossed on the pile of impressionistic and subjectivistic lucubrations, when academic criticism itself has absolutely nothing scientific about it: I came to believe, as I worked on the narrative, that literary science—I repeat, *if it exists one day*—should not be sought in the traditional direction of history and contents but in a science of *forms* in discourse, a point of view that is the working hypothesis of someone like Todorov, as you mentioned.

In *S/Z*, I upset this perspective by rejecting the idea of a model that would transcend several texts, not to mention all texts, in order to suggest, as you said, that each text was in a way its own model, and ought to be dealt with through its own difference, but a difference that should be taken in either a Nietzschean or Derridean sense. Let's put it another way: the text is endlessly and entirely crisscrossed by codes, but it is not the fulfillment of a code (for example, the narrative code), it is not the "speech" of a (narrative) "language." I'm not speaking for the critics or the public here, but I do believe that *S/Z* is an important book for me. When one writes, one has feelings toward one's own books; among the ones I have written, there are some that don't have much importance for me today (which doesn't mean that I disown them), but there are some that are either important or dear to me: for example, I like (and when I say "I like," it simply means "I can live with") a book that is rarely mentioned, *Michelet*, whereas *Writing Degree Zero*, which I am less comfortable with, is nevertheless more deeply imbedded in current histories of criticism and literature. If *S/Z* is an important book for me, it's because I believe that I did indeed effect a change there; I brought off a kind of mutation of my work. Where did this alteration come from? Again, change is often brought about by others: it's because I was surrounded by "formulators," writers like Derrida, Sollers, Kristeva (always the same names, of course), who taught me things, persuaded me, opened my eyes. And I also think that this change in theory, evidenced in *S/Z*, came as a response to pressure, to determination from the critical operation itself. It's because I began to operate on a text—and I almost feel like saying: to operate *a* text—that was relatively short, giving myself, by a stroke of good fortune, the right to spend months on thirty pages and to really go over this text step by step, it's because of this that the theoretical modification took place. If you like, it was my luck (not in relation to the public, I repeat, but personally) to have had the intuition, or the patience, or even the naïveté, to think of a "step-by-step" approach to the text; I think that's what determined the change in theory: I changed the level of perception of the object, and thereby changed the object itself. It's well known that on the order of perception, if the level of perception is changed, so is the object; this is clear, if only from that plate of Diderot's *Encyclopedia* that caused such a sensation at the time, showing a flea seen under a contemporary microscope, magnified to several square feet so that it became something quite other than a flea (it's a surrealistic object). A change in the level of perception multiplies objects like some kind of diabolical mirror. And so, in going step by step over a text, I changed the object, and in that way was led to a change in theory.

> *This change in perspective realized through the "step-by-step" method brings your reading of* Sarrasine *into the world of connotation, and in fact, in the initial chapter of* S/Z, *you speak of connotation as the appropriate instrument for approaching the classical readerly text. In*

so doing, you rejoin what might be considered the general
object of all your studies: systems of connotation, that
social rhetoric and its diverse signifying functions. (Thus,
in reading Sarrasine, you study a mythic return of the
text "to language as nature," and we could think of similar
reversals analyzed in Mythologies.) Two questions:

1. Given that you have proposed the analysis of these
connotative codes (I'm thinking here in particular of your
paper "Rhetorical Analysis" given at the Brussels conference) as a possible subject for fruitful study of the
relations between literature and society, could S/Z be
considered in part a first step in this direction, and what
will the next step be? The establishment of a typology of
readerly texts? (Do you think those codes you discovered
at work in Balzac's text are common to all readerly texts?)

2. I would like to quote here the following passage
from Julia Kristeva's book Semiotiké: "The entire problem of current semiotics seems to be here: do we continue
to formalize semiotic systems from the point of view of
communication (let's risk a blunt comparison: as Ricardo
considered surplus value from the point of view of dis-
tribution and consumption), or do we initiate within the
problematics of communication (which is what any social
problematics inevitably is) that other scene—the production of meaning anterior to meaning. If we adopt the
second course, there are two possibilities: either to isolate
a measurable and thus representable aspect of the signifying system under study against the background of a
nonmeasurable concept (labor, production, or those Derridean concepts of le gramme, la trace, la différence); or
else to try and construct a new scientific problematics (in
the sense . . . of a science that is also a theory) in response
to the inevitable demand created by this new concept."
In the framework of a study of those connotative systems
that make up both the plural and the limit of the classical
readerly text, S/Z would seem to align itself along the
model of that scientific approach you described in your
Elements of Semiology (a scientific metalanguage speak-

*ing of connotative language), but it's clear that S/Z must
itself be read as a text, that is, as you said about* Semiotiké,
*a book in which theory and writing are rigorously ho-
mogeneous. I find it difficult to formulate the question
I would like to ask here, but perhaps it could be expressed
if I ask you to situate S/Z in relation to the passage I
quoted from* Semiotiké.

The first question, as far as I can see, comes down to this: Can
semiology allow us, through the intermediary of the concept of
connotation, to return to a kind of sociology of literature? (We're
not discussing the epistemological problem of sociology, a science
which is presently much criticized from a political and ideological
point of view; I'm not considering this problem; whether it's called
sociology or something else is of no concern to me.) I would say
that there is in fact a possibility of sociological exploitation in
S/Z through the identification of its textual codes, because at least
four of the five codes I identified are, or could be, answerable to
sociology: the proairetic code (actions), the semic code (psychological semes), the cultural code (knowledge), and the hermeneutic code (the search for truth, for a solution to the mystery of
the text). For example, one could reread Balzac seeking out cultural intertextuality (the references to knowledge), a rather dense,
sometimes even nauseating, layer in the Balzacian text. This
would be a good problem to tackle, because then we could doubtless see that these cultural codes have marked each author in a
different way. For example, Flaubert also came to grips with
cultural codes; he was truly bogged down in them, and he tried,
in complete contrast to Balzac, to free himself from them through
ambiguous attitudes, irony, plagiarism, simulation; as a result,
we have that vertiginous book, so amazingly modern, *Bouvard
and Pécuchet*. Thus, it would be possible to base a kind of cultural
sociology on literary semiotics, but once again, even there, it
would have to be a freshly conceived literary sociology, one which
could and should profit from what I would call the intertextual
sensibility, a sensitivity to the intertext. I think that such a sensitivity to intertextuality could lead to new horizons. The first
rule of this intertextual analysis would be to understand, for ex-

ample, that the intertext *is not* a problem of sources, because a
source is a declared origin, whereas the intertext is of indeter-
minable origin.

Having said that, there is a fifth code in *S/Z*, which I called
the *symbolic field*. This code, as its name indicates, is a kind of
catchall, I admit; I would also say, however, that it's probably on
the level of this symbolic code that what could be called the
quality of the work is played out, and even its *value* (giving this
word considerable importance, and an almost Nietzschean ac-
ceptation): the scale of value for literary works would be roughly
the range from stereotype to symbol. We should look at mass
culture, which has at bottom a very impoverished symbolic field,
while its stereotypical or endoxal field is very important (an Aristotelian word: the status of *endoxa*, of strong public opinion);
on the contrary, in classical works (I'm not talking about modern
works, which have another viewpoint on the symbolic, but about
classical texts—and romantic texts, too, of course), it's the symbolic that predominates, not only by its richness, density, and
breadth, but also by its devious character. That is what would
finally permit a kind of qualitative differentiation of works and
would perhaps enable us to answer that formidable question,
whether there is in fact good and bad literature, and if it is possible
to distinguish between them using structural criteria.

As to your second question, it's quite well put, so well put, in
fact, that it's not easy to frame a reply. I'll give you an ambiguous
answer.

I would say that, on the one hand, it's Kristeva's first definition—"We isolate a measurable and thus representable aspect of
the signifying system against the background of a nonmeasurable
concept"—which coincides with *S/Z*, because *S/Z* can be read,
understood, as a representation of Balzac's novella *Sarrasine*. It's
a representation because there is analysis, the enumeration of
codes and terms: it's an analytical representation, but it's still a
representation. Moreover, I offer as proof of this reading of *S/Z*
Sollers's article on *S/Z* as the reading of a representation: it's
because he considered *S/Z* as representation that he was able to
analyze the book, unifying and deciphering it from a political
and historico-ideological point of view, in a powerful and pen-

etrating manner. But, on the other hand, and this is the second part of the ambiguity, *S/Z* is not entirely a representation, that is to say an analytical commentary, because, as you said, *S/Z* is *written*. I don't mean, as I have often explained before, that it is well written; that's not where the problem lies, although one should never be too quick to reject the requirement of style. The fact that *S/Z* conforms to certain stylistic values in the traditional sense of the word is important, because style is a beginning of writing, in that it is a rejection of *écrivance*: to accept style means that one refuses to consider language as a pure instrument of transmission, and that is a beginning of writing. But if *S/Z* belongs to the activity of writing, it's not only on the level of the crafting of sentences, but above all because I labored over what used to be called the composition, i.e., the arrangement, the organization of the lexias and their commentaries, the digressions. If I think back to when I wrote the book (I wrote and rewrote, I took a great deal of trouble over it, with passionate interest), I'd say that I don't remember at all those moments when what are usually called ideas came to me, but I have a vivid memory of the time I spent struggling to piece the book together, and that's why I consider it to be *written*. (That's also why the book *S/Z* is an entirely different object from the *seminar S/Z*, which I gave at the École Pratique des Hautes Études before I wrote the book, even though they both deal with the same conceptual material.) To the extent to which *S/Z* is written, it escapes its own analytical commentary and belongs to textual productivity. I might add that there were two types of reaction to *S/Z* (I mean, *forms* of reaction): there was the traditional reaction, critical articles and reviews in the press, which are absolutely necessary for the book to be able to play, as it must, the social game— and then there was the other reaction, the letters: I received letters from readers, some of whom I didn't know, which linked up with the reading of *S/Z*, multiplying the meanings I had found and finding others; they would tell me, often in a very intelligent— and in any case, by definition, unchallengeable—manner, that I could have found such and such a connotation for this lexia, etc. I would say that, for me, the true justification of my work was not in the reaction of the critics but in these letters, because they showed that I had succeeded, even timidly, in creating an infinite commentary, or rather a perpetual commentary, as one might say a perpetual calendar.

In speaking of the concept of intertextuality, you said that "if literature is a dialogue of writings, then obviously the whole space of history returns in literary language in an entirely new way . . ." Is this the direction of that history of literary forms heralded by Writing Degree Zero?

In a way, what has been done since is a history of writing. The problem is that, at the time of *Writing Degree Zero*, I was thinking of a much more traditional history, I didn't have a new conception of history; I was thinking rather vaguely of a history of writing that would more or less follow the model of literary history, but simply switch objects. Since then, obviously, things have changed: I now feel that we require something else of historical discourse, and that is probably one of the more censored problems of current thought, even of avant-garde thought, which is fighting over history without really rethinking the *discourse* of history. Can we now conceive of a historical discourse—I don't mean a concept of history, but a historical discourse—that would not naïvely offer itself as such? What kind would it be? What resistance would it encounter? And so on. These are the questions that should be asked. In the end, I always feel that history is some sort of bastion that must be taken: not at all to pillage history, as structuralism has been vulgarly accused of wanting to do, but to bring down its walls, to break up historical discourse and transform it into *another* discourse, from which history would not be absent, but which would no longer be historical discourse. What could this other historical discourse be, which would then support the history of writing? I don't know, but I do think that we can already have some sort of idea by looking at the work of Michel Foucault.

The analysis of Sarrasine, *which you intended as textual theory, seems necessarily to have constructed itself as a course in reading (couldn't your entire oeuvre, beginning with* Mythologies, *which was a course in demythicizing*

reading, be defined as a propaedeutics of reading?). Do
you think your research is within the framework of a
general theory of reading, and what would be the prob-
lems and directions for development in such a theory?

In fact, what I tried to begin in S/Z is an identification between
the notions of writing and reading: I wanted to "crush" them into
each other. I'm not the only one, this is a theme now circulating
throughout the avant-garde. Once again, the problem is not to
pass from writing to reading, or from literature to reading, or
from author to reader; the problem is one of a change in object,
as has been said, a change in the level of perception: both writing
and reading should be conceived, worked, defined, and redefined
together. Because if they continue to be separated (often insidi-
ously, perfidiously—we're constantly led to separate writing from
reading), what happens? We produce a theory of literature which,
if reading is isolated from writing, can never be anything but a
theory on the sociological or phenomenological order, according
to which reading will always be defined as a projection of writing,
and the reader as a poor, mute "brother" of the writer. We'll be
dragged backward once more toward a theory of expressiveness,
style, creation, or the instrumentality of language. And so we
must *block* these two notions.

Which doesn't mean that there are not, in the meantime,
reading problems of a reformist nature, if I may put it that way:
there is in fact a real problem, a practical, human, social problem,
which is the question of whether one can learn to read texts, or
whether one can change actual, practical reading in relation to
social groups, whether one can learn to read or to not read or to
reread texts outside of academic and cultural conditioning. I'm
convinced that all these things haven't been studied or even considered as problems. For example, we're conditioned to read literature according to a certain rhythm of reading: we ought to find
out if, in changing the rhythm of reading, we would thereby
obtain alterations of understanding; by reading faster or slower,
we might find that things which seemed opaque could become
dazzling. There is also, for example—here I'm talking about
technical reading problems—the problem of conditioned expec-

tations of development, of the unfolding of a narrated story that must avoid all repetitions. And this is really quite a paradox, the fact that our endoxal civilization, a mass civilization that lives embedded in a world of stereotypes and repetitions, loudly proclaims that it is absolutely allergic to any text that seems to repeat itself, to contain repetitions. We had an example just recently, Guyotat's book *Eden Eden Eden*, which almost all the critics hypocritically declared to be unreadable because it seems to repeat itself. It should be suggested to readers that there are several possible ways of reading, one isn't obliged to read a book in a linear and continuous development; nothing forces us to read Guyotat like a potboiler, or even like Flaubert's *Sentimental Education*, from beginning to end; but people won't accept this. It's amazing: they find nothing wrong with dipping here and there into the Bible, but then they insist that there's no other way to read Guyotat except straight through! So there are problems of conditioned reading that ought to be at least formulated one day, problems that should be given due attention.

> *In 1963 you said: "What I'm wondering now is whether there might be arts that are by nature, by technique, more or less reactionary. I think this is so in literature. I don't think that a literature of the left is possible. A problematical literature, yes, that is to say a literature of suspended meaning: an art that provokes answers but does not give them." Is this definition of literature as more or less reactionary valid for all literature, or only for a particular literary period, as the analyses of* Writing Degree Zero *would seem to indicate?*

Let's say that the word "reactionary," which I have used and occasionally still use, perhaps through a lack of imagination, is really too strong here, too monological ("theological"). I think that literature, even classical literature, is never completely reactionary, just as revolutionary and progressive literature is at bottom, even when it's extremely conservative in its form and contents, a literature that is in part paragrammatical, carnivalesque; it is contradictory by its very structure, which is both servile and contestatory. Its status is contradictory and paradoxical, more-over, in the etymological sense of these words, in a way that has not been well explored.

Today we still continue this literature, we are still caught up in this ambiguity, because we're trapped in repetition: it simply gets repeated—since Mallarmé, we French have invented noth-ing, we repeat Mallarmé, and we're even lucky when it's Mal-larmé we're repeating! There haven't been any great innovative texts in French literature since Mallarmé.

That's the case with James Joyce in English literature.

Yes. It's a problem. I'm very interested these days in this problem of innovative, mutant texts, a problem linked to stereotype and repetition. For example, it's obvious that the writings of Marx were a mutant text, but since then we've been repeating this discourse—there hasn't been a new mutation. Lenin, Gramsci, Mao—all very important, but their discourse is a repetition of Marx.

Foucault speaks precisely of Marx and Freud as founders of discursiveness: whereas someone like Galileo founds a science that develops, extending itself beyond the space of its discourse, Marx, as well as Freud, founds a scientific discourse that is constantly returning toward its source, questioning, analyzing, perpetually rereading it. Would this be close to your conception of the problem of rep-etition?

That's exactly it; moreover, I considered taking as the subject of this year's seminar a text by Freud—considered as a mutant text.

You have said that today "we produce theory and not works . . . I'm talking about what is commonly called literature." Doesn't such a formulation imply the tradi-tional opposition between theory and practice that you have rejected elsewhere (for example, by referring to Julia Kristeva's Semiotiké as a "work," une oeuvre)? Wouldn't

a nontheoretical work belong nowadays to that more or
less reactionary literature that must be challenged by a
theory of writing?

Julia Kristeva's work is considered theoretical; it *is* theoretical.
However, it is considered theoretical in the sense of *abstract*,
difficult, because it is believed that theory is abstraction and difficulty. And her book is criticized in large part with just those
accusations—too abstract, too difficult. But of course "theoretical" doesn't mean "abstract"; from my point of view, it means
reflexive, i.e., turning back on itself: a discourse that looks back
on itself is thereby a theoretical discourse. After all, the epony-
mous hero, the mythical hero of theory could be Orpheus, precisely because he is the one who looks back on what he loves,
even at the risk of destroying it; in looking back at Eurydice, he
makes her vanish, he kills her a second time. This retrospection
must be done, even at the cost of destruction. At that point, theory,
which I personally think of as corresponding to a very definite
historical phase in Western societies, would also correspond to a
paranoiac phase, in the nonpejorative sense of the term, which
is to say a scientific phase, a phase in the wisdom of our society
(a phase eminently superior, of course, to the infantile phase that
coexists with it and consists in not reflecting on language, in
speaking without turning language back upon itself, in manip-
ulating a kind of simpleton's language: obviously, this refusal to
turn language back upon itself is an open invitation to major
ideological impostures).

Do you feel any constraints in connection with such a
view of language, or more generally, of your own work?

Do I feel any constraints? From a certain point of view, I ought
to answer yes, because after all it would be complete madness to
think that I write without constraints. But at the same time, on
an existential level, I can say that I don't feel any constraints in
what I do. Why? Let's just say that I take pleasure (in the strong
sense of the word) in playing the social game, not in a full and
emphatic fashion, but on a more profound level, by virtue of a

certain ethics of the game; which means that at bottom, on the level of what happens to what I write or how it fits into society, I have no personal claims to make: I have neither complaints nor desires to formulate. I write, it's launched into communication: period. I have nothing more to say about it, and I would even say that it's this acceptance that amuses me, because it obliges me to place my own work in the perspective of a certain "paragrammatical" (plural, multiple, ambiguous) status. Because, as always, the main problem—for me at least—is to foil the signified, thwart the law, baffle the father, frustrate repression—I don't mean to explode it, but to *outplay* it. I feel at ease wherever there is the possibility of paragrammatical work, a certain paragrammatical tracing of my own text. If I ever really had to write a critical appraisal of my own work, I would center everything on "paragrammatism."

In general, everything that is revindication, contestation, protestation, always seems boring and flat to me. That's why I feel a bit off to one side, in a way; I don't feel very much in tune with a somewhat newer style, particularly regarding young people. Let's say that everything based on the "happening" in the largest sense of the word seems to me very dull and impoverished when compared to the values and activities of cheating; I will always defend play against the "happening." There is not enough play in the "happening" because there is no superior game without codes. And so one must take on codes; in order to outplay them, it is necessary to enter into them.

> *I think one clearly feels, in* Mythologies, *that you are fascinated by the codes you are outmaneuvering.*

Absolutely. To the point that I'm fascinated by aggressive code forms, such as stupidity.

Moreover, to get back somewhat to the question of constraints, I would say that what we ought to do is retrace not the biography of a writer but what could be called the writing of his work, a kind of ergography. In my case, the history of what I've written is the history of a game, a playful succession of texts that I have tried out: which is to say that I've tried out registers of different models, different fields of citations; *The Fashion System* is, thus, a certain register of citations, of models, one turned much more toward that quasi-scientific writing I call *écrivance* than toward reflexive writing. Why? Because for my work on fashion, the writing was in the fabrication of the system, in the *bricolage*, and not in the account rendered, the scription of the book. There, for once, the writing is really not in the book: it was in what I did alone beforehand, and it's that alone, moreover, that I remember. Whereas for *Empire of Signs*, it's quite different: in this book I gave myself the freedom of entering completely into the signifier, of *writing*, even in the stylistic sense we were talking about earlier, and I particularly allowed myself the freedom of writing in fragments. Obviously, the difficulty is that the role I'm expected to play in the intelligentsia doesn't involve the signifier: I'm expected to contribute support of a theoretical and pedagogical order, I'm assigned a place in the history of ideas, when I'm much more enticed now by an activity that would really delve into the signifier. I would say that the constraint is there, if there is one; not at all a constraint of a truly editorial, economical nature, but a constraint of the *imago*, an imago changed into an economic demand; I'm almost never asked for anything that could be the equivalent for me of what I wrote on Japan. The *imago* brings demands to bear on us that do not correspond to our true desires.

> *Derrida affirms in* Of Grammatology *that "the end of linear writing is indeed the end of the book, even if it is still in the form of the book that new writings, whether literary or theoretical, take shape, after their own fashion." These new writings are the ones you described at the beginning of* S/Z *in your discussion of the* writerly *text. How do you conceive of "the end of the book" Derrida talks about?*

To answer you, I'll play a bit on words. You ask: "How do you conceive of the end of the book"; I'm not sure what to reply to the verb itself. In fact, I don't *foresee* this end of the book, I mean that I can't make it fit into a social or historical programming; at the very most, I might be able to *see* it, insofar as *to see* contrasts with to *foresee* as a utopian and phantasmatic activity. But, in truth, I cannot see the end of the book because that would be to see my own death; which is to say that I can hardly speak of it, except mythically, as something caught up in the Heraclitean play of history.

Having said that, I can add, giving you a more realistic and disquieting answer, that barbarism (that barbarism which Lenin posited as the very alternative to socialism) is always possible. One can therefore have an apocalyptic vision of the end of the book, which would not disappear—far from it—but would triumph in its most abject forms: the book of mass communication, of consumption, the capitalistic book, in the sense in which a capitalistic society would at that point eliminate all possible play of marginal forms, so that no further cheating and evasion would be possible. And that would be complete barbarism: the death of the book would correspond to the exclusive reign of the readerly, legible book and the total defeat of the "illegible" book.

> *You have always defined literary criticism as the deciphement of a text in order to be able to read it within its own truth, its final meaning, thus immobilizing the plural of the text. Your own work (and S/Z is exemplary here) continues, as a textual semiotics, "just this side of" criticism, so to speak—which seems a more radical venture, more critical, in the strong sense of the word. Do you think there still remains an authentic role for criticism? Isn't it fatally implicated in that complicity of the sign analyzed by Julia Kristeva?*

I'm not sure I remember ever having defined criticism as a hermeneutics, but it's always possible; I don't insist on having always said the same thing. But I think that I was in favor, in *Critique et Vérité*, in any case, of a non-alethic function for criticism, a symbolic and polysemic function. What I would like to say here is that a distinction could be made between critical *roles* and critical *activity*. It's always possible to imagine critical roles and their continuation, even the continuation of traditional roles, which will not necessarily be useless; Schönberg said that even after the eventual triumph of avant-garde music—and that was the music for which one ought to fight—it would still be possible to make beautiful music in C major. I would say that it will always be possible to write good criticism in C major.

> *I just wanted to touch on that opposition you seem to establish between criticism and semiology: criticism would be the activity of someone who wants to immobilize signs, to search for a definitive meaning (which could only be ideological), whereas semiology or textual semiotics as practiced in S/Z by you, as a semiologist, would be on the contrary an answer, a response to the plural of the text, which would thus remain in a way just this side of criticism . . .*

Yes, that is what I wanted to do in S/Z. I don't excommunicate what I call criticism in C major, but I distinguish between critical roles and critical activity, which is no longer a critic's activity, but simply the activity of a writer. It's an activity of the text, of the intertext, of commentary, in that at bottom one can conceive of writing infinitely on past texts, or at least I can. Now, one could very well imagine a time when *works* in the traditional sense of the word would no longer be written, and the works of the past would be rewritten endlessly, "endlessly" in the sense of "perpetually": there would be an activity of proliferating commentary, branching out, recurrent, which would be the true writing activity of our time. After all, it's not unthinkable, since the Middle Ages did just that, and it would be better to go back to the Middle Ages, to what is called the barbarism of the Middle Ages, than to accept a barbarism of repetition; it would be better perpetually to rewrite *Bouvard and Pécuchet* than to stay in the unavowed repetition of stereotypes. Obviously I'm talking about a perpetual commentary that serious theoretical analysis would take beyond the stage of paraphrase to "crack" texts and obtain something else.

> *Last year you participated in the Cerisy conference on current problems in the teaching of literature. What do*

you think are the main problems? What valid form could the teaching of literature take at present?

I don't quite know what to answer. I don't know if literature *should* be taught. If one thinks that it should, then one should accept, shall we say, a reformist perspective, and in that case one becomes a "joiner": one joins the university to change things, one joins the schools to change the way literature is taught. In the main, I would be more or less inclined, by personal temperament, to this provisional, localized reformism. In this case, teaching would be directed toward exploding the literary text as much as possible. The pedagogical problem would be to shake up the notion of the literary text and to make adolescents understand that there is text everywhere, but that not everything is text; I mean that there is text everywhere, but repetition, stereotype, and *doxa* are also everywhere. That's the goal: the distinction between this textuality, which is not to be found only in literature, and society's neurotic, repetitive activity. People should be made to realize that we have a right of access to texts that are not printed as texts, as I did with Japan, for example, by learning to read the text and fabric of life, of the street. We should perhaps even redo biographies as writings of life, no longer based on real or historical referents. There would be a whole spectrum of projects, tasks that would be directed roughly toward a *disappropriation* of the text.

Politique-Hebdo, January 13, 1972
From an interview conducted by Jean Duflot

The Fatality of Culture, the Limits of Counterculture

Sade, Fourier, Loyola has just been published, there has been a special issue of Tel Quel, *and appearances on television and in the leftist press . . . Does this return of Roland Barthes to the spotlight herald some new discovery, some new dramatic commitment? Roland Barthes has never really been away, and he continues, within the problematics of culture, what he considers the chief task of present-day subversion: the elucidation of writing "which follows, step by step, the rending of bourgeois culture."*

At a time when great confusion reigns in the field of subversive action, when violence (the language of violence) exhausts itself in often arbitrary and thoughtless sorties, his reflections on the limits of counterculture are of great interest.

> *You have been credited with this paradoxical self-definition: "I am in the rear guard of the avant-garde" . . .*

There is a certain historical dialectic that makes it difficult to be sure of one's position in terms of a rear or an advance guard. In fact, it should be remembered that the notion of an avant-garde is itself historical, dating more or less from the beginning of the twentieth century. Since the First World War, avant-gardes have followed each other in ever more rapid succession in Europe, and a reasonably objective historical picture of this development would show that until now they have almost always ended up by being absorbed by institutions, normal culture, current opinion.

This movement of perpetual recuperation can be quite rapid. I need only mention the way in which French culture has recuperated Surrealism, a movement which for a long time was considered the very prototype of the avant-garde. Nowadays, Surrealism—I'm not making any judgment on its contents, only on the use made of them—is to be found above all in the display windows of big department stores and elegant boutiques.

If you take the example of film, the process of recuperation is even more pronounced. How many films have there been which seemed firmly avant-garde, quite outside the current commercial sector, and which a simple twist of fashion made into fads, popular successes!

Avant-garde activity is extremely fragile, it is destined to be recuperated, doubtless because we live in an alienated and capitalistic society which supports and indeed needs to support the phenomena of fashion for economic reasons. Unfortunately (and unfortunately for our interview), we are not currently able to reflect seriously on all these cultural phenomena as they occur in other societies, historically or socially liberated societies.

The example of Soviet society is not conclusive: it cannot be said that it has produced cultural liberation as we conceive of it. China's example would doubtless be more convincing, but we must admit that we lack information. With the result that, here in the West, the de-alienation of culture can take only a utopian form.

> *Isn't there some confusion between the "avant-garde" and militant extremism?*

The whole problem is to understand whether it is a kind of congenital characteristic of the avant-garde to engage in activities which are violent or spectacularly subversive. This may not be so. I am personally opposed to violence, except in precise political cases. I'm drawing on classic analyses of the Leninist type, where

violence is something that must be directed toward well-defined
tactical ends, not adopted as a permanent ethical attitude. Personally, I feel that there is a great deal of work to be done in a
kind of underground subversion, apart from spectacularly violent
and destructive activities.

> *The counterculture, as it's called, is a phenomenon that
> has its roots in the formation of a new American left and
> in those intellectual sectors close to it. What is your
> analysis of their activities?*

Historical justification can be made for countercultural activities,
which are historically necessary insofar as they exemplify a certain
nihilistic action, which is one of the current tasks of a counter-
civilization. That said, I must add that in the present state of
things these countercultural forms seem to me to be, above all,
languages of *expression*: their main usefulness is in permitting
certain individuals or small social groups to *express themselves*,
to liberate themselves on the level of expression. But I see a very
great difference between the expression and the action of language: between language as expression and language as transformation, as production.

> *But doesn't this expressive activity produce any results?*

I'm trying to ascertain the importance of these movements in a
dialectical fashion, to see how they are useful, but also to understand that they do not necessarily represent, despite appearances, the most radical form of subversion.

> *How do you explain the power this expressive culture
> has over young people, especially through its music?*

There is the corporeal, sensual content of rock music, which is
very important to this countercultural form; it expresses a new
relation to the body, and it should be defended. The example I
find most interesting, however, because it is the most intelligent
(and intelligible), is conceptual art, which aims at the destruction

of traditional art objects—paintings, expositions, museums—and at the same time produces theoretical texts of a high intelligence. What disappoints me somewhat, if I may say so, is that, aside from conceptual art, the other countercultural movements we could mention, such as pop art, rock music, the underground, all end up by destroying discourse, renouncing any attempt at theorization.

Now, in our present society, theory is the subversive weapon par excellence. I'm not saying that this holds true in other countries, in other historical states. One could very well imagine a state—and this is probably true of China—where revolutionary conditions are such that the relations between theory and practice are already completely modified, and the role of theory is, thus, no longer the same there as it is for us. I feel that, in our case, theoretical work is still vital. So I take these countercultural movements more seriously when they take a stab at intelligence, when they accept the responsibility of producing an intelligent discourse regarding their goals and actions.

> *Isn't it the illusion of a certain cultural extremism to believe that one's language is situated outside ideology, as if it were a language cut off and liberated by a division between classes?*

I would like to emphasize two points. The first is my profound conviction (which my work has reflected for twenty years) that everything is language, nothing escapes language, all of society is permeated by language. Therefore, in a certain sense, everything is cultural, and it is impossible to be part of a nonculture. Culture is a fate to which we are condemned. To engage in radical countercultural activity is therefore simply to move language around, and, unless one is very careful, to rely on the same stereotypes, language fragments which already exist.

I would say that violence itself is a code that is quite well worn, one might say time-honored, even anthropological: violence in itself hardly represents an unheard-of innovation. To advocate the radical destruction of culture thus seems to me rather thoughtless, relatively ineffective, and valuable only as a form of expres-

sion. As soon as the problem is considered in terms of a broader
historical task, it becomes clear that the only solution is to accept
the inevitability of culture. One must therefore work for its destruction or transformation from within. From without, such an
attitude is merely decorative.

What do you mean by transformation from within?

Society imposes divided languages on us (we live in a division of
language which is a sign of our society's alienation). But, when
we place ourselves outside certain types of language—we should
do this, and we all do it—we mustn't forget that we always do
this from the standpoint of another language, never a nonlanguage. From then on, in all honesty, we are embarked on an
infinite process of self-criticism, of criticism of our own language.
This is an attitude of reflexivity (we were speaking just now of
theory, to me it's the same thing), which can have an effect on
culture: this attitude is linked to the extremely vigilant perception
of one's own position in language. Any individual, no matter
how revolutionary he claims to be, who does not consider the
position from which he himself speaks, is a counterfeit revolutionary.

*Isn't this position usually that of a mostly marginal petite
bourgeoisie?*

We don't have enough information on that point; moreover, there
are relays between a social class, its determinations, and the meanings (the myths) it elaborates which are poorly understood. So I
don't know what class furnishes the actors of counterculture, but
if they do come from the petite bourgeoisie, it should be remembered that that isn't a disgrace, given that one of the tasks of this
century is to learn how the petite bourgeoisie can itself become
a progressive class. I believe that if we do not find the answer to
that question, history might hang fire for a long time. On the
cultural plane, we can say that petit-bourgeois culture reproduces
bourgeois culture—"as farce," and that ridiculous imitation is so-

called mass culture. So there is no social class, no group that is safe from this general contagion of petit-bourgeois culture.

> *You have written that what characterizes French culture is the aggressive rise of the petite bourgeoisie, which began to challenge the hegemony of grand-bourgeois culture . . .*

Perhaps what dominates this second half of the twentieth century, at least in France, is a great settling of scores between the bourgeoisie and the petite bourgeoisie. The historical problem is to find out if the petite bourgeoisie is going to break through within the general framework of a capitalistic situation (of the Pompidou type) or along the lines of a French Communist Party program.

I should like to add that all these countercultural movements—and here we return to the tenaciously dialectical evaluation we must apply to them—endeavor to promote a kind of nihilism. And it is this which partially justifies their actions, it seems to me. In fact, I believe that nihilism is the only possible philosophy for our current situation. But I must immediately add that I do not confuse nihilism with violent, radically destructive behavior, or—on a deeper level—with behavior that is more or less neurotic or hysterical.

Nihilism is a type of reflection and utterance (because problems must always be framed in terms of language) which demands an effort of intelligence and a certain mastery of language. It should not be forgotten that the philosopher who carried nihilistic thought to its furthest reach is Nietzsche, and remember also that he is still unknown or poorly known in France. The forms of nihilistic theory and action we can imagine at present may often seem discreet, stifled, marginal, even courteous, but that doesn't mean that they may not be more profoundly nihilistic than forms of action which seem more radical.

> *How do you resolve the contradiction between the need for a specific, highly technical language, such as the one you use for your theoretical work, and the need for a*

*politicization of the social strata we've just been discuss-
ing?*

That is a problem, and I'm not the only one who has run into
it. Obviously, our work takes place within small groups. This
work has its esoteric aspects, and it is definitely not meant to
appeal to what are called *the masses*. This should be made very
clear, so that there are no misunderstandings on this point. But
I do feel that this relatively closeted work is necessary to the *mise
en scène* of a destruction of meaning. Our task, as intellectuals,
is not politicization but a critique of meanings, a critique of
meaning itself.

On the cultural level, French society is so dominated by petit-
bourgeois cultural models that one would have to compromise
oneself (and one's actions) within these models in order to reach
the vast majority of people.

Having said that, one could certainly ask oneself, in the wake
of Brecht—and that is the role of *creators* (for example in the
theater, the cinema)—whether one couldn't attempt to build an
art which would have a great power of communication, in relation
to French society as it actually is, in its very alienation, an art
which would also comprise serious elements (I would even say
severe elements) of progressivism, subversion, or nihilism.

It's up to the creators to search and to discover. We might add
that even if these creators were to arrive at an effective result,
they would find a mass of difficulties on the level of the diffusion,
the dissemination of their work. There is incontestable censorship
on the level of cultural institutions (on the radio, the television,
perhaps even at school and at the universities) which would be
automatically reinforced. There has always been a barrage of
resistance as soon as an art form begins to seem subversive. But
it is not the most violent forms which are the most dangerous.

Les Lettres françaises, February 9, 1972
From an interview conducted by Jean Ristat

Pleasure / Writing / Reading

In Sade, Fourier, Loyola *you examine three inventors
of writing, instead of the philosophy of evil, utopian
socialism, or the mystique of obedience. Your analysis
of those three founders of languages continues the undertaking launched so masterfully with* Writing Degree
Zero, *almost twenty years ago.* Empire of Signs *and*
Sade, Fourier, Loyola *introduce a new reflection on the
pleasure of the text. It seems as though we should
"pluralize" the history of your work, perhaps divide it into
two periods . . .*

Your last sentence could stand as the emblem of everything cultural, always multidimensional, springing from a plural history.
On the level of my personal work, this history covers some twenty
years, and in this history, *Sade, Fourier, Loyola* plays an almost
obsessive role: I mean that once again the subject is writing. This
has been my chosen subject since *Writing Degree Zero*, and it
has obviously passed through several avatars. At times, I tried to
formulate my reflections in a seemingly more scientific manner,
as with *The Fashion System*. Fashion language is certainly not a
literary language. But having abandoned the idea of investigating
the system of actual fashion, or photographed fashion, in order
to consider fashion only as it is described in magazines, it is quite
clear that I returned to my obsession: language, particularly written language. *Sade, Fourier, Loyola* continues this research on

secondary discourses or languages. It is only a variation (in the musical sense) of a life's work.

Empire of Signs *is the starting point for a new phase . . .*

I do begin my consideration of the pleasure of the text in that book. I deciphered the text of Japanese life as I saw it. What I described was definitely not the technological, capitalistic Japan but a very phantasmatic Japan. *Empire of Signs* permitted me to liberate what Gérard Genette discerned in my work as "a kind of ethics of the sign." I have no neutral relations to signs: I've always been passionately interested by the decipherment of signs in societies or literature. I should add that this relationship is ambivalent. Sometimes I am liberated by codes because they generate security. Societies like ours, a prey to alienation and anxiety, need the clarity and permanence of signs to reassure themselves. A well-made code is always reassuring, even if it is restrictive. But at the same time I am easily oppressed by signs. I cannot tolerate languages or societies that neutralize signs: they "live" the signs but refuse to proclaim them as such. In other words, they do not experience the signs for what they are: products of history, ideological elaborations of meaning. This intolerance was the spark for my *Mythologies*, for example.

The Japan I wrote about was for me a countermythology, a kind of happiness of signs, a country which, as the result of a very fragile and quite unusual historical situation, finds itself completely plunged into modernity and yet so close to the feudal period that it can maintain a kind of semantic luxury which has not yet been flattened out, tamed by mass civilization, by the consumer society.

And so you found in Japan what you call a "happiness of signs." Would you describe what you mean by that?

On the one hand, very strong and subtle codes are never naturalized (they show themselves off *as* sign systems), and on the other hand, they never refer to ultimate signifieds, to stable, closed signifieds. Perhaps this has to do with the Japanese past, with their religious history, the weight of paganism, or even Zen Buddhism. Japan has not had as close a relation to monological discourse as our Judeo-Islamic-Christian countries have had. Japan gave me a kind of "writing courage." I was happy to write that text. It enabled me to settle a bit farther into that hedonistic space, or rather that erotic space of the text, of reading, of the signifier. Now I am quite tempted to continue along this path, to write texts of pleasure and to include in textual theory a reflection on the pleasure and seduction of the text. One almost has to speak of the Don Juanism of the text. Why does a text seduce, what is the seduction of a text? Is the pleasure of the text purely cultural? Does it depend on cultural levels, or is it more corporeal—and if so, would it then be in a highly mediated dialectical relationship with culture? That's the sort of question I would like to begin asking.

> *It gave you pleasure to read Sade, Fourier, and Loyola. To read Sade with pleasure is inadmissible in our society; a more subtle rejection takes the form of the usual philosophical approach (the philosophy of evil, for example), or a study of Sade as a pathological case. Pleasure does not have the same origin in Loyola as it does in Fourier— where do you find it in your reading of those two authors?*

I have always greatly enjoyed reading Sade, contrary to the current opinion that Sade is a boring author. I read him, like everyone else, in a very casual fashion, skipping passages. Not always the same passages. He is the writer who has given me the greatest reading pleasure. I know of no other writer in our literature beside Proust, on a completely different level, of course, who provides this same kind of pleasure in reading and infinite rereading. From this point of view, Fourier is more anthological. There are pieces by Fourier which have an intense power to caress, but there are also unbearable redundancies. He is much more difficult to read because there is no plot, no novelistic thread. The pleasure of reading him is less syntactic, more semantic, more "poetic" in the classical sense of the term. As for Loyola, it's difficult to speak about this kind of pleasure, above all when one is at a distance from Christian discourse; it's impossible for me to "invest" myself there, even in the guise of revolt. Loyola's discourse neither irritates me nor affords me real pleasure, but he has provided me with the elements of an enthralling linguistic reconstruction. A bit like the pleasure Champollion and all the other language decipherers may have known, the ones Jakobson calls the cryptanalysts.

> *The misunderstandings such a subject can give rise to shouldn't be underestimated, however; to say that one is going to undertake a theoretical consideration of pleasure can or will appear to go against the current of modern thought itself. I can easily imagine the sort of thing that some people would be ready to exploit. Why do you feel that what you're doing now is work that is necessary to the avant-garde?*

To undertake a theoretical consideration of the pleasure of the text has tactical value. For a long time I wrote mostly ideological criticism: *Mythologies*, for example, and *Critical Essays*. These days, the chores of ideological criticism have been taken up to a certain extent by everyone. It is not avant-gardist work; there is much redundancy and mere verbiage in ideological criticism, as it is practiced by students, for example. It must therefore be refined, made more subtle. It's one thing to become aware of ideology, to dissect it is another: subtlety and intelligence are required (by intelligence I mean a quality of operation, not a psychological value). This collective task has already been taken up by a whole section of the French intelligentsia, while a theory of pleasure, on the contrary, is waiting for constructive, combative action.

Why is this the case? Because today the intellectual's idiolect has become politicized; in saying this, I leave aside the problem of political options, and remain on the plane of language. Politicized language takes its terminological and phraseological models from a generally Marxist theoretical literature, which naturally excludes the problem of pleasure. Speaking frankly, it seems to me that in much of the counter-ideological work being done in

France today, work that is indeed necessary, there is nevertheless a law, a censorship, a foreclosure of pleasure. The current promotion of eroticism, even in intellectual milieux, is not very interesting. What must be understood and described is not genital eroticism and its problems of liberation and censorship. Intellectual effort should be directed toward secondary sexuality, and in particular toward the sexuality of language. Language as a sexual or erotic space has nothing to do with the eroticism of mass culture. The work of the avant-garde is to lift the erotic interdiction which unfortunately permeates politicized and counterideological languages, making these discourses gloomy, heavy, repetitious, obsessive, and boring.

> *Would you say something further about the rather enigmatic "site of reading." You write: "This obfuscation appears at the very moment when one vilifies bourgeois ideology the most—without ever asking oneself from what site one is speaking about or against this ideology: is it the space of nondiscourse ('We're through with talking, no more writing—into the streets')? Is it the space of a counterdiscourse ('We should argue against class culture')?"*

Each time there is a vituperative attack against bourgeois ideology, there is conjointly a kind of occultation of the question: *From what position do I speak?* I simply wanted to protest, which all modernity has done since Blanchot, in favor of essentially reflexive discourses that initiate, imitate within themselves the infinite nature of language, discourses that never finish up with the demonstration of a signified. In trying to bring to light a reflection on the eroticism of reading, I am simply countering dogmatic discourse. Nowadays dogmatic discourse and terrorist discourse are lumped together in the same accusation. Dogmatic discourse is based on a signified, and tends to valorize language through the existence of an ultimate signified—which explains the well-known relationship between dogmatic discourse and theological discourse. The signified often takes the form of a Cause: political, ethical, religious, etc. But from the moment discourse (I'm not talking about the options of an individual) lets itself be stopped when it comes up against a signified, it becomes dogmatic. Terrorist discourse has aggressive characteristics one may or may not approve of, but it remains within the signifier: it manipulates language as a more or less ludic deployment of signifiers.

There is no place without language: one cannot contrast language, what is verbal (and even verbose), with some pure and dignified space which would be the space of reality and truth, a space outside language. Everything is language, or more precisely, language is everywhere. It permeates the whole of reality; there is nothing real without language. Any attitude that consists in hiding from language behind a nonlanguage or a supposedly neutral or insignificant language is an attitude of bad faith. The only possible subversion in language is to displace things. Bourgeois culture is within us: in our syntax, in the way we speak, perhaps even in a part of our pleasure. We cannot move into nondiscourse because it doesn't exist. Even the most terrorist, the most extremist attitudes can be rapidly recuperated by bourgeois culture. The only combat that remains to us is not frank, out in the open, but most often muffled, insidious. This combat doesn't always end in triumph, but it must attempt to displace, to shift languages. We are trying to create, with bourgeois language—its rhetorical figures, its syntax, its word values—a new typology of language: a new space where the subject of writing and the subject of reading do not have exactly the same place. This is what modernity is working on.

> *To return to the subject of pleasure, you write: "The pleasure of a reading guarantees its truth." Are the revolutionary tasks we must undertake inconsistent with pleasure?*

The Marxist superego censures pleasure easily; historically, Marx and Lenin had to resolve problems of need, not of pleasure; we should note, however, that in Marx's text there is a great sensitivity to pleasure as the final question of the revolution. But on the question of the pleasure of the text, I have a prestigious supporter on my side: Brecht. No one can deny that Brecht's oeuvre, both theatrical and theoretical, is Marxist criticism of an almost impeccable force and intelligence. And Brecht is a great Marxist author who fought tirelessly on behalf of pleasure, he wanted his theater to be one of pleasure, and he never thought that pleasure was in any way contradictory to revolutionary responsibilities.

In his plays there are compassionate, almost affectionate illustrations of the value of pleasure. Consider his fondness for cigars, and the fact that he used to remind people that Marx was also a cigar lover . . . There's an entire hedonistic dimension to the progressive camp which really ought to be looked into.

I'm always sorry that the dimension of pleasure is not more perceptible in the language of students, who have in other regards such a true impression of life and society. It has been remarked, with a glance in my direction, I believe, that *these residues of hedonism should be liquidated*. Not at all, they should not be eliminated, pleasure should not be reduced to this residual status in the first place. Revolutionary practice, on whatever scale it takes, is a polyphonic practice: a vast syncretism of behaviors, discourses, symbols, actions, determinations—a plural activity. The problems we are discussing are linked not only to a class situation, that goes without saying, but also to a caste situation: and there also we must learn to consider the intellectual's role. He is not a proxy, he doesn't speak in the name of the proletariat: he must speak in his own name, in a revolutionary perspective, to account for what he needs, what hinders his intellectual activities, the alienations imposed upon him as an intellectual by our present society. He will be all the more a revolutionary if he measures the extent of his own alienation, and not just that of others.

> *Would you clear up a few misunderstandings on another subject: science, particularly a science of literature, the possibility of which you seem to doubt, in the opinion of some people . . .*

It's true that the image of myself I receive from others presents that ambiguity. Because I was one of the first semiologists, and that carries with it an aura of scientificity. And yet, on the contrary, I am sometimes judged to be insufficiently rigorous and scientific, too subjective and impressionistic.

In fact, to go straight to the crux of the matter, I don't believe in scientific *discourse*. I leave aside the problem of science itself, and the problem of a science of literature. I never said such a science existed, contrary to what was said about *Critique et Vérité*. I had written: *The science of literature (if it exists one day)*. The message (one of doubt) was the parenthesis. There are doubtless researchers whose attitude toward literature is resolutely scientific, for example Todorov: I wholeheartedly approve, I think it's very useful, but in all these projects regarding a literary science, the essential problem is never resolved: the *discourse* of science. In what discourse will a literary science express itself? There could only be one scientific discourse which could claim to escape the bad faith of all discourse: algorithmic discourse. Whence the strong and more or less conscious temptation to put the literary text into logical equations, to have recourse to formalizations. At this point, in fact, the problem of the discursiveness of science has been resolved: algorithmic discourse offers itself immediately and completely as *without signified*, as the expression of pure relations. As soon as you rejoin the national idiom, you can't escape the cultural and in a way psychoanalytical necessity of connotations, multiple meanings, the roles of the image-repertoire: and then scientific discourse no longer has the virtues required of science.

If there is one day a science of literature, it can only be a formal, formalized science: only in that way can it escape the ideological necessity which inhabits all language. I feel there is a scientific image-repertoire, *un imaginaire scientifique*—"*imaginaire*" in the Lacanian sense (a language or set of languages functioning as a misunderstanding of the subject by itself). You have only to read all the social-sciences journals, which are written in a so-called scientific or parascientific style: it would be quite possible to dissect the image-repertoire of these schools. Writing (*écriture*, as opposed to the *écrivance*, the unself-conscious writing of these discourses) is the type of practice that allows us to dissolve the image-repertoires of our language. We make ourselves into psychoanalytical subjects by writing. We conduct a certain type of analysis on ourselves, and at that point the relationship between subject and object is entirely displaced, *invalid*. The old opposition between subjectivity as an attribute of impressionistic criticism and objectivity as an attribute of scientific criticism becomes uninteresting.

> *You do research, for example at the Centre National de Recherche Scientifique, on what are called literary texts. Does the* institution *require that you adopt the role of a scholar?*

That's where the bad faith begins. If you agree to play that role, you're going to opt for a type of activity which is labeled scientific, a type of scientific discourse I call *écrivance*. And you're going to miss the text, because you won't be in a transferential relationship of self-analysis with the text. You simply won't be reading the text. You'll treat it as a semiological or historical document, for example; you'll be practicing an orthodox literary semiology, you'll try to reconstruct narrative models, narrative syntaxes, or poetics in the Jakobsonian sense. But you'll remain outside reading. You will not be part of an activity which displaces the reading subject through contact with the text, and so you will not displace the writing subject: you will be condemned to consider the subject who wrote the text under study as an *author* in the traditional sense of the word, a *subjectivity which expressed itself in a work*. The only remedy against this would be to *rewrite* the work.

> *And now we come to the question of the subject. "If I were a writer, and dead, how I would like my life to be summed up, through the care of a friendly and unself-conscious biographer, in a few details, a few tastes and interests, a few reflections—call them 'biographemes.' " This and other things you have written lead me to suppose that you are delicately reintroducing, subtly or perhaps inadvertently (please excuse the suggestion), the notion of the subject-author taught to us by classical, humanistic tradition . . .*

I am the product of an education that believed in the subject, in the humanistic and classical sense of the word. In the profound transformation of the metaphysical subject begun by Marx, Nietzsche, and Freud, a transformation now diversified into many different directions, my place is only a transitory one, not right on the cutting edge. I'm still fascinated by all the ways the subject can be dispersed, that fragile moment when the classical subject of writing is in the throes of change, of destruction, in the midst of entering into an arrangement, so to speak. It is this fleeting moment of a very delicate explosion that interests me. My relation to what is called the modern text is ambiguous: it is a passionate critical attachment, but the relationship is not always one of pleasure.

> *And when you say: "The pleasure of the text also includes an amicable return of the author"?*

To me, that sentence seems rather avant-garde! It really would be a wonderful liberation to be able to take up the authors of the past again as agreeable, charming bodies, traces which still remain seductive. There are writers who point the way for us: Proust, Jean Genet (I'm thinking of his novels)—he is in his books. He says *I, Jean*. It would never occur to anyone, however, to say that his books express a subjective experience: Genet is in his books as a *paper character*. That is the success of his work: he is there as a completely disinherited character, unencumbered by any heredity in relation to himself as a *referent*.

> *How did you organize* Sade, Fourier, Loyola? *This grouping of three authors is surprising, it could be taken as a provocation.*

I have already said no provocation was intended, which doesn't mean that there may not be an *effect* of provocation. Motives are situated on a different plane.

> *Sade, Fourier, Loyola: materialist authors?*

Apropos of these authors, I used the expression "materialist rite," and perhaps that is the greatest provocation. I did not take into account the fact that Loyola was a believer, for example. I considered all three of them outside any content whatsoever. The more an author is engaged in writing, the more he "materializes" himself, the more he jettisons the idealist baggage there may be in the contents he proposes; of course, that burden may be so heavy that no one can see anything else for a long time; and yet, if Diderot is for me a materialist author, it's not because he has been assigned that role on some chart of philosophers through the ages. *Jacques le Fataliste* is one of the greatest texts which "think" modern writing, by subjecting the relationship between language and reality to a kind of insatiable, unstoppable discursiveness: that is when he is a great materialist writer.

> *You say that Sade, Fourier, and Loyola all theatricalized. What theatricality do you mean?*

In the idea of theatricality, there are two notions which must be distinguished: hysterical theatricality, which has given rise, in our Western theater, to post-Brechtian and counter-Brechtian theater, more or less in the wake of "happenings." There is another theatricality connected with the idea of *mise en scène*, in the almost etymological sense of the expression. Its referents should be sought either in the direction of the Freudian scene, "the other scene," or in the direction of Mallarmé, of *le livre à venir*: a theatricality based on mechanisms of mobile combinatives, conceived in such a way that they completely and constantly displace the relationship between the reader and the listener.

> *And you also speak of them as scenographers?*

The metaphor of scenography is still quite fertile, it hasn't been completely mined-out yet. It would consist of giving primacy to the director instead of the actor. Our theater is traditionally a theater of actors.

Am I correct in my judgment that the texts devoted to Sade play an important part in the overall structure of the book?

You are the first to bring up that point, which I feel is an important one. There are two quite obvious replies, the first of which is that Sade frames the argument. And so the book is not a trilogy, a simple parade of authors. A certain perspective is set up: Sade before and after. The second reply is that "Sade I" was written as an article, along a certain discursive line. "Sade II" is composed of fragments. I had the feeling that I had not completely exhausted my reading of Sade after having written "Sade I"; I felt that I had written a rather ethnological description which neglected the intriguing points of Sadean language. I reread Sade. I redid my reading notes. Then I realized that Sade was an enigmatic experience for me, an exaltation and a disappointment: in fact, I saw that I thought the same way about Sade as when I was writing "Sade I." And so, with "Sade II," what is interesting is the decision to write a fragmented Sade, a decision related to the Sadean text itself. I'm very interested in these chopped-up repetitions.

In "Sade I" and "Sade II," you talk about the Sadean secret. Shouldn't you explain what you mean by the word "secret" in this case?

There's no need to make a fuss about the word "secret": this word is a little dangerous because it suggests a certain hermeneutic vision of the writer and the work, it implies the idea of decipherment. In fact, there are two Sadean secrets, the first of which I considered in "Sade I," the second in "Sade II." The first secret turns out to be the secret of Saint-Fonds: a libertine shuts himself away for mysterious purposes he refuses to disclose to his closest friends. We know what he does in this hideaway: he blasphemes, he rails at God. The libertine's secret is thus to have a relationship with God, which is inadmissible. The second secret is alleged in those moments when Sade, after having described erotic practices in such extreme detail that one can't imagine that there could be anything further to say, says: "And then other extraordinary things went on which I cannot relate to you." This is a false secret, because what was speakable has already been exhausted. It's simply a way of including a provision of purely verbal extraordinariness in the discourse. The first Sadean secret will greatly appeal to all those who try to fit Sade into a dialectic with the divine. The second is attractive to those who, like myself, try to reinstate Sade within the instance of discourse.

> *Is Sade an erotic author? Isn't his eroticism, as you have shown, totally different from our allusive eroticism, exemplified by the "complete-incomplete" form of the striptease? In "Sade II" you speak of a porno-grammar— I think that is the important point.*

Sade established the total number of erotic figures possible with one, two, or several partners, and constructed the system of these figures. On the contrary, the eroticism of mass culture takes the striptease as its model, an allusion which unfolds but is never resolved. Sade takes things to a different level. The striptease is already long past when he begins his description. I've always been struck by the smooth and irreversible circulation between erotic figures and grammatical, rhetorical figures. In "Sade II" I spoke of a porno-grammar. "Pornography" is a word that demands attention. In Greek, *pornè* is lewdness, prostitution. What interests me in "pornography" is the writing, *graphē*, of lewdness: the fact that it can be written. There are erotic "sentences" in Sade, eroticism is constructed *stricto sensu* as a sentence: there are units, a combinative, development just as in a verbal sentence.

Why is Sade a hidden author?

Sade's writing is censured more than his eroticism, which is censured by law, legislation. His writing is censured more subtly in the fact that he is not mentioned in any history of French literature. He's not considered a writer, his books are categorized as the works of a madman. There are many intellectuals who claim that Sade is boring!

> *May we come now to Fourier? It was perhaps this part*
> *of your book where I sensed the most happiness, this*
> *pleasure in writing we were talking about earlier. Doubt-*
> *less because you experienced a certain happiness in writ-*
> *ing this section. There are in these pages what could be*
> *called biographemes . . .*

This text is not perfect. On the one hand, there are small recon-
stitutive essays, purely taxonomic (scraps of Fourier's systems of
hieroglyphics, numbers, etc.): thus, they do not spring directly
from the hedonistic vein you mentioned, they are semiological.
But it is true that I have a real attachment to certain Fourierist
themes: sybaritic themes, voluptuous in the etymological sense
of the word. Food, for example: Fourier speaks of food with the
avidity of hunger; he adored French fruits, and so do I. There is
a linkage between his tastes and mine. I thoroughly enjoy his
descriptions of lemonade, pears, tiny pastries, melons.

Equally important to me is the phalanstery as an organized,
closed place where pleasure circulates. A sanatorium, for example, at least when I was in one, much resembled a phalanstery.
I was happy there. The organization of a lived-in space, a habitable place, a sociality which is both affectionate and "well-
aired," at ease—this is an important theme in human life.

There is also the third great Fourierist pleasure: praise of neologisms.

> *So you're very attentive to all the systematics of writers*
> *or founders of languages: systematics that, although quite*
> *structured, are not closed by God. I'm thinking, for ex-*
> *ample, of what you write about Fourier: "Fourierist con-*
> *struction posits the rights of a baroque semantics, i.e.,*
> *open to the proliferation of the signifier: infinite and yet*
> *structured."*

If the study of language has taken on such importance nowadays,
it's because language offers us the image of a structured and
decentered ensemble, or set (a voluntarily neutral word). The
dictionary, I repeat, is the concrete object that best accounts for

this contradictory quality of language. A dictionary refers to a structure of language, but it is at the same time without a center. Structuralism is not new because it returned to the idea of structure. We had the concept of a closed structure, a circular, centered structure, whereas now we're beginning to work on decentered structures. I refer you here to all those contemporary authors who are usually grouped together, even if they find each other uneasy company.

And Fourier's utopia?

We must not forget Marx's critique, which more or less disposes of Fourier, but neither should we forget that Fourier says some things that Marx left out.

> *Here I'll quote you, to be more precise: "Simplism (a Fourierist passion) would today be either the censure of Need or the censure of Desire; which would be answered, in Harmony (in Utopia?), by the combined science of both."*

Utopia is the state of a society where Marx would no longer critique Fourier.

Gulliver, no. 5, March 1973

The Adjective Is the "Statement" of Desire

This interview with Roland Barthes took place before the publication of The Pleasure of the Text, *which was of course the major subject of discussion. The idea behind the interview was not to "explain" Barthes, or to summarize his new book—it is to be hoped, rather, that those intrigued will read* The Pleasure of the Text *and form their own opinions. Barthes's first formulations of the idea of pleasure appear in the preface of* Sade, Fourier, Loyola, *but his wonderful text on Japan,* Empire of Signs, *was already, in the full sense of the term, a book of pleasure.*

> *The question of aesthetic pleasure hardly seems original: it was raised, for example, by the generation of Valery Larbaud, Schlumberger, etc. But is it really the same question? Or, to be more precise: what changes when the terms are manipulated ever so slightly, replacing "literary pleasure" with the "pleasure of the text"?*

Nothing is new under the sun, everything comes back—it's an old complaint. What is important is that the return should not occur at the same place: substitute the (dialectic) spiral for the (religious) circle. The pleasure of reading has been recognized and commented on for a long time, and I see no reason to argue against it, even if it has been expressed within the framework of what might be called elitist thought. Pleasures, too, are finite in number, and if ever we achieve a de-alienated society, it will have to take up again, *but in another place, in a spiral,* certain remnants of bourgeois *savoir-vivre*.

Having said that, the expression "pleasure of the text" can be new in two ways. On the one hand, it lets us establish the pleasure of writing and the pleasure of reading as equals, and I would even say *as identical* (the "text" is not a vectorial object, it is neither active nor passive; it is neither an object of consumption, presupposing a passive subject, nor a technique of action, presupposing an agent; it is a production, whose irretrievable subject circulates perpetually).

On the other hand, "pleasure," in such an expression, is not an aesthetic value: it's not a question of "contemplating" the text, or even of "projecting" oneself, of "participating" in it; if the text is an "object," it is in a purely psychoanalytical sense: caught up in a dialectic of desire, and—to be more precise—perversion, it is an "object" only long enough to put the "subject" into question. There is no erotics without an "object," but neither can it exist without the vacillation of the subject: everything is in this subversion, this perturbation of grammar. Thus, the "pleasure of the text," to my mind, refers to something entirely unknown to aesthetics, particularly literary aesthetics, which is: bliss, a mode of vanishing, of annulment of the subject. Then why say "pleasure of the text" and not "bliss of the text"? Because in the textual practice there is a gamut of dispersions of the subject, which may go from consistence (when there is contentment, plenitude, satisfaction, pleasure in the proper sense) to loss (when there is annulment, fading, bliss); unfortunately, there is no word in French which covers both pleasure and bliss, so the ambiguity of the expression "pleasure of the text" must stand, sometimes specific (pleasure versus bliss), sometimes generic (pleasure and bliss).

> *In your personal critical method, "pleasure" has appeared in an explicit manner only recently (Sade, Fourier, Loyola). But before the focus of this word, there was already an activity, or at least an obsession, something latent and widespread enough to innervate even your first writings. It's as if the question had begun to resolve itself (in prac-*

> *tice) even before it was asked (in theory): you chose a*
> *sensual, sensuous language, which was already passing*
> *on, through your writing on a text, some of the pleasure*
> *you had experienced in reading it . . .*

The pleasure of the text is a value of long standing with me:
Brecht was the first to provide me with a theoretical right to
pleasure. If I explicitly affirmed this value at any certain time, it
was under the tactical pressure of a particular situation. It seemed
to me that the almost wild and uncontrolled development of
ideological criticism called for a certain corrective adjustment,
because it threatened to impose on the text, on textual theory, a
kind of father-figure whose vigilant function would be to forbid
blissful enjoyment: the danger would thus be twofold: to deprive
oneself of a capital pleasure and to wrongly abandon this pleasure
to apolitical art, to right-wing art. I'm too Brechtian not to believe
in the need to make criticism and pleasure coexist.

> *You enjoy sprinkling your texts with metaphorical in-*
> *cidental clauses which seem to exceed any pure and*
> *simple function of explanation or ornament. And the*
> *adjective, that affliction of bourgeois criticism, enjoys an*
> *indulgent redundancy in your writings. But how far can*
> *one go without falling into subjectivism? Isn't it risky to*
> *maintain such a precarious balance between two irrec-*
> *oncilable relations to a text—the "scientific" and the*
> *"loving"?*

To speak and write smoothly without adjectives would just be a
game. In fact (what a discovery!), there are good adjectives and
bad ones. When an adjective enters the language in a purely
stereotyped manner, it leaves the door wide open for ideology,
because stereotype and ideology share an identity. In other cases,
however, when it escapes repetition, the adjective, as a major
predicate complement, is also the main path of desire: it is the
statement of desire, a way of affirming my "will to bliss," of
establishing my relation to the object in the mad adventure of
my own loss.

> *There's something oppressive in the discourse of all those, from Sollers (in the militant camp) to Todorov (in the academic camp), who are more preoccupied with the laws of a text than with its pleasure. The generation schooled in that particular discipline runs the risk of lapsing into a certain sterile frigidity in the more or less near future. Already (could this be the "tightening up" we were promised after the student revolt, that pleasure party of 1968?), students are as stuffed with theory as they are ignorant of the latest novelistic inventions . . .*

A text by Sollers is a multiple, heterological text and *all its threads must be held in a single hand.* He's one of the few writers who must not be fetishized (and he doesn't lend himself to this), i.e.: cut up, weighed, picked over, and sorted out—he should be taken like a torrent, a powerful aspersion, the overwhelming flood of language's *complete plural*; a selective, distributive way of thinking would be, with regard to Sollers, a thought of pleasure, not of bliss. As for "scientific" or "academic" pronouncements, it's true that they usually spring from *écrivance*, that instrumental writing, in that they reject the most immediately effective signifier, which is on the whole the stylistic signifier (with its figures); but writing cannot be limited to such a signifier; in fact, even without "style," there may be "writing": it's enough that there is an energy and singularity of thought sufficiently powerful to give rise to a new cutting-up (a new mapping) of reality (for example, of literary discourse): to sort out and classify, vigorously and *on one's own*, is always to write. A writer (an *écrivant*, not an author) who classifies is on the way to writing, because he risks himself in the signifier, in the utterance, even if he gives himself "scientific" alibis.

> *Does the pleasure of the text depend on cultural levels? Or is it, on the contrary, essentially more corporeal? This is a question you yourself raised in a recent interview. In short, can we legitimately speak of an "erotics of reading"?*

There is probably nothing more cultural, and thus more social, than pleasure. The pleasure of the text (which I here contrast to bliss) is tied to an entire cultural training, or, if you prefer, to a situation of complicity, of inclusion (aptly symbolized by the episode in which the young Proust shuts himself up in the lavatory, with its smells of orrisroot, to read novels, cutting himself off from the world, enveloped in a kind of paradisiac milieu). The bliss of the text is on the contrary atopical, asocial; it is produced in an unforeseeable fashion in families of culture, of language: one cannot account for one's own bliss, no one can classify it. An erotics of reading? Yes, on the condition that perversion—and I would almost say: fear—is never erased.

> *At this point in your work, when theory is transformed into writing—and in the most rigorous continuity, like the recto and verso of one language—the ultimate metamorphosis, the leap into the void, would be a work of fiction. Do you ever think about this?*

We've reached a stage of modernity where it is very difficult to accept innocently the idea of a "work of fiction"; from now on, our works are works of language; fiction can pass through them, contacted obliquely, indirectly present. I will probably never write a "novel," a story fitted out with characters and events; but if it's so easy for me to deprive myself of this activity (after all, it really must be quite enjoyable to write a novel), it's doubtless because my writings are already full of the novelistic (which is the novel minus the characters); and it's true that at present, looking ahead to a new phase of my work as straightforwardly as possible, what I would like to do is to *try out* novelistic forms, to essay them, in such a way that none of them would be called a "novel," but each one would keep, and if possible renew, the title "essay."

Le Monde, September 27, 1973
From an interview conducted by Jean-Louis de Rambures

An Almost Obsessive Relation to Writing Instruments

Do you have a method of working?

It all depends on what you mean by method. As far as methodology is concerned, I have no opinion. But if you're talking about work habits, obviously I have a method of working. And on that basis your question interests me, because there is a kind of censorship which considers this topic taboo, under the pretext that it would be futile for a writer or an intellectual to talk about his writing, his daily schedule, or his desk.

When a great many people agree that a problem is insignificant, that usually means it is not. Insignificance is the locus of true significance. This should never be forgotten. That is why it seems so important to me to ask a writer about his writing habits, putting things on the most material level, I would even say the most minimal level possible. This is an anti-mythological action: it contributes to the overturning of that old myth which continues to present language as the instrument of thought, inwardness, passion, or whatever, and consequently presents writing as a simple instrumental practice.

As always, history clearly shows us the way to understand that actions which are secularized and trivialized in our society, such as writing, are actually heavily charged with meaning. When writing is placed in its historical or even anthropological context, it can be seen that for a long time writing was attended by great ceremony. In ancient Chinese society, one prepared oneself for writing, for handling the ink brush, through an almost religious asceticism. In certain Christian monasteries of the Middle Ages, the copyists began their work only after a day of meditation.

Personally, I call the set of those "rules" (in the monastic sense of the word) which predetermine the work—and it is important to distinguish the different coordinates: working time, working space, and the action of writing itself—the "protocols" of work. The etymology is clear: it means the first page glued to a manuscript in preparation for writing.

> *Do you mean that your own work is inscribed in a ceremonial?*

In a certain manner, yes. Take the gesture, the action of writing. I would say, for example, that I have an almost obsessive relation to writing instruments. I often switch from one pen to another just for the pleasure of it. I try out new ones. I have far too many pens—I don't know what to do with all of them! And yet, as soon as I see a new one, I start craving it. I cannot keep myself from buying them.

When felt-tipped pens first appeared in the stores, I bought a lot of them. (The fact that they were originally from Japan was not, I admit, displeasing to me.) Since then I've gotten tired of them, because the point flattens out too quickly. I've also used pen nibs—not the "Sergeant-Major," which is too dry, but softer nibs, like the "J." In short, I've tried everything . . . except Bics, with which I feel absolutely no affinity. I would even say, a bit nastily, that there is a "Bic style," which is really just for churning out copy, writing that merely transcribes thought.

In the end, I always return to fine fountain pens. The essential thing is that they can produce that soft, smooth writing I absolutely require.

Because you write all your work by hand?

It's not that simple. In my case, there are two stages in the creative process. First comes the moment when desire is invested in a graphic impulse, producing a calligraphical object. Then there is the critical moment when this object is prepared for the anonymous and collective consumption of others through transformation into a typographical object (at that moment, the object is already beginning its commercialization). In other words—first I write the text with a pen, then I type the whole thing on a typewriter (with two fingers, because I don't know how to type).

Up until now, these two stages—handwriting, typewriting—were, in a way, sacred for me. But I should note that I am trying to change my ritual.

I have just bought myself a present: an electric typewriter. Every day I practice typing for a half an hour, in the fond hope of acquiring a more "typewriterly" writing.

I was led to this decision by personal experience. Since I'm often very busy, I have sometimes been obliged to have things typed for me by others (I don't like to do this, but it has happened). When I thought about this, it bothered me. Without going into a big demagogical speech, I'll just say that to me this represented an alienated social relationship: a person, the typist, is confined by the master in an activity I would almost call an enslavement, when writing is precisely a field of liberty and desire! In short, I said to myself: "There's only one solution. I really must learn to type." Philippe Sollers, to whom I mentioned this resolution, reassured me, moreover, that once you learn to type well enough, writing directly at the typewriter creates a kind of unique spontaneity which has its own beauty.

My conversion, I admit, is far from accomplished. I doubt that I'll ever completely stop writing things out by hand, outmoded and eccentric though that may be. In any case, that's my situation. I'm making an honest effort to change with the times. And I've gotten a little bit used to my new regime.

Do you attach equal importance to your workplace?

I simply cannot work in a hotel room. It's not the hotel itself that bothers me. It's not a question of ambiance or decor, but of spatial organization (it's not for nothing that I'm called a structuralist!).

To be able to function, I need to be able structurally to reproduce my usual work space. In Paris, the place where I work (every day from 9:30 a.m. to 1 p.m.; this regular workaday schedule for writing suits me better than an aleatory schedule, which supposes a state of continual excitement) is in my bedroom. This space is completed by a music area (I play the piano every day, at about the same time: 2:30 in the afternoon) and by a "painting" area— I say "painting" with lots of quotation marks (about once a week I perform as a Sunday painter, so I need a place to splatter paint around).

In my country house, I have faithfully reproduced those three areas. It's not important that they're not in the same room. It isn't the walls but the structures that count.

But that's not all. The working space itself must also be divided into a certain number of functional microplaces. First there should be a table. (I like it to be of wood. I might say that I'm on good terms with wood.) There has to be a place on the side, another table where I can spread out the different things I'm working on. And there has to be a place for the typewriter, and a desk for my different memos, notes, "microplannings" for the next few days, "macroplannings" for the trimester, etc. (I never look at them, mind you. Their simple presence is enough.) Finally, I have my index-card system, and the slips have an equally strict format: one quarter the size of my usual sheet of paper. At least that's how they were until the day standards were readjusted within the framework of European unification (in my opinion, one of the cruelest blows of the Common Market). Luckily, I'm not *completely* obsessive. Otherwise, I would have had to redo all my cards from the time I first started writing, twenty-five years ago.

> *Since you're an essayist rather than a novelist, what part does documentation play in the preparation of your books?*

What I enjoy is not the scholarly work. I don't like libraries. I even find it very difficult to read there. What I do enjoy is the excitement provoked by immediate and phenomenological contact with the tutor text. So I don't try to set up a preliminary library for myself, I'm content to read the text in question, in a rather fetishistic way: writing down certain passages, moments, even words which have the power to move me. As I go along, I use my cards to write down quotations, or ideas which come to me, and they do so, curiously, already in the rhythm of a sentence, so that from that moment on, things are already taking on an existence as writing.

After that, a second reading isn't indispensable. On the other hand, from then on, I'm plunged into a kind of frenzied state. I know that everything I read will somehow find its inevitable way into my work. The only problem is to keep what I read for amusement from interfering with reading directed toward my writing. The solution is very simple: the books I read for pleasure, for example a classic, or one of Jakobson's books on linguistics, which I particularly enjoy, those I read in bed at night before going to sleep. I read the others (as well as avant-garde texts) at my worktable in the morning. There is nothing arbitrary about this. The bed is the locus of irresponsibility. The table, that of responsibility.

> *And these unexpected comparisons that are your specialty, how do you arrive at them? Do you make an outline before you begin writing?*

Correspondences are not a question of writing but of textual analysis. Some people have the structural reflex and see things in oppositive terms. Others don't have it. Period.

As for the sacred outline, I admit having sacrificed at its altars during a certain period in the beginnings of semiology. Since then there has been that whole movement challenging the dissertation and its format. My university experience has also shown me the very oppressive, not to say repressive, constraints brought to bear upon students by the myth of the outline and syllogistic, Aristotelian development (this was even one of the problems we attempted to examine this year in my seminar). In short, I opted for an aleatory cutting-up, a *découpage* (into what I call "miniatures"). My aim is to deconstruct the dissertation, to deflate the reader's anxiety, and to reinforce the critical part of writing by fracturing the very notion of the "subject" of a book. But don't make the mistake of thinking that because I tend more and more to produce my texts in fragments I have renounced all constraint. When one replaces logic with chance, it must be closely watched lest it become, in its turn, mechanical. Personally, I proceed according to a method I would call, inspired by certain Zen definitions, "controlled accident." In the second part devoted to Sade in *Sade, Fourier, Loyola*, for example, chance intervenes only in the initial constructive action of giving a title to each fragment. In *The Pleasure of the Text*, these fragments are chosen according to letters of the alphabet. In the end, each book requires a search for its own appropriate form.

Have you never thought about writing a novel?

A novel is not defined by its object, but by forsaking the serious temper, *l'esprit de sérieux*. To cross out or correct a word, to watch over euphony or a figure of speech, to discover a neologism, all this has for me a gourmand savor of language, a truly novelistic pleasure.

But the two aspects of writing that give me the keenest pleasure are, first, to begin, and second, to complete. Frankly, it's so that I can multiply my pleasure many times over that I've decided (provisionally) in favor of discontinuous writing.

Le Nouvel Observateur, December 17, 1973
From an interview conducted by Hector Bianciotti

The Phantoms of the Opera

> *Whether we like it or not, the most dynamic aspect of contemporary French literature is also the most "theoretical," and it is the only one to have any real influence abroad. Roland Barthes is a central figure in modern French criticism, a figure whose every move is followed with the greatest interest. If he takes up a new word, or invents one, a new light is immediately cast on old problems, and new questions come to mind. If he publishes a magazine piece on singing, the rumor quickly spreads that he's going to "take on" opera. In fact, at the request of his students, he will be giving a seminar on "The Voice" at the École Pratique des Hautes Études.*

Many sciences and disciplines are interested in the voice: physiology, aesthetics of course, but also psychoanalysis, semiology (how can a voice signify, independently of what it says?), and even sociology (the connection between social classes and voice types). There is ideology in the voice, as well as fashion, which often affects supposedly natural objects. Each year, a particular body becomes fashionable, while others go out of style. But what interests me the most in the voice, to begin with, is that this very cultural object is, in a certain way, an absent object (much more absent than the body, which is represented in a thousand ways by mass culture): we rarely listen to a voice *en soi*, in itself, we listen to what it says. The voice has the very status of language, an object thought to be graspable only through what it transmits;

however, just as we are now learning, thanks to the notion of "text," to read the linguistic material itself, we must in the same way learn to listen to the voice's text, its meaning, everything in the voice which overflows meaning.

> *And it's this elusive element that you called, in one of your articles, "the grain of the voice"?*

The *grain* of the voice is not indescribable (nothing is indescribable), but I don't think that it can be defined scientifically, because it implies a certain erotic relationship between the voice and the listener. One can therefore describe the grain of a voice, but only through metaphors.

> *Would you give me an example? Did you recently hear Gundula Janowitz in* The Marriage of Figaro?

That voice does indeed have a grain (at least to my ears); to describe this grain, I find images of a milkweed acidity, of a nacreous vibration, situated at the exquisite and dangerous limit of the *toneless*. Her voice, moreover, had the only grain of the entire evening.

> *And Callas?*

Hers is a *tubular* grain, hollow, with a resonance that is just a bit off-pitch (a voice can be in tune while its grain is out of tune); it's a grain I don't like.

> *In your article on singing, you spoke with great admiration of the singer Charles Panzera, and your remarks on his artistry in forming consonants and vowels touched on the very spirit of French language . . .*

I have said this before, Panzera's art (I think that I may now say, quite simply: his voice) was of exemplary value to me, a value that went far beyond simple aesthetic enjoyment: he initiated me, if I may say so, in the materiality of the French language. I studied a little with him, as an amateur, of course, about thirty years ago. Panzera sang French *mélodie*, a genre that is somewhat discredited nowadays, but, for me, this type of melody (from Duparc to Fauré), despite its "salon" origins, is a wonderful *mise en scène* of the French language, and that's why it's important to me. *La Bonne Chanson*, Verlaine's words set to Fauré's music, and sung by Panzera, is a veritable linguistic text: it represents the French language to me, unencumbered by either the naturalness or the hysteria that fatally blemish traditional performance art. Panzera, for example, gave a mellow sheen to his consonants and an extreme purity to his vowels, which allowed him to substitute for vulgar expressivity of feeling a kind of musical clarity which had (which still has, since we have several recordings of his art) a truly sovereign nature: the entire language, in itself, became *evident*.

After all, perhaps it's time to return to the "genius" of our language: not its logical genius, which has gone the way, I hope, of the bourgeois myth of French clarity, but its phonic genius, if I may put it that way. It seems to me that one of the current aspects of the cultural crisis, in France, is precisely that the French as a whole take no interest in their language. A taste for the French language has been completely mortgaged by bourgeois schooling; to be interested in our own language, in its musicalness (which is not superior to any other, but which is at least specific), has become in the course of things an elitist, pretentious attitude. And yet there have been moments when a certain contact was maintained between the "people" and their language, through popular poetry, folksongs, or even a popular ground swell that changed the language despite the guardianship of language pundits. It seems that contact has vanished, certainly from today's "popular" culture, which is nothing more than a fabrication (by radio, television, etc.). If I regret this loss of contact, it isn't for humanistic reasons but because, if contact with the music and phoneticism of one's own language is lost, the relationship between language and the body is destroyed. Historical and social censorship denies the bliss, the *jouissance* of language.

There's a great movement in modern mise en scène *to highlight the pure theatricality of each spectacle, beyond the text itself. Doesn't it seem to you that this theatricality finds its culmination in opera, which most young people today think of as a somewhat ridiculous art form?*

Opera is total spectacle, and perhaps for that very reason it is off-limits: to go to the opera is a complicated enterprise, you have to reserve seats well in advance, the tickets are expensive, and so you feel you must stay until the end of the performance. I would like to see an opera as free and as popular as a movie theater or a wrestling arena: you could go in and out according to your mood, you'd spend part of your evening taking a "hit" of opera—but this opera did exist once, the aristocratic opera, the opera of Balzac's novels. In short, I dream of a box at the opera, or of a ticket costing only as much as a movie ticket.

Have you been to the Paris Opera recently?

I just saw the ballet put on by Merce Cunningham and John Cage.

And what did you think of it?

I thought it was a tender, delicate spectacle; but beyond the ballet itself, I was overwhelmed once more by the almost imperial sensuality of the operatic spectacle: it shines from everywhere, from the music, the visual spectacle, the perfumes of the audience, and what I will call the Venus-like beauty of the dancers, the emphatic presence of bodies in an immense and brightly lit space.

Do you think we might be about to see a general rediscovery of opera?

Yes, there might be a certain return to opera—its popularity is fed by recordings of opera music, and once again opera stars and conductors have many admirers among the general public. Nevertheless, opera remains, for the moment, a spectacle for a distinct social class, first of all because tickets are expensive, and also because the enjoyment of opera requires certain cultural reflexes—of background, *ambiance*, sophistication—which are still class reflexes. And yet opera itself contains many progressive elements: it's a total spectacle, mobilizing many of the senses, many sensual pleasures, including the possibility for the public to enjoy *itself*, in a way, and this all-encompassing, spectacular theatricality has been much sought after by our culture, from ancient theater to rock concerts.

And opera is very well suited to avant-garde interpretations: everything is possible, the stage is a blank canvas, the technical means are there. Finally, the operatic performance can divide into two spectacles in a curious but quite enjoyable fashion: I recently saw Gluck's *Orpheus*, and aside from the wonderful music, it really was a silly thing to watch, an unconscious parody of its own genre, but not only did this element of kitsch fail to upset me, it positively entertained me: I enjoyed the double truth of both the spectacle and its parody: laughter (or a smile) which is not destructive—perhaps that is one form of the culture of the future.

Le Figaro, July 27, 1974
From an interview conducted by Claude Jannoud

Roland Barthes versus Received Ideas

The recent issue of L'Arc *devoted to Roland Barthes shows the astonishing richness of his work, the consistency of his intellectual interests, and the integrity of his approach. Thanks to him, the connections between the act of writing and social practice are laid bare. Not only has Roland Barthes presented us with new and fascinating images of Michelet, Sade, Fourier, and many others, but he has also rehabilitated and brought into the limelight that misunderstood but vital character, the reader.*

In this interview with Roland Barthes, it wasn't possible to touch on every aspect of his work. We asked him about his personal tastes, the current state of literature, its future, the avant-garde which claims him for its own. His opinions run counter to many received ideas, but they also form a magnificent discourse on the latest metamorphoses of writing.

> *You are a "reader." You have renewed the art of reading. What you have said about Bachelard could apply very well to yourself: "For Bachelard, it is as if writers have never written: by a strange lacuna, they are only read." You seem to relish writers so much that you almost swallow them whole.*

Allow me to clarify your remark. I must admit that I am not a great reader; I read very little, and I have elsewhere explained why: either the book excites me and I keep interrupting my reading to muse or reflect on what it says, or else it bores me, and I abandon it shamelessly. Of course, I do sometimes read avidly, even gluttonously, as you say, but this is reading outside of work, usually authors of the past (from Apuleius to Jules Verne). The reason for this is quite simple: in order to read, if not voluptuously, at least "greedily," there must be no attendant critical responsibility. When a book is contemporary, then I, as a reader, feel responsible, because it draws me into formal or ideological problems that concern me. The pleasure of free, happy, gluttonous reading, the pleasure you're thinking about, always involves a taste for the past; it's probably that pleasure which Bachelard knew and described: his favorite poets, whose lines nourish his reverie and his writing, are above all poets of the past.

Bachelard's relation to reading is thus very limited, and that is what I wanted to say. That quotation from *The Pleasure of the Text* is critical in intention: I indirectly express my regret that Bachelard never went beyond rather passively consuming texts that came to him as if ready-made, since he never wondered *how* they had been made.

Now, I am convinced that a theory of reading (that reading which has always been the poor relation of literary creation) is absolutely dependent on a theory of writing: to read a text is to discover—on a corporeal, not a conscious level—*how it was written*, to invest oneself in the production, not the product. This movement of coincidence can be initiated either in the usual fashion, by pleasurably reliving the poetics of the work, or in a more modern way, by removing from oneself all forms of censorship to allow the text the freedom of all its semantic and symbolic excesses; at this point, to read is truly to write: I write—or rewrite—the text I am reading, even better and more searchingly than its author did.

> *Avant-garde literature is no longer the pride of the bourgeoisie, and it isn't read by the general public. It is the prerogative of a mandarin caste, an intellectual elite. Couldn't that form the basis for new alienation?*

That is an objection often made against avant-garde literature, which is accused of both revolutionary pretensions and social impotence. This objection usually comes from the bourgeoisie, and their idea of revolution is, paradoxically, more sovereign than that of the revolutionaries themselves; this might be true in politics, where the event can be sudden and brutal, but in the field of culture, no revolution can avoid passing through a long period of contradictions. One of these contradictions, inevitably, is that in our nonrevolutionary society the avant-garde writer's role is not to please the vast majority of the public, which by the way should not be purely and simply equated to the proletarian class, because in order to please this public the artist would often have to adopt the art and shibboleths of a petit-bourgeois ideology, which are not revolutionary at all (and that's another of the contradictions which must be worked through). Brecht himself tried to construct a theater that was both popular and critical; let's admit that he failed.

Shut off from the "larger" public, the avant-garde writer is even forbidden—and this is an even sharper paradox—to believe that his task is literally to prefigure the art and culture to be created by the future revolution.

A revolution opens up a zone of availability which remains subject for a long time to political constraints, and no one can foresee what form these may take because they are determined by circumstances of the revolutionary struggle (this is the meaning of what is going on today in China): politics may obscure for many years a clear vision of what culture will be like. Consequently, as things stand now in Western society, the role of the avant-garde is limited: *to liquidate and theorize*, as Brecht said—and that's about what it's doing.

As for a "mandarinate" of the avant-garde, the word is inappropriate. Perhaps avant-garde writers make you think of Chinese mandarins because they often work in a separate, enclosed milieu, and because they use a difficult and refined language (even in the interests of subversion), but there is a fundamental difference between them: unlike the mandarin, the avant-garde writer is not on the side of power, he derives no benefit from its privileges and protection, and he is not compromised. His natural support is neither the dominating nor the dominated class, but the third class, the ones who are neither producers nor proprietors nor their accomplices: students, for example, and certain classes of young people.

> *You're often rather enigmatic on the subject of avant-garde literature. You say that it can be effective even without being read! One gets the impression that you find the pleasure of the text in writers hostile to formal research in itself even though, in their own way, they may have advanced its boundaries in their works—for example, Michelet, Brecht, or Zola.*

In my opinion, we can find what we call text, writing, and therefore avant-gardism, in writers of the past such as Proust, Michelet, Brecht; it's not a question of "form" (still less of "formalism") but of impulse: whenever it's the *body* which writes, and not ideology, there's a chance the text will join us in our modernity.

If it's rather difficult to talk about the current avant-garde, it's because there has been a change of objects over the years. Today the avant-garde object is essentially *theoretical*: the double pressure of politics and intellectuals ensures that it is now *theoretical positions* (and their exposition) which are avant-garde, and not necessarily creative works themselves.

Not that there is any lack of these works (more unpublished than published, though), but as it is difficult to judge them by that antiquated criterion of "taste," one ends up judging them less according to their textual effect (besides, why shouldn't there be a great deal of attrition and loss in the avant-garde, as there is elsewhere?) than by the theoretical intelligence they display. And we must remember that "theory," which is the decisive practice of the avant-garde, does not have a progressive role *in itself*; its active role is to reveal as past what we still believe to be present: theory mortifies, and that is what makes it avant-garde.

> *Envisaging the future of literature, you announced that it is heading for disaster. What do you mean by that?*

I can only say (and I'm not alone in saying this) that *literature* has been historically defined by a certain type of society. When society changes, inescapably, either in a revolutionary or a capitalistic direction (because the death of cultural objects does not determine the direction of political change), then so does *literature* (in the institutional, ideological, and aesthetic sense that this word had not long ago): it can either disappear completely (a society without literature is perfectly conceivable) or so change its conditions of production, consumption, and writing, in short its *value*, that it will have to change its name as well. After all, what is left of the *forms* of the old literature?

A few modes of discourse, publishing houses faced with growing economic difficulties, a fragile and unfaithful public weakened by mass culture, which is *not* literary . . . The great *mainstays* of literature are passing: when Aragon and Malraux have gone, there will be no more "great writers." The Nobel ideology is forced to take refuge in authors who live in the past, and even those must be supported by a political trend.

> *You have written a magnificent book on three logothetes, three founders of a linguistic style: Sade, Fourier, Loyola. Louis-Jean Calvet, in the edition of L'Arc which was devoted to you and your work, refers to you as a logothete in your own right.*

In a general manner, I am unable to say who I am—or that I am this, that, or whatever, because in saying it, I would only be adding one more text to the others I have written, without any guarantee that this text would be "truer" than any other. We are all, especially when we write, *interpretable* beings, but it is the other, and never ourselves, who possesses the power of interpretation. As a subject, I cannot apply any predicate, any adjective to myself—except by disregarding my unconscious, which is unknowable by me. And not only are we unable to conceive of ourselves through adjectives, we cannot even authenticate the adjectives applied to us by others: they leave us *mute*; for us, they are critical fictions.

What I can say here is that a *logothete* is not only and not even necessarily a writer who invents words, sentences that bear his stamp, in short, a style; a logothete is someone who knows how to see in the world, in his own world (social, erotic, or religious), elements, traits, "units" in the linguistic term, which he combines and arranges in an original fashion, as if he were producing the first text of a new language.

I doubt that one can say, in this sense, that my work is that of a logothete; Calvet's generous appraisal referred more modestly, I believe, to the liberty I sometimes take (which pleases Calvet, but annoys others) of creating neologisms.

> *You are very sensitive to the physical aspect of writing, to its development in space. Balzac's interlinear notations on his galley proofs delight you no end. You have written on Japanese calligraphy. I would very much like you to comment on something you once said: "The body passes into writing."*

Yes, I love writing, but as this word has taken on a metaphorical sense (it's a way of stating things, close to style), I will take the aforementioned liberty of risking a new word: I love *scription*, the action by which we manually trace signs. Not only do I cherish the pleasure of writing my texts by hand, using a typewriter only in the final phase of preparation, but also and above all, I love the traces of graphic activity, wherever they are: in Oriental calligraphy, in a certain kind of painting we might call "semiographic" (for example, Masson, Réquichot, or Cy Twombly).

Writing is the hand, and thus the body: its impulses, controlling mechanisms, rhythms, weights, glides, complications, flights— not the *soul* (graphology is unimportant), but the subject with its ballast of desire and the unconscious.

> *You are also a teacher. You have described teaching as being half drudgery, half pleasure. What is the relation between your activities as a teacher and as a writer?*

I am not a professor, but I am Director of Studies at the École Pratique des Hautes Études, which means that I don't give courses but I hold seminars—and that means that I'm not obliged to lecture, to dispense an already formulated body of knowledge; my role is rather to work along with my students to create a space for research, for mutual listening, and—why not?—for pleasure. A seminar fosters knowledge, or the search for knowledge, in a community both amicable and intellectual; more than a class or even a course, it rather resembles what used to be called, in the eighteenth century, in the provinces, an "academy."

Thus, there is no direct relation between seminar and book; for this relationship to exist, the book would have to become a collective enterprise. The idea has been considered, but such a book is difficult to manage. We'll get there, however.

> *You say somewhere that Proust is a reference work for you. Tell us about the pleasure of reading Proust.*

Proust is a complete world-reading system. This means that if we accept this system even in the slightest degree, if only because it is so seductive, then there is no incident in our daily life, no encounter, no trait, no situation which doesn't have its reference in Proust. Proust can be my memory, my culture, my language; I may constantly *remember* and *refer* to Proust, as the narrator's grandmother does with Madame de Sévigné. The pleasure of reading Proust—or rather of rereading him—is like consulting the Bible, abstraction made of the sacred and the respect it demands: it's the encounter between a present and what must be called, in the complete sense of the word, a *wisdom*: a knowledge of "life" and its language.

Naturally, there are many other possible reading systems; that one is dependent on very specific givens (social, psychoanalytical, philosophical, neurotic) and I certainly don't keep it constantly in mind: I'm not "Proustian."

> *What have you become in relation to the author of* Writing Degree Zero?

Have I evolved? One would have to know both terms, what I was, what I am. Again, I can't make that judgment: no one can authenticate either his being or his becoming. Still, if you would accept an "imaginary" answer, I will say that I don't think I've changed much. I love and comment on the same things, the same values that appeared in *Writing Degree Zero*: language, literature, and that very notion of "degree zero" which refers to the utopia of a lifting of signs, an exemption from meaning, an indivision of language, a transparency of social relations. What has changed in me, fortunately, has been other people, because I am also that other who speaks to me, to whom I listen, who lures me on. I would be so happy if these words of Brecht could be applied to me: "He thought in the heads of others; and in his own, others than he were thinking. That is true thought."

Le Monde, November 15, 1974

What Would Become of a Society That Ceased to Reflect upon Itself?

The following questions were submitted to twenty well-known intellectuals:

1. There is in France a large and outspoken intellectual class. Do you feel a part of this community?

2. Intellectuals are accused of blending irresponsibility with snobbery, superficiality with "terrorism." In your opinion, do these accusations have any foundation in reality?

3. What do you feel is the principal function of the intellectual? How well do you think the French intelligentsia performs this function?

Here is Roland Barthes's reply.

The suit that is periodically brought against intellectuals (since the Dreyfus affair, which occasioned, I believe, the birth of the word and the idea) is a witch hunt: the intellectual is treated as a sorcerer might be by a small, primitive tribe of merchants, businessmen, and lawyers, because he disturbs ideological interests. Anti-intellectualism is a historical myth, doubtless connected to the rise of the petite bourgeoisie. Poujade put this myth into its rawest formulation: "A fish starts rotting at its head." Such a witch hunt can periodically stir up the grandstand, such things always do, but its *political* danger should not be overlooked: quite simply, it is fascism, which always and everywhere takes the liquidation of the intellectual class as its first objective.

The obligations of an intellectual are defined by those menaces themselves, by their point of origin; Brecht addressed himself to these obligations many times: to dissect bourgeois (and petit-bourgeois) ideology, to study the forces which move the world, and to make theory progress. Within these formulations, there must obviously be room for a great variety of writings and languages (since the intellectual assumes himself as a being of language, and that disturbs the assurance of a world that arrogantly opposes "realities" to "words," as if language were only the futile decor of man's more substantial interests).

The intellectual's historical situation is not an easy one—not because of the laughable accusations brought against him, but because his situation is dialectical: his function is to criticize bourgeois language under the very reign of the bourgeoisie. The intellectual must be both an analyst and a utopian, he must calculate the world's difficulties, and also its wild desires; he strives to be a philosophical and historical contemporary of the present. What would be the worth of a society that ceased to reflect upon itself? What would become of it? And how can we see ourselves except by talking to one another?

Les Nouvelles littéraires, January 13, 1975
From an interview conducted by Jean-Louis Ézine

The Play of the Kaleidoscope

Since the publication of Writing Degree Zero *in 1953, Roland Barthes has remained in the forefront of modern criticism, a brilliant and tireless participant in the theoretical work of the avant-garde. He has shown no sign of flagging during some twenty years of literary production: this trajectory through our modernity might remind us of Zeno's arrow, "which quivers, flies, and yet flies not at all," for it seems to be always just on the point of hitting its target. An illusion, no doubt: Roland Barthes assures us he has no objective destination in mind.*

And yet each of his books seems to offer the first fruits of a future completion—which becomes a kind of dalliance. Though intimately marked with the desire of writing, his work appears to decline its most natural invitations. In short, he refuses to compose. He prefers to show the public the writer's other side, not the busy scribbler in academic portraits, pen in hand, but that other hand, the empty one that seems to hold the weight of creation in its nonchalant repose. Roland Barthes's talent is always to be present at the birth *of a work, and never to show the text other than* in labor: *in the most Socratic sense of the word, he is a midwife for texts, for literary adventures and emotions.*

Roland Barthes has just published The Pleasure of the Text, *incontestably one of the great books of the decade.*

You are a reader, but doubtless in the sense meant by
Spengler, who claimed that reading as a great art
perished in Goethe's time, and that from then on the
reader demoralized *books. You place yourself doubt-*
less at the extreme vanguard of this enterprise of de-
moralization, which is poorly sustained, moreover, by
an army of obscure little scholars and other buzzing
academics . . .

In French, "to demoralize" has two meanings. In the nineteenth
century it meant "to remove morality," to champion amorality.
The current meaning is "to discourage." Do we discourage reading? Or do we "amoralize" it? Ideally, we should do nothing to
discourage reading, but everything to make it immoral . . . For
five years, the problem of reading has been at the center of the
critical stage, and now we have the appropriate epistemological
tools to help us. There are two methodologies that should allow
us to think of reading in a new way: ideological criticism and
Freudian psychoanalysis, both of which will force us to conceive
of a new subject-reader through their radical new philosophies
of the human subject.

Each of us is part of a generation, part of a culture and its
habits . . . When I read the books of other writers, what char-
acterizes me as a reader, I feel, is my unself-consciousness, my
casualness. When I'm complimented for being a reader, I'm very
touched, on the one hand—there is no compliment more beautiful than that—but on the other hand, I feel unworthy: in fact,
I read very little, and rather casually, as I said. If a book bores
me—and I'm easily bored by books—I drop it. I don't have much
time to read, except perhaps at bedtime . . . and what I want to
read then are old books, ripe with age, from a culture that has
since vanished . . .

Oh, I wouldn't say that you were a casual reader. Twenty
years ago, you stated that "writing is not at all an instru-
ment of communication, it is not an open path along
which travels the intention of language." And now?

I think one should never either deny or affirm systematically any written sentence. Today that sentence would have a different connotation. What remains true is the constancy of a paradoxical theme, the need continually to protest the usual reduction of language to a simple instrument of communication. That sentence was ahead of its time insofar as it is becoming more and more difficult to maintain that language is merely an instrument of expression and communication, because psychoanalysis, semiology, and structuralism have entered the fray. When someone speaks, we know that much more is going on, in both the speaker and his listener, than the simple message studied by linguistics.

> *Onto the severe stock of a scientific project—semiology— are being grafted the pleasure, even the* gourmandise *of language, and the exercise of style seems to be overtaking scientific practice in your work.*

You speak of style as if it were a pretty but superfluous decoration. I don't agree. Style is a very complex adventure. For centuries, the work of style has been alienated within ideologies that are no longer ours. Despite everything, what we call writing—the work of the body which is a prey to language—passes through style. There is always a stylistic phase in the work of writing. Writing even begins with style, which is not what is well written: style is drawn, as I was already saying in *Writing Degree Zero*, from the depths of the body, and cannot be reduced to a petty aesthetic desire for prettiness.

> *But you do have a pronounced taste for neologisms and other metaphors . . .*

That's true, I admit it.

> *I won't go so far as to claim that I wouldn't be surprised to hear you'd joined Oulipo [a literary group founded in the 1950s by Raymond Queneau and Georges Perec], but still . . .*

No, but writing is quite enjoyable, that dimension should not be forgotten. Style is definitely a kind of pleasure that comes along for the ride. We were talking about communication—I'm going to reverse myself now and speak for communication: in the present state of our civilization and culture, a text that is thought out with the help of style has a better chance of communicating, because style is an instrument of diffusion and percussion. Style must be accepted, if only from a tactical point of view . . . I refuse to be trapped in the opposition that sets style on the one hand and something more serious on the other. What is serious is to be within the signifier, i.e., within style, because that is where writing begins.

> *The shadow thrown by signifiers is starting to grow shorter, though.*

The word is becoming worn out in the course of things, but it is still serviceable. It's a matter of opinion.

> *You yourself have been putting a few signifiers on the shelf, lately . . .*

I'm very sensitive to the freshness of words, and also to their wearing out—thus, my taste for neologisms: I live constantly in a restless relation to language, and I very quickly take the measure of my taste or distaste for certain words. In fact, I spend my time taking up certain words and getting rid of others. So I don't always live with the same ones, which allows for those periodically necessary, and very useful, deflations of language.

> *Michaux said that the more an investigator discovers, the less time he has to realize his new ignorance. What is the extent of your ignorance these days?*

Like everyone, I go through phases of appreciation and depreciation in self-esteem; in any case, I don't always have the same idea of my tasks, my aptitudes, not even of my pleasures.

*You have always possessed the secret of being forgiven
for your boldness, which some might call impudence.
Hermetism, for example, when you wrote: "I write criticism, not in order to make things intelligible, but in
order to learn about the unintelligible."*

That was the structuralist phase: the goal was to understand what
understanding is. So that proposition wasn't a paradox, it was
even epistemologically well-founded. A writer never becomes aware
of the increasing obscurity of his language with a light heart;
language is not an infinite translation system. There is a complete
register of ideas, of clause-sentences, which can be produced only
in a certain obscurity. We have to accept this, to trust history,
even the sidelights of history, which will get things moving again
sooner or later. Besides, obscurity itself can be a theatrical tool
of writing, one needn't necessarily give it up . . . even if one
catches the classicist virus and begins envying a kind of formulation that has the appearance, in any case, of clarity.

*You're the leader of a school of criticism. What does this
mean to you?*

For a writer, nothing is more difficult than obtaining a precise
idea of his own role and image: your image comes to you only
in fragments, and it's almost impossible to know precisely what
happens to the work you do. Besides, I haven't the vocation to
be a *chef d'école*.

*When one of your innovations starts showing up all over,
like some kind of nervous tic, how do you feel about it?*

I'm very philosophical and tolerant about that. It's inevitable, and
it doesn't bother me.

*Are you a "repressed" novelist? I almost said a novelist
manqué . . .*

Perhaps a future novelist, who knows. Your question is a good one, not because I have an easy answer ready, but because it touches on something absorbing to me, which is the problem, if not of the novel, at least of the novelistic. In daily life, I feel a sort of curiosity for everything I see and hear, almost an intellectual affectivity, which is on the order of the novelistic. A century ago, I suppose I would have strolled through life with the notebook of a realist novelist. But I can't see myself today composing a story, an anecdote, with characters who have names; in short, a novel. For me, the problem—a problem for the future, because I would very much like to begin working in this vein—will be to discover, slowly, the form which would separate the novelistic from the novel, but would assume the novelistic more profoundly than I have been able to do up until now.

> *You can't really disapprove of an atmosphere you yourself were among the first to help fashion. Besides, what use would be a theory that wasn't put into practice?*

There's a kind of eros of language in me, an impulse of desire regarding language, which has made me into a being of language. It was through an accident of history that this being came into existence at a time when the sciences and philosophies of language had begun to enjoy a very great, profound, and new importance. I and my enthusiasm were carried along by the times, and I was able to make a place for myself, so that it's no longer easy to determine whether I am entirely a product of these times or whether I helped shape them, even if only a little . . . Moreover, theory must lead to practice, and at every point in theory there must be the thought of practice. I think that theory can mark time now, and that there should be a new "working" phase, I would almost say an experimental phase. That's where one comes up against social reality, and the problem is to learn where these textual experiments can lead.

> *The revenge of the signified?*

No, the signified is a constant danger, especially in the "scientistic" areas of literature—and even in the name of the signifier. Semiology itself is beginning to engender some "scientism" here and there. What counters the risk of theological recuperation— by a signified—is to emphasize the pleasure of production, to make oneself a producer, which is to say an amateur. The great figure of a liberated civilization would be the amateur. Currently, the amateur has no status, no viable role, but one can imagine a society where those who wanted to could produce. It would be splendid.

> *For the last thirty years, literature has seemed to draw away from the world.*

No longer able to master historical reality, literature passed from a system of representation to one of symbolic games. For the first time in its history, the world overflows literature. At bottom, literature is in a constant state of surprise at a world even more profuse than itself.

> *If you write a novel in the near future, people will say that you have taken the plunge . . . and that your critical work has given you a considerable running start.*

I like that image, but it would give credence to the idea that my life's work has had a meaning, an evolution, a goal that would define the truth of this work. I don't like the idea of a unitary subject, I prefer the play of the kaleidoscope: you give it a tap, and the little bits of colored glass form a new pattern . . . If I were to write a novel, the most difficult thing for me would not be the problems linked to a lengthy literary form but quite simply to give names to the characters, for example, or to use the past historic tense.

> *Do you still find it difficult to choose a name for a cat?*

Well . . . one can always write, as Chateaubriand did in his *Life of Rancé*, that the cat was yellow . . . and it's already a novel.

Le Magazine littéraire, February 1975
From an interview conducted by Jean-Jacques Brochier

Twenty Key Words for Roland Barthes

From familiar themes—analogy, doxa, sign —to the irruption of the pleasure of the text, to the fragments of Roland Barthes, Barthes talks to us here about some key words and several of the authors who have been, and remain, important to him.

The irruption of the word "pleasure"

The word "pleasure," the subject of your latest work, has appeared fairly recently in your writing.

That word appeared in what I would call a tactical fashion. I felt that today's intellectual language was submitting too easily to moralizing imperatives that eliminated all notion of enjoyment, of bliss. In reaction, I wanted therefore to reintroduce this word within my personal range, to lift its censorship, to unblock it, to *un-repress* it.

In the order of ideas, a tactical movement finds ample reasonable explanations with which to surround itself. The first reason is that I give a certain importance on the subjective level to what can be grouped under the somewhat outmoded label of hedonism, and I give particular importance to the theme of the art of living. These are things to which I have already drawn attention, indirectly; for example, when I have spoken of Brecht and his beloved cigars. Moreover, there is an extensive consideration of pleasure in all of Brecht's undeniably Marxist oeuvre.

In my case, I have taken on the responsibility of a certain hedonism, the return of a philosophy discredited and repressed for centuries: first of all by Christian morality, then again by positivistic, rationalistic morality, and unfortunately once again by a certain Marxist ethic.

The second justification for this return of the word "pleasure" is that it permits a certain exploration of the human subject. When one tries to make a distinction between "pleasure" and "bliss," when one considers the problem of *jouissance*, one takes up a very modern and timely thematics, one quite familiar to psychoanalysis and interesting to what is called the avant-garde.

> *You set up a relation, and often an opposition, between "pleasure"* [plaisir] *and "bliss"* [jouissance].

The opposition "pleasure/bliss" is one of those voluntarily artificial oppositions for which I've always had a certain predilection. I've often tried to create such oppositions: for example, between *écriture* and *écrivance*, "denotation" and "connotation." These oppositions shouldn't be taken literally; for example, by asking if such and such a text belongs to the order of pleasure or of bliss. These oppositions are intended above all to clear more ground, to make headway—just to talk and to write.

Having said that, let me add: the difference between the two words is still quite real, and I'm not the only one to insist on it. Pleasure is linked to a consistence of the self, of the subject, which is assured in values of comfort, relaxation, ease—and for me, that's the entire realm of reading the classics, for example. On the contrary, bliss is the system of reading, or utterance, through which the subject, instead of establishing itself, is lost, experiencing that expenditure which is, properly speaking, bliss.

If one wanted to establish a provisional classification of texts according to these two words, it would be clear that the great majority of texts we know and love consist roughly of texts of pleasure, while texts of bliss are extremely rare—and there's no assurance that they are also texts of pleasure. These are texts that may displease you, provoke you, but which, at least temporarily, in the flash of an instant, change and transmute you, effecting that expenditure of the self in loss.

This theme of bliss skirts other themes, for example, not drugs in the proper sense, but "addiction," or certain forms of perversion.

> *Without getting involved in a distribution of prizes, if you had to offer examples of texts of bliss, which ones would you mention?*

Let's say, texts of the avant-garde, texts that don't tend toward the probable and the realistic. As soon as a text submits to a code of verisimilitude, no matter how incendiary it may be . . . I'm thinking of Sade, for example: it's tempting to put Sade with the texts of bliss, and he belongs there on many counts, not because he speaks of bliss, but by the manner in which he does so; but despite all this, the Sadean text, because it is subject to a code of verisimilitude through the constraint of its period, remains aligned with texts of pleasure. The text of bliss should be on the side of a certain illegibility. It should unsettle us, not only on the level of our imagination, but on the level of language itself.

> *Then the work of Severo Sarduy, for example, would be closer to* jouissance.

Completely. And Sollers's writings. But this is difficult to explain because the criteria for judging texts of bliss are still obscure, whereas those for judging texts of pleasure are readily imaginable.

> *Especially since time has a tendency to turn texts of bliss into texts of pleasure.*

Of course. Culture recuperates. Recuperation is the great law of history.

Analogy, nature, *imaginaire*

> *There is a series of concepts you seem to detest in particular: analogy, nature, and* imaginaire, *the image-repertoire.*

As for analogy and nature, that's quite true, and my distaste is of long standing; I have always been hostile to analogical forms of thought and art. And it's for the opposite reason that I have so loved, if I may say so, the linguistic sign: because I discovered, reading Saussure so many years ago, that there is no analogy within the linguistic sign, that there is no relationship of resemblance between the signifier and the signified. That's something which has always intrigued me in the linguistic sign and in all its transformations into written sentences, texts, and so on.

Further analysis leads us to understand that the denunciation of analogy is in fact a denunciation of the "natural," of pseudo-nature. The social, conformist world always bases its idea of nature on the fact that things resemble each other, and the resulting idea of nature is both artificial and repressive: the "natural." Common sense always considers things that resemble each other "natural." I thus went very easily from analogy to this theme of the "natural," of "what seems natural to most people." And it's a very familiar theme in my writing, one already at work in *Mythologies*, which present themselves as a denunciation of "what goes without saying." It's also a Brechtian theme: "Underneath the rule discover the abuse." Under cover of the natural, discover history, uncover what is not natural, discover abuses.

As for the image-repertoire, it's a more recent term, since it's now used in a Lacanian sense, and no longer in a Bachelardian sense.

> *Or in a Sartrean sense.*

No, although it would be rather interesting to go back someday to those first writings of Sartre, a wealth of material that is now completely ignored. The Sartrean question should be reopened. And I think that this will come about on its own.

What Lacan means by *imaginaire* is closely related to analogy, analogy between images, since the image-repertoire is the register where the subject adheres to an image in a movement of identification that relies in particular on the coalescence of the signifier and the signified. Here we reencounter the theme of representation, figuration, the homogeneity of images and models.

> *And you challenge that way of thinking with an understanding of the signifier.*

We must be careful of that word, it's beginning to wear out. I'm interested, if not in the signifier, at least in what is called *signifiance*, which is a regime of meaning, of course, but one that never closes upon a signified, and where the subject, when he listens, speaks, writes, even at the level of his inner text, always goes from signifier to signifier, through meaning, without ever ending in closure. Whereas analogy closes itself off, and justifies this closure by pointing to an identity between the two parts of the sign.

The fragment, the *dictée*, the haiku

> *Isn't this interest in* significance *linked in your work to a taste for bits and pieces, beginnings, a fondness for fragments of writing like the haiku?*

I have long had a taste for discontinuous writing, a tendency reactivated in *Roland Barthes*. Rereading my books and articles, which I had never done before, I noticed that my mode of writing was never lengthy, always proceeding by fragments, miniatures, paragraphs with titles, or articles—there was an entire period of my life during which I wrote no books, only articles. It's this taste for the short form that is now becoming systematic. The implication from the point of view of an ideology or a counter-ideology of form is that the fragment breaks up what I would call the smooth finish, the composition, discourse constructed to give a final meaning to what one says, which is the general rule of all past rhetoric. In relation to the smooth finish of constructed discourse, the fragment is a spoilsport, discontinuous, establishing a kind of pulverization of sentences, images, thoughts, none of which "takes" definitively.

Anarchic writing, in a way.

I would be delighted if that were so, but only on the condition that "anarchy" not be the signified of this system. The complication in this system of forms is that they must be kept from "taking," from solidifying. This position is a bit paradoxical in relation to avant-garde style, but perhaps the best way to prevent this solidification is to pretend to remain within an apparently classical code, to keep the appearance of a writing subject to certain stylistic imperatives, and thus to attain the dissociation of an ultimate meaning through a form that is not spectacularly disorganized, that avoids hysteria.

The ruse of writing after the ruse of history?

Yes. I'm not at all sure that such is the result of what I do, but if I wanted something, that would be it.

There are two completely established styles, however, which you seem very fond of: the dictée *and the haiku.*

In *Roland Barthes*, there are indeed several "dictations." I was very interested in the problem of the *dictée*. When I wanted to recount a childhood memory, it would take a certain form of writing on its own, which is roughly the writing of our schooldays, the way we were taught to write, the form of the dictation or composition. The natural discourse of memory is the scholastic discourse, the discourse of dictation. Instead of completely foreclosing this mode of expression, I decided to assume it, to give myself an occasional composition subject or dictation. As if I were giving a future selected excerpt to a schoolbook anthology. This is perhaps very pretentious of me, but I did this in an essentially playful spirit, without imagining at all that I would end up one day in a French textbook.

I thus implicitly placed quotation marks around certain fragments in *Roland Barthes*—but I trust this is quite obvious.

But you carefully avoided doing pastiches of dictées.

You're right to mention that, I did not want to do pastiches. When I started working on this book, I thought that I was going to parody myself, writing literary criticism of someone who by accident just happened to be myself. Then I realized, after the first excitement of a gag project, a practical joke, that it wasn't working, it was boring. And then I'm perhaps not very gifted in parody.

It's at that point that my project changed, and I gave up the idea of an intentional parody, while still remaining vaguely within a citational, intertextual area.

The haiku is something else again: it's the essential, musical future of the fragment, its form of becoming. I encountered it in its real and historical nature during my travels in Japan. I have a profound admiration, that is, a profound desire, for this form. If I imagine myself writing other things, some of them would be on the order of the haiku. The haiku is a very short form, but unlike the maxim, an equally short form, it is characterized by its matteness. It engenders no sense, but at the same time it is not non-sense. It's always the same problem: to keep meaning from taking hold, but without abandoning meaning, under the threat of falling into the worst meaning, nonmeaning.

In *Roland Barthes*, there are fragments like a haiku, not in a poetic form, which I called "anamneses": memories of my childhood and youth, given in a few sentences at most, which have the characteristic—at least I hope so, it's difficult to bring off— of being absolutely matte. Not solidified.

The haiku is a bit of an anti-*dictée*. That's why it was legitimate to link the two notions together.

The three arrogances

> *You speak at one point of the three arrogances:* doxa
> *(opinion, consensus), science, and militancy. Now, lin-*
> *guistics is a science, after all, and it has been one of the*
> *mainstays of your critical thought and approach.*

That's true. But to begin with, I have not always had the same
intolerance for scientific arrogance. Science, or rather scientificity, used to fascinate me. What separates me today from linguistics is that it wants to be a science of language, but it remains
glued, in an almost analogical or imaginary manner, to a scientific
metalanguage, thus rejoining the world of the signified. What I
currently challenge in linguistics, and in the other human sciences, is that they are incapable of putting into question their
own type of utterance, their own mode of discourse.

At present, it seems difficult to avoid this problematics of utterance, because we have known very well for some thirty years
that utterance is affected by two factors previously unknown to
us: ideology and the awareness of ideology, and the unconscious
and an awareness of the unconscious, if I may put it that way.
The entire problem of utterance, of discourse, whatever its site,
must now pass through a consideration of these two factors—
which by definition elude the subject who writes, who does not
know exactly in which ideology he is entrapped and who does
not know his own unconscious.

The problem of the human sciences is that they are ignorant
of ideology and the unconscious. Now, if I may be permitted
a play on words, although it is not unusual for these two
forces to be misunderstood, it is quite unusual for them to be
ignored.

But this is a problem of general history: we cannot do everything
at once. And the distance I keep with regard to the linguistic—
even the semiological—sciences is not at all a distance in regard to these scientists themselves. Let's just say that, personally,
I no longer feel the need to proffer an orthodox linguistic discourse. In any case, I was never more than an amateur in
linguistics.

Isn't this distrust of science a very Sartrean attitude? Even if he never expresses it directly, Sartre is characterized by a certain distance in regard to science.

When I began to write, after the war, Sartre was the avant-garde. The encounter with Sartre was very important to me. I have always been, not fascinated, the word is absurd, but changed, carried away, almost set on fire by his writing as an essayist. He truly created a new language of the essay, which impressed me very much. Sartre's distrust of science, however, came from the standpoint of phenomenological philosophy, a philosophy of the existential subject, whereas mine is rooted in a psychoanalytical language, at least at present.

But psychoanalysis is also a philosophy of the subject.

Which is why I repeat that Sartrism should be reexamined, and so to speak rewritten, at least in the Chomskian sense.

You speak of the arrogance of science and militancy, yet Chomsky, precisely, wants to be scientific and militant.

I have no humoral fellow feeling for Chomsky. Obviously, I admire him. But the linguist for whom I feel the greatest affinity is Benveniste. We owe a great deal to Saussure, of course, to Jakobson, to others. But in the end, only a small number of people make a lasting impression on you. In my case, there was Sartre. There was Brecht, and there still is, I still feel a close tie to Brecht. And there was Benveniste.

Isn't it also because there is a novelistic side to Benveniste, an aspect of imagination in philology? Noms d'agents et Noms d'actions en indo-européen *is also a wonderful novel.*

What is so beautiful in Benveniste is that he's a scholar not only of language, of the language function, but also of languages. He tackled languages themselves, and it is these that are important, more so than language in general. Benveniste was thus led to deal with extremely concrete matters, through nouns, names, words. Which gives that almost novelistic aspect to his work.

There is also a writing in Benveniste, a style, both of thought and form, that is extraordinary. This is not simply *écrivance*, the instrumental writing of a scholar recording his thoughts. There is a specific relation between Benveniste's body (even though it may struggle to appear absent) and what it writes, the manner in which it writes. What I love in Benveniste is this aspect at once burning and discreet, the total absence of intellectual vulgarity, his tact—all the aesthetic values I find infinitely seductive. Moreover, almost the same palette of values can be found in Brecht.

Since this interview will be published, I think I ought to say this: a few of us are scandalized at the current plight of Benveniste; he is now a very sick man, enduring his illness under extremely difficult material circumstances, totally ignored not only by the fashion of today's culture but also by its official aspects as well, and this is a man who is without a doubt one of the greatest scholars in France today. His situation, unhappily not limited to physical misery—he was struck four or five years ago by illness, a terrible illness, especially for a man of language—should make society ashamed.

Names, personal pronouns

> *You attach great importance to names. Your Proustian ancestry?*

Again, this is going back rather far, because the only text I wrote on Proust was one on proper nouns. It's true that my relation to proper nouns is mysterious to me, on the order of *signifiance*, desire, perhaps even of bliss. Psychoanalysis has paid a great deal of attention to these problems, and we know very well that the proper noun is, if I may say so, an open road for the subject and desire. I acknowledge that loving and enigmatic attachment to proper nouns, particularly those of my childhood. I spent my childhood and part of my adolescence among the bourgeoisie of a small provincial city, Bayonne, and I was constantly exposed to the names of Bayonne's bourgeois families, which have always interested, amused, and intrigued me by their consonance, their pure poetic phonetism, as well as their social and historical weight.

And a second direction of interest—when I read novels, novels of times gone by, or memoirs, I am very sensitive to proper nouns. I've even thought now and then that the success of a novel depended on the success of its onomastics.

> *As proof, you wrote an article on Pierre Loti called "Aziyadé."*

The name "Aziyadé" was a very good find.

> *Let's go on from names to pronouns. In your latest book there is a game, a very subtle movement between "R.B." and "I." A sentence in which R.B. is the subject, in the third person, might very casually include a possessive adjective in the first person.*

In *Roland Barthes* there are four regimes: "I"; "he" (I speak of myself by saying "he"); "R.B.," my initials; and sometimes I speak of myself by saying "you." I explained myself somewhat on this point in a fragment, but explications, being essentially imaginary, do not exhaust a subject. It's up to the reader to go beyond what I say.

Roughly, let's say that the pronoun "I" is really the pronoun of the image-repertoire, the self. Every time I say "I," I can be sure, like now, by the way, that I am within the image-repertoire. I wanted to weave a kind of moiré with all those pronouns in order to write a book that is in fact the book of the image-repertoire, of *l'imaginaire*, but an image-repertoire that tries to undo itself, unravel itself, to dismember itself, through mental structures that are no longer only those of the image-repertoire, without being, for all that, the structure of truth. There's a back-and-forth movement, a kind of Brownian movement, between different neurotic dominants.

"I" is the pronoun of the image-repertoire; "he," which I use rather often, is the pronoun of distance. It can be taken in several ways, the choice is up to the reader: either as a sort of inflation, as if I gave myself such importance that I say "he" in speaking of myself—or as a kind of mortification: to say "he" in speaking of someone is to absent him, mortify him, turn him into something just a little bit dead. It could also be—but this would be a too-lucky hypothesis . . . let's offer it anyway—the "he" of distance in a Brechtian perspective, an epic "he" through which I criticize myself.

As for the "you," there also we have two possible interpretations. I rarely say "you" to myself, but it happens occasionally. "You" can be taken as the pronoun of accusation, self-accusation, a kind of decomposed paranoia, but also in a much more empirical, unself-conscious manner, like the Sadean "you," with which Sade addresses himself in certain notes. It's the "you" of the writing operator, who puts himself—which was so modern and brilliant at the time—in position to disengage the scriptor from the subject.

"R.B." is not very important. He appears mostly in sentences where "he" would be ambiguous.

> *Doesn't R.B. designate, in a rather rhetorical manner, the character who remembers? The source of indirect discourse: R.B. said that . . .*

There is certainly retentivity, in the textual music, of the very lovely piece Philippe Sollers wrote about me in *Tel Quel*, entitled "R.B."

The amateur

> *Another word I picked out is "amateur," a word often used by Roger Vailland. What does "amateur" mean to you?*

This theme interests me. I can take it in a purely practical and empirical fashion: when I have the time, I paint or play music in the completely assumed role of a simple amateur. The enormous benefit of the amateur's situation is that it involves no image-repertoire, no narcissism. When one draws or paints as an amateur, there is no preoccupation with the *imago*, the image one will project of oneself in making the drawing or painting. It's thus a liberation, I would almost say a liberation from civilization. To be included in a utopia à la Fourier. A civilization where people would act without being preoccupied with the image of themselves they will project to others.

This theme, so important on a practical level, is converted into theory, insofar as I can imagine a society to come, completely de-alienated, that would no longer know anything except amateur activity on the level of writing. Particularly on the order of the text. People would write, make texts, for pleasure, they would benefit from the bliss of writing without any concern for their *imago*.

> *What is your relation to music? You say that you play music as an amateur, but playing the piano involves regular practice, a continuous effort.*

I studied piano when I was a child. My father's sister, who lived in Bayonne, was a piano teacher. And so I lived in an atmosphere of music. But I haven't studied since, I have no technique, no speed. I did learn to read music at an early age, and my fingers follow as best they can. So I can sight-read music, but I don't really know how to play. Which is fine for amateur playing. Despite lagging tempi and false notes, I still manage to attain the materiality of the musical text, because it passes into my fingers. The sensuality of music is not purely auditory, it is also muscular.

The amateur is not a consumer. Contact between the amateur's body and his art is very close, imbued with presence. That's what is beautiful about it, and that's where the future lies. But here things open onto a problem of civilization. Technical development and the evolution of mass culture reinforce the division between producers and consumers to a frightening extent. We are a consumer society, and not at all a society of amateurs.

History has its repercussions, its mishaps, that famous bell curve familiar to statisticians. There have been periods of alienation (monarchical or even feudal societies) where there was a real amateurism in the heart of the ruling classes. What we should do is find that amateurism again elsewhere than in the "elite" of society. At present, we're at a bit of a low point on the curve.

> *That's why you speak somewhere of the (discreet) charm of bourgeois culture. Because there is no other culture besides bourgeois culture.*

There is a petit-bourgeois culture, which is a degraded bourgeois culture, and that's normal, historically speaking.

Politics

> *What is the place of politics? In what you write, your relation to politics is extremely discreet.*

Discreet, but obsessed. I would first like to make a distinction which may seem somewhat specious to you, but it is quite valid to me: between "the political" and "politics." To me, the political is a fundamental order of history, of thought, of everything that is done, and said. It's the very dimension of the real. Politics, however, is something else, it's the moment when the political changes into the same old story, the discourse of repetition. My profound interest in the attachment of the political is equaled only by my intolerance of political discourse. Which doesn't make my situation very easy. My position is somewhat divided, and often guilt-ridden. But I think that I'm not the only one, and that at present most people, at least most intellectuals, have a guilty relation to politics. One of the essential duties of today's avant-garde would be to address this problem of the intellectual's guilt in regard to politics.

The situation is complicated because this problem should be dealt with in a dialectical manner: it's impossible to liquidate politics in favor of a pure and simple depoliticization. What we need is a mode of presence within the discourse of the political which would not be repetitive.

My methods are obviously discreet, obscure. What I'm looking for is a kind of deflation, because I feel surrounded and menaced by the inflation of political discourse.

But politics is not just discourse, it's also activity.

That's a big problem: is it really an activity, is it anything else besides discourse?

> *When one reads* Mythologies, *the texts seem directly political. Not only the article on Poujade, but also the ones on Bardot, or the Eiffel Tower. And then, in what you wrote afterward, the political environment becomes both more and more discreet and ever more menacing. Your* Michelet *is by its very subject linked to the political, and even to politics.*

Although that is one of the aspects that I doubtless underestimated: his ideology.

> *But you say that you took care of that in one page, the first page.*

It's perhaps not one of my better efforts.

> *In* Roland Barthes, *it seems that the political is constantly present, but hidden, as a potential for aggression.*

Yes, as a discourse. Which doesn't imply any ambiguity regarding the practical options available to the French at this time. What is in question is the relation to discourse. If the problem has evolved, become more complex, it's because arrogant discourse came only from the right when I wrote *Mythologies*, whereas now we can see the growth of arrogance in the left. The heart of my personal problem is that there is an arrogant leftist discourse: I'm divided between my situation within a political site and the aggressions of discourse coming from this site.

> *And yet, if we go back to the period of* Mythologies, *which is around the time when intellectuals like Edgar Morin were expelled from the Communist Party, the*

> *arrogance of Stalinist discourse was much stronger than*
> *it is now.*

Yes, that's true. There is more discursive arrogance today in leftism than in communism. But, if I may say so, things aren't any the better for it. Because it means that communist language is passing into the somewhat sticky language of *doxa*, opinion, the natural, the obvious, the "it goes without saying." We're still caught between these two languages; I outlined their mode of domination in speaking of the reign of one and the triumph of the other. We're caught between the two, and that's why the current situation is difficult to live in.

> *Thus, the movement of many on the left toward the*
> *right, because it's easier to live there.*

Of course, but I don't want any part of it. I'd rather be accused of a "precarious position" than be complacent.

> *The real* bête noire *is* doxa *(majority opinion), and "the*
> *pleasure of the text" is a new attack against conformity.*

Yes. When *doxa* appears as a censorship of pleasure, of *jouissance*, then the counter-offensive is reinforced by an impulse of *jouissance*, exploding in that passion which is, if not violent, at least tenacious in the struggle against consensus, majority opinion.

Reading

> *One thing strikes me: you're one of the few critics who*
> *says: "I love to read."*

I wouldn't want to deprive you of an illusion, all the more so in that I do love to read. But I am not a great reader, I'm a casual reader, casual in the sense that I very quickly take the measure of my own pleasure. If a book bores me, I have the courage, or cowardice, to drop it. I'm freeing myself more and more from any superego in regard to books. So, if I read a book, it's because I want to.

My reading schedule is not at all a regular and placid ingestion of books. Either a book bores me and I put it aside, or it excites me and I constantly want to stop reading it so that I can think about what I've just read—which is also reflected in the way I read for my work: I'm unable, unwilling, to sum up a book, to efface myself behind a capsule description of it on an index card, but on the contrary, I'm quite ready to pick out certain sentences, certain characteristics of the book, to ingest them as discontinuous fragments. This is obviously not a good philological attitude, since it comes down to deforming the book for my own purposes.

> *You said somewhere that you have written only commissioned books. Is this true of* The Pleasure of the Text?

No, that is an exception. The subject was not proposed to me, I obviously decided upon it myself. What I meant was that a commission is often a good incentive, and for a very long time I wrote because people asked me to. The only text I wrote without being asked for it was the first one I showed to Nadeau, through a friend. After that, texts and subjects were always more or less proposed to me.

At present, this is changing. I'm feeling a bit cooped up by commissions, and I'd rather write books on my own initiative. For the pleasure of writing them, fashioning them, feigning them (in the etymological sense).

The country, the café

> *You speak of the country in* Roland Barthes; *perhaps it's my lack of imagination, I can't see you "out in the country" at all! You say that the arrangement of things—desk, piano, pens—is the same as in Paris. But the environment is so different.*

Not at all. In the southwest of France, I live in my house. The country is my house. The opposition isn't between the city and the country but between an apartment and a house. Which doesn't mean that the environment doesn't exist for me (I particularly love the light of the southwest).

> *Cafés are very important to you . . .*

They are where I have my rendezvous, and I love cafés because they are complex spaces. When I'm in a café, I'm completely involved with those who are at the same table with me, I'm all ears to what they say to me, and at the same time, as in a text, a paragram, a stereophony, there is a field of diversion all around me, people entering and leaving, triggering something novelistic. I'm very sensitive to this stereophony.

Whereas the country is solitude. One's dream would be to arrive in the country to spend a month or two, but with some intellectual work already well laid out, so that one could putter away at it, like a civil servant, or a roadmender.

> *But the country is also a place of dissipation: you talk*
> *about all those little things—eating a pear, going to look*
> *at a plant—that distract you from work.*

It's just that work is boring, which should never be denied.

The novelistic

> *I was struck by that sentence where you say "I think of*
> *myself not as a critic but as a novelist—not of the novel*
> *but of the novelistic. I love the novelistic, but I know*
> *that the novel is dead."*

The novelistic is a mode of discourse unstructured by a story; a mode of notation, investment, interest in daily reality, in people, in everything that happens in life. The transformation of this novelistic material into a novel seems very difficult to me because I can't imagine myself elaborating a narrative object where there would be a story, which to me means essentially verbs in the imperfect and past historic, characters who are psychologically believable—that's the sort of thing I could never do, that's why a novel seems impossible to me. But at the same time I would like very much to work more on the novelistic experience, the novelistic utterance.

You've never written a novel, started a novel?

Quite frankly, no, never.

You were saying that every biography is fictive, novelistic, a novel that doesn't dare speak its name. Isn't Roland Barthes, *which is a biography, also a novel?*

It's a novel, but not a biography. The detour is not the same. It's intellectually novelistic—novelistic for two reasons. First of all, many of the fragments concern the novelistic surface of life, and in addition, what is presented or staged in these fragments is an image-repertoire; i.e., the very discourse of the novel. I put myself on stage as a character in a novel, but one without a name, in a way, someone who wouldn't have any adventures suitable for a novel.

The book's discourse is novelistic rather than intellectual, which is why it doesn't mind being a bit stupid sometimes . . . insofar as it isn't the intellectual subject who identifies with his utterance, but another subject, a novelistic subject, who thus occasionally tosses off ideas or judgments that the first subject finds a little silly, but out they come all the same because they belong to the image-repertoire.

The place of stupidity in your world is a curious one, moreover. It's everywhere and nowhere, somewhat like God for you.

Let's hope for God's sake that the converse is not true. I do find stupidity fascinating. And nauseating, of course. It's very difficult to talk about stupidity, since the discourse of stupidity is a discourse from which one cannot *simply* exclude oneself. I don't mean that one can't be innocent of it, that would be bad faith, but one can't be innocent of it *simply*.

We've known this since Flaubert, whose attitude toward stupidity is quite complex—apparently critical, but falsely so, that's obvious. An attitude of uneasiness.

In any case, stupidity's mode of being is triumph. One can do nothing against stupidity. One can only internalize it, take a small homeopathic dose of it—but not too much.

> *Whereas* Mythologies *was completely directed against stupidity.*

Mythologies was based on a much simpler political, or counter-ideological consciousness, for the historical reasons I mentioned.

A few important names

> *Sade?*

Yes, and for an immediate reason: I love to read Sade. Perhaps I don't read him as one should—but who knows how one should read Sade? I read him in a very novelistic fashion. I think he is a very great writer, in the most classical sense of the word; he constructed marvelous novels. That's what I love in Sade, and not so much the transgressive aspect—although I understand its importance. I love Sade as a writer, as I love Proust.

> *Marx?*

Each time I read or reread him, I experience, not the wonderment one might feel before the founder of an important vulgate in today's political game, but the astonishment one feels before someone who has effected a break in discourse, in discursiveness. On each page of Marx, there is a detour into the unexpected and the penetrating, even outside his system, and I'm very alert to that sort of thing.

> *Brecht?*

Yes, Brecht: I've always loved his theater, and his intellectual work perhaps even more. His last essays constitute an admirable book, *Writings on Politics and Society*, translated four or five years ago. A book both just and violent. A text I constantly want to quote. While writing *Roland Barthes*, I wasn't sure at one point that I'd have enough to say, and I considered—if only as a fantasy—inserting passages from Brecht.

I discovered Brecht in 1954, when the Berliner Ensemble came to present *Mother Courage* at the invitation of the Théâtre des Nations, and I remember very well being up in the balcony of the Sarah Bernhardt Theater with Bernard Dort, where I was literally inflamed with enthusiasm for that production, but, let me add right away, inflamed also by the twenty or so lines of Brecht printed in the theater program. I had never read a language like that on theater and art.

> *What did you discover?*

It's a discovery that has evolved. First of all, I was captivated by the alliance of extremely vigilant, informed, and firm Marxist thought with a sense of pleasure, of forms, colors, lighting, materials, all that artistic materiality so extraordinarily thought out. I understood that the product of these two constraints was the very thing to do, the object to be desired. Then I read more Brecht, and discovered in him that ethic of both pleasure and intellectual vigilance, responsibility, an ethic wasting no time with pathos, with humanist or free-will sentimentality.

There is also a sly side to Brecht, and if I may say so—the word also has the connotation of excessive subtlety—a certain Chinese aspect.

> *You don't reduce Brecht to his theater, as many others do?*

No. He is a great writer of ideas. In *Writings on Politics and Society* the essay takes on a thousand forms. Not just dissertations, but bits of dialogue, projects, announcements, notes, schemes: everything that makes things lively.

> *In the end, Sartre was wrong to say, during the 1950s,*
> *that Lukàcs was the only Marxist who knew how to read.*
> *There was also Brecht . . .*

Obviously. As for Lukàcs, I couldn't say, I don't know his work
very well, and he doesn't interest me very much. In the end, his
criteria aren't very systematic. There is, if I may say so, an aesthetics of the intellect.

Gide

> *In* Roland Barthes, *you speak of Gide as your "Ur-suppe,"*
> *your primordial literary broth.*

We no longer talk enough about Gide. He was important to me
when I was young. Doubtless, this masked other things: I didn't
have any literary contacts with Surrealism, whereas I had numerous contacts with Gide. And I've always felt greatly drawn to
Gide. He wrote at least one great book, a great modern book:
Paludes, which should be reevaluated today, without a doubt.
And the *Journal*, which I always particularly liked, in connection
with the themes that interest me: that authenticity which out-
maneuvers itself, twisting, until it is no longer authenticity. The
thematics of the *Journal* is very close to that of the fragments of
Roland Barthes.

Criticism

> *Let me put things in the proper context: you had written*
> *a series of prefaces to the plays of Racine, which were*
> *collected and published, with an introduction, as* On
> Racine. *Then a Sorbonne professor, himself the writer*
> *of a thesis on Racine, wrote a pamphlet entitled* New
> Criticism or New Imposture, *a pamphlet directed against*
> *several writers, you in particular. To which you re-*
> *sponded with your text* Critique et Vérité. *Aside from*
> *the fact that Picard had written a huge historical thesis*
> *on Racine that few people had read, whereas everyone*

> *had read your book, what was really at stake in this*
> *polemic?*

That goes back a long way. Speaking objectively and, if I may use the word, historically, even if "history" seems a big word for this small affair, the stake was strictly academic at first, in my opinion. A vocabulary from my prefaces on Racine was doubtless infiltrating the dissertations of Sorbonne students—because the question is essentially one of terminology—and the professor, finally, simply had enough. There was probably a quite understandable feeling of intolerance on the professor's part: the outrage one feels at seeing a language taking over center stage in a massive and endless wave.

I think that the pamphlet by this professor, who was moreover a talented man, sprang from that personal intolerance he felt at seeing over and over in theses on Racine a vocabulary that wasn't the vocabulary of traditional criticism of great works of the past— and this is where the academic stake is redoubled by an ideological stake. Traditional criticism continued to be either positivistic criticism of literary history, of sources, of influences, or else aesthetic criticism—and such was the case with that professor, who tried his hand at an aesthetic criticism reminiscent of Valéry in his prefaces to Racine's theater. Another traditional school of criticism offered a psychology completely outmoded today because it ignores psychoanalysis.

In this somewhat artificial duel, there was the traditional struggle between the old and the new. What was new, in a modest fashion, was that I was using, in connection with texts as classical as Racine's plays, a language unlike those of psychological or aesthetic criticism, or the criticism of sources.

> *But hadn't psychoanalytical criticism already gained ac*
> *ademic respectability through such people as Charles*
> *Mauron?*

True. But there were two languages in *On Racine*, two epistemologies, to use big words: on the one hand, psychoanalytical language, or at least its vulgate, and on the other, an attempt at structuration. Structural language was beginning to enter criticism, and I had analyzed Racine's characters not in psychological terms but according to their position in a structure: relations of authority, subjection, etc. So there were these two elements that, in the eyes of a Sorbonne professor, were unduly fashionable: a psychoanalytical language and a structuralist language.

Psychoanalysis could enter Academe through people like Mauron because Mauron's brand of psychoanalysis is old-fashioned, quite orthodox in relation to the first stirrings of psychoanalytical literary criticism; this criticism anchors the work in relation to the author's early childhood. If you included the author's life or early childhood in your critical work, the Sorbonne made no objection at all.

But structural criticism (Lucien Goldmann, for example, although his work is quite different from mine) met with hostility and contempt. And I wonder if it wasn't the structuralist or pre-structuralist aspect of *On Racine*, rather than its psychoanalytical aspect, that shocked the university.

> *All that seems far away. Nowadays it's hard to understand that kind of objection.*

Yes. And yet, and this goes beyond Picard and myself as people, the Sorbonne professor is a figure to be reckoned with. One who can always return, even in another form.

Japan

> *You say that, of all your books,* Empire of Signs *is "the most happily written."*

I allowed myself to say that. Why? Why shouldn't one say what one thinks about one's own books? Especially since those very subtle affective bonds one has with them do not necessarily coincide with the evaluation of critics, of friends and colleagues. Thus, I haven't any close, personal, corporeal ties to a well-known book like *Writing Degree Zero*, or even *Mythologies*, whereas I feel very close to a lesser-known book of mine, *Michelet*.

As for *Empire of Signs*, when I wrote that book I felt a pleasure unmixed with anxiety, untainted by the *imago*. And I said so, in a fragment, a note of discretion that I will not overstep here: namely, that this happiness was related to the happiness of sexuality, a happy sexuality that I found in Japan more than anywhere else. And I think I'm right to put the two things together.

> *It seems to me that you are a bit Asiatic, that there's an affinity between you and the Japanese way of life.*

I'm very drawn to it, and once again we find Brecht waiting for us at the crossroads, because Brecht was one of the first Westerners to become interested in Chinese theater, at a time when China was absolutely not in fashion.

> Empire of Signs *is one of the few books (the other being your essay on Fourier) where you talk about food, where there is not a theory but an extremely sensual description of dishes.*

True. Japan greatly liberated me on the level of writing by furnishing me with quite ordinary subjects, daily occasions, that are happy subjects, in contrast to those of *Mythologies*. Because in Japan, precisely, the quotidian is aestheticized. At least that's how things appeared to me, and that's what seduced me. The art of living is a very important theme for me, one to which I should like to return one day, I'm not sure in what form. And it is situated in a globally Asiatic aesthetics of distance, discretion, a certain emptiness, yet at the same time a fine sensuality: the principle of delicacy in Sade, if you like.

> *And yet the frenetic, hyperindustrialized Japan of the modern world doesn't appear at all in your book.*

Of course, but I never claimed to be offering a photograph of Japan.

> *You censored that aspect very well on your own.*

It's the beginning of the uncoupling that became more evident in *The Pleasure of the Text*.

> *Under the circumstances, it was also the pleasure of the site.*

I've always enjoyed my trips to Japan; each time I lived the life of an ethnologist, as it were, but without the bad faith of the Western ethnologist who goes to examine foreign customs. In Japan I even behaved contrary to my character, with impulsive energy that I wouldn't have at home: nocturnal wanderings, in a huge city, the largest in the world, a city completely unfamiliar to me, and I don't speak a word of Japanese. But I always felt entirely at ease. At four in the morning, lost in out-of-the-way neighborhoods, I was always very happy. Whereas, if I were to go wandering here, at the same late hour, in Bagnolet—I could certainly go, but it would never have the same fascination for me.

As for what interested me in Japan—that's why I speak of being an ethnologist—I was constantly on the alert for all the tips I might receive, and I investigated all of them. If I was told about a place I might like, even in rather vague terms, I didn't give up until I'd found it. That's the ethnologist's attitude: exploration lured by desire.

> *You also say that you're an ethnologist in Racine, in Sade, or Proust.*

In that fragment I explain what I like about ethnology. Not the ethnology of primitive peoples, which has run out of territory and dried up, but the ethnology of modernity, of the big city, or the ethnology of France, introduced by Michelet. And Proust, Sade, Racine, they are entire populations, societies.

Cruising

> *I would like you to define this fabulous word, which appears several times in* Roland Barthes: *"cruising."*

In talking about it, perhaps I'll arrive at a definition. It's an important theme for me. Cruising is the voyage of desire. The body is in a state of alert, on the lookout for its own desire. And then, cruising implies a temporality that accentuates the meeting, the "first time." As if the first meeting possessed an unheard-of privilege: that of being withdrawn from all repetition. Repetition is a baleful theme for me—stereotype, the same old thing, naturalness as repetition. Cruising is anti-natural, anti-repetition. Cruising is an act that repeats itself, but its catch is absolutely fresh.

That's why cruising is a notion I can easily move from the order of the erotic quest, which is its origin, to the quest of texts, for example, or the search for novelistic features. What offers itself in the surprise of the "first time."

> *Cruising the text is also very sensual.*

Yes, all this should be related to the capture of sentences, citations, turns of phrase, fragments. The theme of the short text, obviously. When I try to produce this short writing, in fragments, I put myself in the situation of an author who will be cruised by the reader. It's the happiness of chance, but chance that is wished-for, quite thought-out: spied-upon, in a way.

Perversion

> *This sentence of yours: "Perversion, quite simply, makes one happy."*

Quite simply.

> *Aside from the opposition* perversion/simply, *what does that mean, "perversion"?*

In the fragment to which you refer, I used the word "perversion" after two allusions, to hashish and homosexuality. I mean that "perversion" doesn't have a psychoanalytical rigor here—for psychoanalysis, drugs would not be classifiable, properly speaking, among the perversions. Perversion is the search for a pleasure that is not made profitable by a social end, a benefit to the species. It is, for example, the pleasure of love that is not accounted for as a means of procreation. It's on the order of bliss that exerts itself for nothing. The theme of expenditure.

We can, however, reintroduce a psychoanalytical specificity into the generality of the term. Thus, for Freudian thought, one of the major perversions is fetishism (a theme we find again in the wish for a *cut-up* writing). And insofar as perversion is disengaged from neurosis, Freudian thought accentuates the fact that the pervert is, after all, happy.

What I've written from *Empire of Signs* up to certain fragments of *Roland Barthes* is under the sign of a kind of perverse writing.

Perversion is the pleasure principle.

Perversion, through the relay of fetishism, implies a particular relation to the Mother; another theme now rears its head, one that interests me very much these days: the theme of the image-repertoire, *l'imaginaire*. Moreover, *Roland Barthes* is in a small way a hinge between a way of thinking about fetishism and a way of thinking about the image-repertoire. And that's why *Roland Barthes* could finally be considered more chaste than *The Pleasure of the Text*, since its main theme is not the problem of bliss but that of the image, the image-repertoire.

What currently interests me is this field of the image-repertoire, which *Roland Barthes* introduced into my work. And I'm beginning a seminar at the École Pratique des Hautes Études on the lover's discourse, which for me is even more closely tied to these problems of the image-repertoire.

Pratiques, no. 5, February 1975
From an interview conducted by André Petitjean

Literature / Teaching

You have written that you don't like the spoken interview which is tape-recorded and then transcribed: "The interview is a discount article," as much for the "thought"/ "form" disjunction it implies as for the repetition it sanctions, since the interviewee must talk about what he has already "written."

So we have chosen the format of a questionnaire in the hope that your answers will help bridge the gap between our position (the teaching profession) and yours (to be defined?). We would like to draw out your image-repertoire on a subject that, though covered by many discourses, is as yet largely unexplored: the teaching of literature.

1. Can "literature" be taught? If we provisionally define the teaching function as the transmission of a collected body of knowledge, we can ask ourselves:

—If this knowledge exists, as a collected body of information

—If it does exist, of what type is it

—If it does exist, is it useful to students, and in what way

2. The pleasure of the text. What could be the pleasure of the text in a relation involving the teacher and his knowledge (?), the student and his knowledge (?), confronted by a text as the object of work to be done?

3. The teaching relationship. Pleasure/knowledge/

reading: taking this triple stake into account, how do you
view the teaching relationship, concretely, in today's
schools?

4. Writing/reading. You have written that there is today "a divorce between the reader and the scriptor." What
do you mean by that? How does one articulate, in teaching practice, the apprenticeship of both reading and writing?

5. You have spoken of "the (collective) edification of
a theory that liberates the signifier" (S/Z). Could you be
more explicit about this project?

6. Literature/school/society. You have written that "the
reader should be made into a writer," and that "this
requires a transformation of society." What specific role
can school, and the teaching of language, in particular,
play in the process of social change?

Before I answer your questions, I feel that some preliminary
remarks are in order.

These remarks may appear to be mere oratorical precautions,
but they have the advantage of pointing out eventual problems,
and so perhaps have an important part to play in our discussion.

First of all, a few personal remarks: I am, in fact, quite removed
from schoolteaching now. I was a young teacher during the war,
in a lycée where I taught French and Latin. The fact that this
was so long ago (1939–40) leaves me with few memories; and
even if I did remember that time quite well, teaching conditions
and the institutional environment have certainly greatly changed.

Afterward, I devoted myself to theoretical or, rather, para-
theoretical writing, because this writing does not have the relation
to theory that a philosophical reflection might have. At the same
time, I became a "writer," someone who should not be defined
as a sacred individual but as a person who enjoys writing and
enjoys renewing this pleasure.

There is thus a hiatus, a gap, between your experience as
secondary-school teachers and mine as an intellectual writer.

We shouldn't try to gloss over this hiatus with hollow propositions that, launched from the theoretical into the practical,

would remain completely rhetorical. That would not be a good way to answer your questions. On the contrary, this hiatus must be assumed, as one assumes a responsibility, because it is important that we realize, on the one hand, that the theoretical is, in a way, uninhabitable in our current society (we cannot be comfortable there), whereas it could be quite habitable for a nineteenth-century philosopher—and we must not erase this uninhabitable character while, on the other hand, as a corollary, we must assume the fact that a writer's activity is "for nothing." The writer is, at least in large part, useless, which pushes him to develop a utopia of pure expenditure "for nothing." The writer sustains himself in our present society only as a pervert who lives his activity as a utopia, who tends to project his perversion, his "for nothing," into a social utopia.

Thus, I'm unable to address the concrete, practical problems of your profession; I will therefore be, as you are, within the indirect, and our meeting will be that of two uninhabitable positions. I don't think we should give in too quickly to the myth whereby theory puts practice back on an even keel, and practice, in turn, straightens out theory. This dialectic, which holds true for politics, could never be that simple for language.

And so you'll doubtless ask me what my function could possibly be, insofar as I have one. My answer is that I must tirelessly assert that language is not simply communication, that it is not a *straight* communication.

My second preliminary point is this: people are usually concerned with content in the teaching of language and literature. But the task involves more than content; it also involves the relation and shared presence of living bodies, a presence directed and in large part falsified by the institutional space itself. The real problem is to learn how a class in language or literature can be filled with values or desires that haven't been provided for by the institution, when they're not actively repressed by it. Indeed, how do we instill *affect* and *delicacy*, in the Sadean sense? Today these things are left to the teacher in the classroom and are quite ignored by the school itself.

When the world of students is discussed, the repressive character of school is always emphasized. But a pure and simple protest

against repression is superficial. It seems to me that if I were
facing a classroom of students, my chief anxiety would be to find
out what is desired. It would not be a question of wanting to
liberate desires, or even of learning what they might be (which
would be an enormous undertaking in any case), but of asking
the question: "Is there desire?"

Today, in France, when I look around, I have the impression
that the real problem is not so much repression as the absence
of blissful impulses: what psychoanalysis calls *aphanisis*, lack of
desire. This is logical, in fact, because there is an alienation even
more profound than constraint: castration. France is a world in
which there is a language of contestation, but this language may
not harbor the impulses of *jouissance*. This is the most profound
of all alienations: in mythology, beneath the slave, there is the
eunuch.

I'll conclude this second preliminary observation by evoking
my experience of a totally anomic space, that of my seminar,
which people attend because of desire. At this level, for nine-
tenths of the students, the thesis is an alibi for a fantasy. There
is always, deep inside, a desire for writing. People come because
I have written. Of course the semiological or methodological
motivation should not be ignored, but it is overdetermined.

First question: Can literature be taught?

To a point-blank question, a point-blank answer: *Only literature
should be taught*.

"Literature" is the name for a corpus of texts sanctified but also
classified by a metalanguage ("literary history"), a body of past
texts stretching from the sixteenth to the twentieth century, with
a restriction (a misdeal) limiting "literature" to "good literature,"
thus excluding other texts as unworthy or dangerous, "bad cards"
such as Sade, or Lautréamont . . .

Until the twentieth century, this literature formed a *mathesis*:
a complete field of knowledge. It brought into play, through very
diverse texts, all the knowledge of the world at a given moment.
It's obvious that this is not scientific knowledge, even though it
is articulated on the scientific codes of different periods. It would

be very interesting to excavate the knowledge invested in Balzac, for example. In this regard, structuralism can be reproached for not having been sufficiently interested in the codes of knowledge, especially since it had the means with which to investigate them. "Literature" is, of course, a metaphorical, narrative code, but it is also the site of immense political knowledge. That is why I affirm paradoxically that only literature should be taught, because all knowledge could be approached within it.

There is also a very dangerous ideological prejudice that must be dealt with, the belief that literature *lies* and that knowledge is divided between disciplines that tell the truth and others that are, then, considered disciplines of fiction, amusement, and vanity. "Literature" does not tell the truth, but truth is not to be found only where there are no lies (there are other sites for truth, if only the unconscious): the opposite of lying is not necessarily telling the truth. The question must be shifted: what is important is not to elaborate and disseminate knowledge about literature (in "literary histories") but to show literature to be a mediator of knowledge. It is more useful to see how knowledge is invested in a work than to learn that Racine was preceded by a theory of the *vraisemblable*.

At present, things are changing. "Literature," the text, can no longer coincide with this function of *mathesis* for three reasons:

1. Today our world is a global village. It's a profuse world, and what we learn about it is made known immediately, but we are bombarded by fragmentary, controlled bits of information. Since knowledge of the world is no longer filtered, this world would not fit easily into a *literary mathesis*.

2. The world is too surprising, its unexpectedness is so excessive that it goes beyond the codes of popular wisdom. Thus, Brecht noted correctly that no literature could deal with what happened in the Nazi concentration camps of Auschwitz and Buchenwald. Excess and astonishment make literary expression impossible. Literature, as *mathesis*, was the closure of a homogeneous body of knowledge.

3. It's banal to say that knowledge has a relation to science, but science is plural today: there is not one science but many sciences, the old dream of the nineteenth century has collapsed.

In fact, it is impossible to maintain frontiers between sciences, all leadership is precarious. The leadership of linguistics, which lasted about twenty years, is being replaced by that of biology, and so on.

The fact that literature can no longer be a *mathesis* can be seen in the absence of the realistic novel, although the political conditions of society haven't fundamentally changed. In the nineteenth century, realistic novels gave an account of class division; these divisions still exist in our century, yet realistic novels—even those of socialist realism—have disappeared, at least in France. Texts seek instead to constitute a *semiosis,* a *mise en scène* of *signifiance.* The avant-garde text (Lautréamont, Mallarmé, Joyce . . .) brings into play a knowledge of signs.

For centuries, literature was both a *mathesis* and a *mimesis,* with its correlative metalanguage: reflection. Today the text is a *semiosis;* that is, a *mise en scène* of the symbolic, not of content but of the detours, twists, in short the bliss of the symbolic. Society will probably resist *semiosis,* resist a world that would be understood and accepted as a world of signs, without anything behind it.

> *Isn't every text a* semiosis *in your sense, an operation of significations producing effects of meaning?*

Yes, of course; there is text in classical works, we can even say that there is writing in style. In the present state of things, moreover, writing begins with style. From this perspective, we can say that literature is a field of texts, a corpus, to be valorized as a body. It's possible to pulverize and fragment this corpus—even the classical works—to play (with) it, to consider it as a fiction of fictions, to make it into a space where one can begin to desire.

> *Isn't it tactically important to defend teaching as the dissemination of knowledge that is backed up by different theoretical practices?*

Yes, we must affirm, in the face of ignorance, a wisdom of the text: the "knowledge of the symbolic," to be defined as psychoanalytical knowledge or, let me put it this way, as the science of *displacement*, in the Freudian sense. Obviously, the "knowledge of the symbolic" cannot be positivistic, because it is itself caught up in the utterance of this knowledge. This is the problem of the social sciences and humanities that have not begun to consider the problematics of utterance. In Geneva, for example, a student delivering a paper on the symbolic order, apropos of a passage in *Bouvard and Pécuchet*, remained within the bounds of "untutored symbolism," the association of ideas. Now, that paper was spontaneous but banal, the characteristic of the spontaneous being that it is bad, banal. At the time, it was difficult for me to present a counter-argument; I should have explained to the student that there are avenues of the symbolic with which one must be familiar. When one opens literature to the symbolic field, one renounces old values ("taste" . . .), but without being in a position to postulate new values, nonrepressive values. So things are very complicated, but that's the way it is.

> *Second and third questions: The pleasure of the text, the teaching relationship.*

Can one make work into pleasure? We should think about this, because what stifles pleasure isn't so much work as it is its environment. In other words, I'm pessimistic. It seems to me almost impossible to introduce pleasure into the classroom, because if work requirements are maintained there, the work/pleasure conjunction will demand a long and patient elaboration.

A priori, children should be given the opportunity to create complete objects (which homework assignments cannot be) over a long period of time. We should almost imagine that each pupil will create a book, and will set himself all the tasks necessary to its completion. It would be a good idea to consider the idea of a model-object, or the idea of production while the product is not yet reified. In any case, the problem is to bypass the *given* of the exercise (assignment-composition) and to offer the student a real possibility of structuring the object to be created. The pupil must become once again, I won't say an individual, but a subject who directs his desire, his production, his creation. On the institutional level, that would of course presuppose that there are no national curricula.

> Schoolwork does in fact play an important role in the students' creative passivity. At first, the desire to write is officially sanctioned through composition, but it comes up against the moral and aesthetic norms of the teacher who will not tolerate, for example, a student writing about a funeral in a humorous way. Afterward, compositional writing is not permitted, only a reductive critical discourse in the form of dissertations, explications de texte. Isn't the problem, as you emphasize elsewhere, to "make a writer of the reader," which would require an entire "education," different exercises and so forth?

You're quite right. Going back to what was said about the pleasure of making something, we may ask ourselves why creation implies a certain amount of work. Speaking for myself, this is so because I must consider, unlike the avant-garde, the problem of *effects*. "Effectiveness" implies the idea of work but also the desire to seduce, to communicate, to be loved. A pedagogy of effects is thus possible: students would be made aware of and sensitive to the production and reception of effects.

> Fourth question: Writing and reading.

It's a banality to say that there are more people who read than there are people who write. But this phenomenon isn't normal or natural: it is historically determined. We know of societies with privileged sectors where there was more or less numerical equality between authors and their public. Until the nineteenth century, for instance, the audience for classical music was composed largely of people who played it. This is no longer the case, which is why I give such importance to the role of the "amateur," who must revalorize the productive function that has been reified by commercial circuits. The reader is cut off from any relation to the world of production. Enmeshed in a world where he projects himself, he projects not his doing, his making (his body), but his psychology. This reader who cannot write projects his image-repertoire (the narcissistic zone of the psyche) very far from his muscular, carnal body, the body of *jouissance*. He is drawn into the trap of the image-repertoire.

Is it still possible to learn how to read? Yes, if the function of institutional codes is clearly identified. To begin with, the accomplishments of liberal secular schooling must be maintained, but redirected toward the exercise of *l'esprit critique*, the decipherment of codes, supported by semiological studies.

> *Reading, in fact, must be considered as a critical apprenticeship of codes, as the detection of the organized behind the natural on all levels of reading (novels, comics, films . . .); we must establish what you call a new "regime of readerliness."*

Yes, a reader must learn to demystify appearances, to flush out the transcendental, idealist signified. There ought to be an ethics of semiology, which would explain how semiology can sharpen the critical spirit. As for psychoanalysis, it can teach us to read meaning *where we never looked before*. We read while noticing the unforeseen, what we didn't expect to notice. Psychoanalysis teaches us to read *elsewhere*.

> *"The (collective) edification of a theory that liberates the signifier."*

The "theory that liberates the signifier" must help liberate the text—all texts—from theologies of the transcendental signified. Today I would speak of *signifiance* rather than of a "signifier": the text sends us from signifier to signifier without ever closing itself off.

> *Literature/school/society.*

What is the specific role of school? It's to develop that critical spirit I mentioned before. But we must also know whether we should teach something on the order of doubt or truth. And how can we escape this alternative? We must teach not skepticism but doubt bolstered by *jouissance*. Even better, we must turn to Nietzsche, to where he speaks of "shaking up truth." The ultimate goal is still to make difference shimmer, that plural in the Nietzschean sense, without ever letting it decline into simple liberalism, preferable though that may be to dogmatism. We must question the relation of meaning to "naturalness," and shake up this "naturalness" that is a blow struck against social classes by power and mass culture. I would say that the task of schooling is to make sure that this process of liberation, if it occurs, does not pass through a return of the signified. Political constraints must never be considered as a purgatory demanding total submission. On the contrary, the claims of the signifier must constantly be put forward to prevent the return of the repressed. It isn't a question of making schools into sites for the preaching of dogmatism, but of preventing repercussions, the return of monology, and the tyranny of imposed meaning.

Le Quotidien de Paris, May 1975
From an interview conducted by Daniel Oster

The Surrealists
Overlooked the Body

*Do you consider surrealist texts to be "texts of pleasure"
or "texts of bliss"? Is there a* Kamasutra *of surrealist writing?*

Textual pleasure and/or bliss are not attributes to be attached
objectively to this or that type of text; it's impossible to set up
some sort of definitive prize list of such texts: these affects don't
determine what label should be assigned to a work. Nothing
prevents the Surrealist text from being a text of pleasure or bliss,
but nothing obliges it to be one or the other.

*It would seem that the Surrealists were not very con-
cerned with "deconstructing" language. But why
weren't they?*

I suppose that if the "Surrealists" (but shouldn't we first "deconstruct" this label?) didn't deconstruct language, or only very little,
it was because at bottom they had a normative idea of the body—
of sexuality, to be blunt. The "corset" imposed on syntax (an
enormously complicated garment, in Breton's case) and sexual
constraint come down to the same thing. The "dream" they
conceived of offered no access to bodily madness (except in Artaud's case, but I presume you put him in a category all his own),
but rather entrance to a kind of cultural vulgate, to "oneirism,"

a rhetorical release of images. It seems to me that the Surrealists *missed* the body. For this reason they left behind *too much* literature.

> *You write in* The Pleasure of the Text: *"The text has a human form, which is a figure, an anagram of the body"; and farther on: "The pleasure of the text is that moment when my body starts following its own ideas." Couldn't we compare this representation of the body with automatic writing? And aren't you proposing a kind of automatic reading?*

I don't like the notion of *automatic writing* at all. Without becoming involved in a now classic and purely art-historical debate ("Did they really perform automatic writing?"), I'll just say that automatism—supposing that we retain this vague notion for the time being—is not rooted at all in the "spontaneous," the "savage," the "pure," the "profound," the "subversive," but originates on the contrary from the "strictly coded": what is mechanical can make only the Other speak, and the Other is always *consistent*. If we were to imagine that the Good Fairy Automatism were to touch the speaking or writing subject with her wand, the toads and vipers that would spring from his mouth would just be stereotypes. The idea of automatic writing implies an idealist view of man divided into a speaking subject and a profound inner subject. As for the text, it can only be a braid, woven in an extremely twisted and devious fashion between the symbolic and the image-repertoire. One cannot write without the image-repertoire—this is my conviction, at least. The same holds true for reading, of course.

> *Do you feel that Breton and the Surrealists truly fulfilled the promise articulated by Breton: "to return with one bound to the birth of the signifier"?*

The signifier has no "source." It's always this idea of origins, of depth, of primitiveness, in short of *nature*, that bothers me in Surrealist discourse.

> *Again, from* The Pleasure of the Text: *"What is important is to equalize the field of pleasure, to abolish the false opposition of practical life and contemplative life." To abolish oppositions . . . We seem to hear Breton. In your search for the "atopia of bliss," would you perhaps be a Surrealist?*

In my eyes, that is perhaps what is best in the Surrealists: to understand that writing doesn't stop with the written, but can transmigrate into behavior, actions, activities, into private life, daily life, *what is done*: there are writings of life, and we can make certain moments of our life into actual texts, which only our friends may read. It's probably this idea—its presentiment— that gives the *friendship* of the Surrealists an almost textual importance (whereas their banding together is usually interpreted as an act of terrorism): the Surrealist group was itself a textual space. What still bothers me, however, is that this "lived" textuality (where the opposition between book and life, practice and speculation was abolished) took on in their case, as far as we know, a *literary* allure: when acted out, Surrealism was always a *gesture*, not a *fiction*.

> *You speak of "writing out loud." You mention Artaud, Sollers. But* Champs magnétiques, *Desnos?*

Of course, why not? When one speaks of literature in general, one always forgets someone. Ignorance? Carelessness? Or perhaps instead the impossibility, in literary matters, of matching the performance of science: perfect and complete adequation of rule and example, language and speech? Behind my omission, there is doubtless a snake in the grass: infinite difference.

Le Magazine littéraire, January 1976
From an interview conducted by Jean-Jacques Brochier

The Crisis of Truth

> *In a way, isn't Flaubert's* Bouvard and Pécuchet *the same undertaking—but inverted—as Mallarmé's* Le Livre à venir? *Flaubert wants no one to dare write anymore after* Bouvard and Pécuchet, *while Mallarmé hopes to create the book that would contain all possible books.*

The encyclopedias of the eighteenth, nineteenth, and even the twentieth centuries are encyclopedias of knowledge, or bodies of knowledge. Now, in the midst of this history, there is a Flaubert moment, a *Bouvard and Pécuchet* moment, which is the farce-moment. The encyclopedia is then treated with derision, as a farce. But this farce carries with it, behind the scenes, something very serious: encyclopedias of knowledge are replaced by an encyclopedia of languages. What Flaubert is recording and identifying in *B and P* are languages.

Obviously, insofar as the relation to knowledge is a farcical one, and where the problem of language is dissimulated, the book's tone and *ethos* are very uncertain: one never knows whether to take the book seriously or not.

> *Flaubert says in one of his letters, moreover, that the reader will never know whether he's being made fun of or not.*

And that's the unanimous opinion on *B and P*: if you choose to take the book seriously, it doesn't work. If you choose not to take the book seriously—it still doesn't work. Simply because the language is neither on the side of truth nor on the side of error. It's on both sides at once, so you can't tell whether it's serious or not. Which explains why no one has been able to pin down the Flaubert of *B and P*, a book that seems to me the very essence of Flaubert. He appears there in an "enunciatory role" both perfectly distinct and perfectly uncertain.

> *Isn't it this same mixture that Flaubert calls stupidity?*

It refers to stupidity, but we mustn't let ourselves become hypnotized by this word. I was myself fascinated while studying stupidity in Flaubert's works, and then I realized that the important things were perhaps elsewhere. In *B and P*, but also in *Madame Bovary*, and even more in *Salammbô*, Flaubert seems to be a man who literally stuffs himself with languages. But of all these languages, finally, there is not one that prevails, there is no master language. I would therefore say that Flaubert's favorite book was not the novel but the dictionary. And what is important in his *Dictionary of Received Ideas* is not "received ideas" but "dictionary." That's why the theme of stupidity is a bit of a trap. The great book implicit in Flaubert is the phraseological dictionary, the phrase book, like one finds, for example, in the entries in Littré.

> *And the dictionary is linked to the theme of copying, which opens and closes* B and P. *Because what else is a dictionary except copying the sentences of others?*

Of course. The theme of copying is an important theme, by the way. There have been some very interesting copy dictionaries, such as Bayle's *Critical Dictionary* at the end of the seventeenth century. But in Flaubert, copying is an empty act, purely reflexive. When Bouvard and Pécuchet go back to copying at the end of the book, there's nothing left but the gestural activity. They'll copy anything at all, as long as the manual gesture is preserved.

This is a historic moment in the crisis of truth, which is equally manifest in Nietzsche, for example, even though there is no relation between Flaubert and Nietzsche. It's the moment when one realizes that language carries no guarantees. There is no instance, no security for language: it's the opening rift in the crisis of our modernity.

In the telling words of Lévi-Strauss, there is "something amiss with meaning" in everything written. This doesn't mean that production is simply insignificant. There is something amiss with meaning in production: there is no meaning, but there is something like a dream of meaning. It's the beginning of the unconditional loss of language. One no longer writes for this or that reason, but the act of writing is racked by the need for meaning, what we call today *significance*. No meaning in language, but meaningfulness.

> In B. Maurice's novel Les Deux Greffiers, which was Flaubert's initial inspiration, the two clerks finally return to copying, like Bouvard and Pécuchet. But, unlike those two, each of Maurice's characters dictates to the other what is to be copied. That would be a kind of reappearance of language, in the form of dictation.

This brings up a second characteristic of *B and P* that is both mysterious and—to some people—repulsive. You know that it's a book many people don't like, including Sartre himself. I think that the uneasiness many readers feel comes from the fact that in *B and P* there is no allocutory plane, to use linguistic terms: no one is talking to anyone, and one never knows where the message is coming from or where it's going. The two characters themselves form a loving couple, but they mirror each other— indeed, it's quite hard to tell them apart. If you look closely at the book, you realize in fact that they never speak to each other. And you can't even project yourself into this loving couple that is so distant, so glacial, never speaking to the reader. The book doesn't address us, which is precisely what bothers someone like Sartre, who wrote these remarks about the *Dictionary of Received Ideas*: "A strange work: more than a thousand entries, and at whom are they directed? No one, unless it's Gustave himself." I would go further: not even Gustave himself is addressed, he is not a "subject." To me, it's this loss of allocution, of destination—

an intercommunication that exists in every book, even those written in the third person—that is fascinating, because it is, in seed form, the discourse of a psychotic.

When he speaks, the psychotic does not address himself, and that's why *B and P*, underneath completely traditional trappings, is a crazed book, in the proper sense of the term. In the same line of thought, what strikes us in this book is the lack of gifts: Bouvard and Pécuchet never give anything. Even excrement, today considered the very model of the gift, is recuperated to make manure: it's a famous episode in the book. Everything is always exchanged, everything is anticipated, spoken as an exchange, but this exchange always fails. It's a world without expenditure, without echo, matte. Flaubert's art, in *Bouvard and Pécuchet*, is an elliptical art, and therefore classical, but an art where the ellipse never hides any implications. Ellipses with no remainder. This is unthinkable for a classical, humanist consciousness, and even for today's ordinary way of thinking. It is, literally, an avant-garde work.

> *It's as if men had ceased to exist but language still continued on its own.*

Yes, and what you're describing is something very modern.

> *Flaubert may reach all the way to psychosis with* Bouvard and Pécuchet, *but all his suffering over style and phrasing is perfectly neurotic.*

In accepting the classical heritage, Flaubert placed himself within the perspective of stylistic labor, which had been the writer's rule since Horace and Quintilian: the writer is someone who works on his language, who labors over its form. Flaubert carried this work to the point of madness. There are a thousand examples: when he says it took him eight hours to correct five pages, that four pages of *Madame Bovary* cost him a week, that he'd spent a full two days trying to perfect two lines, etc. This kind of work on form belongs to the category of the *excruciating*, which represents the complete, and obstinate, sacrifice of the writer: Flaubert shut himself away in Croisset at the age of twenty-five. And this incarceration is symbolized, emblematized by that indispensable piece of furniture in his study, the divan, where he would fling himself when his ideas ran dry: he called this his "marinade."

In this stylistic travail, Flaubert carried two especially heavy crosses: a maniacal obsession with transitions and with the repetition of words. And the justification for this agonizing work was the substitution of prose for poetry as the standard of value. It was Flaubert who first claimed that prose was as complicated to produce as poetry.

All this work took place around an object that became, through Flaubert, most singular: the sentence. The Flaubertian sentence is complete: it is at once a unit of style—it is thus not only linguistic but rhetorical—and a unit of work, since he measured his days in numbers of sentences, and also a unit of life: his life is summed up in his sentences. Flaubert learned to elaborate, in theory and in practice, a concept clearly understood by Proust, who called it the *special substance* of the sentence, a substance, Proust also notes, that is lacking in Balzac. The Balzacian sentence is not that incredibly recognizable object that is the Flaubertian sentence. The practical proof of this is that, among Proust's pastiches, those wonderful theoretical analyses of style, the pastiche that outshines all the others is the one of Flaubert. One could play on the ambiguity of the expression and say that Flaubert spent all his life as a "phrasemaker." A Flaubertian sentence is a perfectly identifiable object. At one point, Flaubert says: "And so I will again take up my poor life, so tranquil and dull, where sentences are adventures." Why did that sentence of Flaubert's play the role of destiny in his life, and in the history of our literature? Because it presents, as if on a pedestal, the very contradiction of all language. Which is that the sentence is structurable (linguistics, up until Chomsky, has shown this) and since it has a structure, it presents a problem of value: there are good and bad structures, which explains why Flaubert searched so obsessively for the right structure; and what's more, the sentence is infinite. There is no obligation to end a sentence, it is infinitely "catalyzable," one can always add a little something to it. And so on, until the end of our lives. Something that Mallarmé, for example, postulated in his *Coup de dé*. The entire Flaubertian vertigo springs from these two marching orders, contradictorily but simultaneously maintained: "We must work on finishing the sentence"; and then again: "It's never finished."

Flaubert, through his stylistic labors, is the last classical writer, but because this labor is out of proportion, monstrous, neurotic, it bothers classical temperaments, from Faguet to Sartre. Flaubert thus becomes the first modern writer: because he accedes to madness. A madness that is not of representation, imitation, realism, but a madness of writing, a madness of language.

Le Magazine littéraire, June 1976
From an interview conducted by Jean-Jacques Brochier

A Great Rhetorician of Erotic Figures

Roland Barthes does not hesitate to place Sade alongside Fourier and Loyola, because these three are inventors of language, and their works are a combinative of original signs: for passions, erotic figures, and prayer. Like Loyola and Fourier, Sade is a great writer. What is more, he provides French literature with a dimension it lacks: the picaresque novel.

> *I believe it was in the twentieth century that Sade was first recognized as a writer. In the nineteenth century he was simply the Devil, omnipresent but hidden, and at the end of the eighteenth century he was considered just another pornographic writer. Why this appearance of Sade in the literary scene in our century?*

A study should be made of the mythology, the fortunes of Sade, somewhat like Étiemble did for Rimbaud: just as there is a Rimbaud mythology, there is one for Sade. Sade began to emerge from his purgatory at the end of the nineteenth century. I remember reading some remarkable lines of Léon Bloy on Sade, and yet the ideologies of these two were poles apart. Even though there was nothing in Bloy's character to lead him toward an understanding of Sade, he was a very interesting thinker, a curious man, in the two senses of the word. And then there was Apollinaire.

One could say there is a mythological filiation that starts with Bloy, proceeding through many deformations to Klossowski, who considers Sade a kind of absolute writer. And there is another mythological vein, the most prolific these last years in particular, that considers Sade the Transgressor, the one who brings together the themes of transgression and writing, and makes transgression fall upon writing, in the end.

That filiation would begin with Blanchot?

Yes, and it would pass through Bataille, *Tel Quel,* even if there are enormous distinctions to be made between them. But we're simplifying things here. There should be a kind of literary history that historians never attend to, a mythological history, covering the semi-collective images of the writer within each period.

> *You wrote an essay on Sade that you added to analyses of Loyola and Fourier, all in one book. Why did you choose Sade, rather than Restif de La Bretonne, for example?*

What interested me in Sade was not his transgressive aspect, or his "Nietzschean" aspect (Nietzschean in quotation marks, because in fact they have little in common), but an outstandingly scriptural aspect: a man who, through writing, constructs extremely well-made novelistic structures that are also erotic structures. The figures are erotic figures, postures, and rhetorical figures, all at the same time. Sade is, in a way, a great rhetorician of erotic figures.

When one speaks nowadays of Sade as a writer, it must be made clear that Sade is still not generally recognized as a writer: he is perceived as a producer-transgressor of writing, but society still refuses to admit him to the pantheon of writers. He doesn't figure at all, or very rarely, in histories of literature.

> *The famous reservations: Sade is very boring, Sade is unreadable, etc.*

Sade is very boring, that's what Pompidou said. Obviously, there's a repetitive aspect in Sade. But, without speaking of the *120 Days of Sodom*, of which only a quarter has been completely edited, I consider *Juliette* a very great novel. It's the great picaresque novel that French literature has never produced—aside from Sade and perhaps Proust, who can also be considered a picaresque novelist, a novelist of the fragment, the infinite voyage, the anecdote leading on to other anecdotes. That's what I love in Sade, the never-ending novelistic flow, this autarchic world into which we are plunged. We also had these grand cosmogonies in the nineteenth century, Balzac or Wagner, for example, but they were always "right-thinking" cosmogonies. Sade produced a novelistic cosmogony at once repetitious, heavily structured, and very original, and it takes its place in the great debate of contestatory philosophy.

> *Why is Sade still not recognized as a writer? Is it his morality that is still so scandalous?*

Yes, I think so. Quite simply. And his recognition as a writer should be twofold: as a fine composer of stories, which I think is obvious, and as the producer of a typical sentence, the Sadean sentence. In its erotic developments, this sentence has an incredible beauty and precision. One need only compare Sade with pornographic novels to see that the difference is in the style. And one would thus experience what it is that makes a great writer.

> *Perhaps the difference is that Sade uses the appropriate words in an erotic sentence, in the appropriate cadence, with the precise tranquillity of someone writing: "The Marquise went out at five o'clock."*

Sade does produce something very rare in literature and rhetoric: a perfectly denotative writing. When he describes an erotic act, there is absolutely no connotation. The sentence is so matte that no symbolism can intervene. For example, there is no sly, knowing wink at the reader. If symbolism is an escape, a flight, Sade's eroticism is perfectly anti-symbolic. The proof is that when symbolism needed an original matrix to establish its discourse, it invented the word "sadism."

> *These days there is a reading of Sade—I'm thinking in particular of Philippe Roger's book* La Philosophie dans le pressoir—*that I feel is restrictive, because it reduces Sade to a rhetorician and neglects his novelistic ingenuity, his invention of stories.*

I don't share your reticence. I think it takes courage and a sense of what is necessary to intervene in the Sadean debate while abandoning the usual "modernist" reading or commentary. After Blanchot, Bataille, and a few others, one can do nothing else in that direction but repeat them or oneself. Philippe Roger broke with that tradition. Not by ignoring it, because he is obviously quite familiar with it, but he did not derive, if I may put it this way, his "jargon" from it. In addition, his study has sociological value, in the good sense of the word, since he put Sade back in the literary and rhetorical context of his time. One would wish that all works of literary history could be of this quality. And that instead of establishing influences and schools, literary historians would reconstruct the literary ideological climate of a period, the rhetorical apprenticeship of writers, without of course neglecting the contributions of other traditions.

> *But it's a pity to leave aside Sade's extraordinary talent for telling stories.*

I don't think that is what Philippe Roger had in mind. But it would indeed be very interesting for a semiologist to study the structures of the Sadean narrative in detail.

> *Without ever forgetting that the machine of desire and the storytelling machine are one and the same.*

. . . with that unique representational rhythm between the erotic scene and the dissertation, which draw their meaning from each other, alternating perpetually like the warp and woof of the narrative fabric. One would have to study carefully the function of these constantly alternating large sections of language.

Why did you put Sade in with Fourier and Loyola?

There were circumstantial motives, of course, but the explanation I did give is not artificial: all three writers fabricated a language, i.e., a system of units, of figures, and their entire oeuvre is the representation of this system. The inventor of a language must take semantic units and establish a combinative, a syntax, which is what they did.

Loyola combined figures of meditation, which were mostly more or less mystical phantasms, to produce the language of his mysticism, which is not the same as the mysticism of St. John of the Cross, for example. The great classical mystics cross through language to attain a region beyond language, their enemy. Loyola's aim, on the contrary, is to produce language and images, to give language to those in contemplative seclusion. Loyola produces the language of spiritual retreat.

As for Fourier, he's obviously a combiner of passions (he counted 1,620 of them), and from these combinations he derived more complex units, series, sentences. The phalanstery is like a discourse.

In Sade we also find the foundation of a language.

> *Is there not also in these three writers—and it's perhaps the same thing—the same classicism, the same rejection of romanticism: classicism being defined as that deliberate construction of a language beyond which one cannot go.*

It would be interesting to see if there are any structural works, i.e., works that create languages, in romanticism understood in the larger sense. At first glance, that does not in fact seem to be a concern of romanticism, which is more metaphorical than metonymical, and which consequently does not emphasize combination.

And which, above all, thinks that any combination is insufficient to account for what it has in mind.

There is one romantic adventure that should be examined, however, and that is Wagner's, because the Wagnerian universe displays that obsession with themes, with the leitmotif.

There is a writer who seems eminently classical to me, in the heritage of Sade: Robbe-Grillet.

Yes, except that Robbe-Grillet's universe, which is a combinative, offers itself explicitly as a universe of perversion, whereas the Sadean universe is not reducible to any erotic perversion whatever, it is unclassifiable on the neurotic chart. Sade upsets psychiatry, he upsets psychoanalysis, and that is what defines his radicality.

For Sade, as for Fourier and Loyola, you used the word "phantasm."

It's a word I often use—perhaps too often—in the sense defined by Laplanche and Pontalis in their dictionary of psychoanalysis. What makes the word easy to use for writers is that the phantasm is a scenario in which the subject situates himself in terms of his desire. This very simple definition is quite suitable for scenes— one passes easily from scenario to scene. Ignatian scenes, Fourierist scenes, Sadean scenes are all in fact scenarios where the subject performs in terms of his desire, with a view to the satisfaction—fantasized, of course—of his desire. Sade, Fourier, and Loyola, even if they are completely separated by ideology, have one strong feature in common: they write in terms of their desire. And they produce languages according to their desire, languages of desire.

Le Nouvel Observateur, January 10, 1977
From an interview conducted by Bernard-Henri Lévy

Of What Use Is an Intellectual?

Roland Barthes, the father of French literary structuralism and semiology, has just been inducted into the Collège de France, following Michel Foucault and Pierre Boulez. Barthes has formulated new methods of literary and philosophical criticism that have acquired a solid following. Professor at the École Pratique des Hautes Études for many years, a teacher at heart but protective of his private life, he agreed to speak with Bernard-Henri Lévy shortly before delivering the inaugural address of the Chair of Literary Semiology he will hold at the Collège de France.

> *Roland Barthes, we see very little of you, and you rarely speak in public: aside from your books, we know almost nothing about you . . .*

Supposing that to be true, it's because I don't much like interviews. I feel trapped between two dangers: either one enunciates positions in an impersonal manner, leading people to believe one considers oneself a "thinker," or else I constantly say "I" and end up accused of egotism.

> *You speak of yourself, however, in* Roland Barthes. *But there, loquacious on the subject of your childhood and adolescence, you remain strangely silent about what fol-*

> *lowed, the mature Barthes, your growing fame and lit-
> erary achievements . . .*

It's just that—like everyone else, I believe—I remember my childhood and youth quite well, I know the dates and can point out
the landmarks. And after that, strangely enough, I don't remember any more, I can't recall the dates, the dates of my own life.
As if I had a memory only at the beginning, as if adolescence
formed the exemplary, unique time of memory. Yes, that's it:
after adolescence, I see my life as an immense present, impossible
to take apart or put into perspective.

> *Which means that you literally don't have a "biogra-
> phy" . . .*

I do not have a biography. Or, more precisely, from the first line
I ever wrote, I no longer see myself, I'm no longer an image for
myself. I can't imagine myself, can't crystallize myself in images
anymore.

> *That explains the absence, in* Roland Barthes, *of pho-
> tographs of you as an adult?*

I have hardly any such pictures. My book is by necessity in two
parts. I don't recount anything of my youth, which is reflected
in photographs, because that is the true age and time of memory,
of images. As for the rest, on the contrary, I say nothing more
with pictures, because I have none, and so everything passes
through writing.

> *This dividing line is also one of illness. They are con-
> temporary, in any case . . .*

The correct word is not "illness," in my case, but "tuberculosis."
Because at the time, before chemotherapy, tuberculosis was truly
a way of life, I would almost say an election. One could even,
at the outside, imagine a conversion to that way of life, somewhat
like Hans Castorp, you know, in Thomas Mann's *The Magic*

Mountain . . . A person with tuberculosis might seriously consider, as I did, the possibility of living all his life in a sanatorium
or in a parasanatorial profession . . .

> *A life outside time? Beyond the reach of temporal haz-*
> *ards?*

Let's put it this way: a life with a certain resemblance to the
monastic regimen. The savor of a regulated life, of a strict schedule, as in a monastery: a disturbing phenomenon that pursues
me even today, and I intend to touch on this in my course at the
Collège de France this year.

> *We always speak of illness as something that mutilates,*
> *diminishes, or amputates. We rarely consider what it*
> *brings of a positive nature, even to the practice of writ-*
> *ing . . .*

Exactly. As for myself, I did not find it too difficult to spend those
five or six years away from the world: my character was doubtless
predisposed to "inwardness," to the solitude of reading. What did
I gain? A form of culture, surely. An experience of "living together" characterized by an intensification of friendships, the
assurance of having one's friends constantly close by, of never
being separated from them. And also, much later, the strange
feeling of being always five or six years younger than I really am.

> *Did you write?*

I read quite a lot, in any case, since, after all, it was during my
second stay in a sanatorium that I read all of Michelet, for example. On the other hand, I wrote very little. Just two articles,
one on Gide's *Journal* and the other on Camus's *The Stranger*,
which was the seed for *Writing Degree Zero*.

> *Did you know Gide?*

No, I never knew him. I saw him once, from a distance, at the restaurant Lutétia: he was eating a pear and reading a book. So I never knew him; but there were a thousand things about him that interested me, along with many other adolescents of the time as well.

For example?

He was a Protestant. He played the piano. He talked about desire. He wrote.

What does being a Protestant mean to you?

It's difficult to say. Because when faith is gone, only the imprint, the image, is left. And the image belongs to other people. It's up to them to say whether I "seem" Protestant.

What I meant was, what did your religious apprenticeship instill in you?

I might say, very cautiously, that a Protestant adolescence can provide a certain taste for or a certain perversion of inwardness, the inner language, the subject's constant dialogue with himself. And then, don't forget that to be a Protestant means not to have the slightest idea what a priest is, or prayer-by-formula . . . But these things should be left to the sociologists of mentalities, if French Protestantism still interests them.

You're said above all to be a "hedonist." Is this a mis-understanding?

Hedonism is considered "bad." Not nice. Poorly understood. It's unbelievable how pejorative this word can get! No one, no one at all, no philosophy, no doctrine, dares to take up hedonism. It's an "obscene" word.

But you, do you champion it?

Perhaps it would be better to find a new word. Because if hedonism is a philosophy, the texts that constitute its foundation are exceptionally fragile. There are no texts, really. Barely a tradition. So it's very difficult to situate oneself where the texts are so inconsistent and the tradition so tenuous.

> *Still, there was Epicureanism.*

Yes, but that's been censured for a long time now . . .

> *But you do have a "morality" . . .*

Let's say, a morality of affective relations. But I can't say anything about that, because I would have so much to say—as the Chinese proverb tells us: "The darkest place is always under the lamp."

> *One thing you never talk about: sexuality . . .*

I speak rather of sensuality.

> *To be exact, you sometimes talk about sexuality, but in order to minimize its importance. This sentence, for example, culled from one of your books: "The formative problem for me was not so much sex as it was money" . . .*

What I meant by that was that I never really suffered from sexual prohibitions, even though they were much stronger forty years ago than they are now. Frankly, I'm sometimes surprised at the indignation of some people at the iron grip of normality. I'm not denying the power of that regime, of course, but there are always gaps to slip through.

> *By what miracle did you escape?*

I didn't escape. It's just that I've always given priority to being in love, and consequently the notion of the "forbidden" has always been replaced by the notion of the "refused." What made me suffer wasn't to be forbidden something but to be refused something, which is entirely different.

> *Let's stay with this "sensuality." You speak of literature, music, or the opera, a dish of food, a trip, or a language, all with equal happiness, as if they were equal pleasures . . .*

Not always. Music and opera, for example, are quite different, after all. I love listening to music, and I listen to it often. But real enjoyment, to me, is making music: at one time I sang, now I play the piano. Opera is something else again. How shall I put it—opera is a festival, a festival of the voice; I enjoy it, but I'm not an opera fanatic.

> *Opera is also a "total spectacle."*

Agreed. But I should say that my personal enjoyment of opera is not rooted in that particular aspect of it; there are probably two types of opera lovers: those who are enthralled by the music, and those who love the opera itself, and I belong to the first group. There are two privileged moments in opera for me, discontinuous moments: the immediate surprise of the *mise en scène*, which I view almost as a voyeur, and the internalized pleasure of the music and the human voice—it's this second moment alone that permits me to close my eyes and enjoy the music.

> *You seem to be saying both that opera is not music and yet that it's the music that you enjoy in opera.*

Yes, and that's the very reason why I don't think of myself as an opera lover . . . This summer, for example, I went to Bayreuth for the first time; it was fascinating, but during the week I spent there I actually missed hearing music, because there were no other concerts aside from the opera.

> *Do you like traveling, aside from this or that particular attraction?*

I used to, quite a bit, but not so much these days. There was a time when I would take off at the drop of a hat, to different countries that appealed to me at various times. I enjoyed Holland, then Italy, afterward Morocco. Recently, Japan . . .

> *Your enjoyment varied, I suppose, according to what*
> *you found there . . .*

Of course. But I never cared very much for monuments, cultural landmarks and such, except for Dutch painting. When I travel, what interests me the most are those wisps of the art of living I can seize in passing. The feeling of plunging into a world that is both easy and opaque (everything is easy, for the tourist). Not a vulgar dip into slumming, but a voluptuous immersion into a language that I perceive only as sounds, for example. It's a very restful thing, not to understand a language. All vulgarity is eliminated, all stupidity, all aggression.

> *In the end, you think of traveling as a form of relaxed*
> *and inspired ethnography . . .*

It's something like that. A city like Tokyo, for example, is in itself an amazing mass of ethnographic material. I went there with all the enthusiasm of an ethnologist.

> *I suppose that this attitude carries over into human re-*
> *lations.*

I'll give you a direct answer: traveling is also an adventure for me, a series of possible adventures of great intensity. Traveling is obviously linked to a kind of amorous awareness, one is always on the alert . . .

> *There's one trip you don't talk about, however, a quite*
> *recent trip . . .*

Yes, I know, China. I spent three weeks there. The trip was tightly organized, of course, along the classic format. Even though we did receive some special attentions.

> *When you got back, you wrote hardly anything about this trip. Why?*

I wrote very little, but I saw and listened to everything with close attention and interest. Writing demands something else, however, some kind of piquancy in addition to what is seen and heard, something that I didn't find in China.

> *And yet China is certainly full of signs!*

That's true, of course. But you have a point: signs are important to me only if they seduce or irritate me. Signs in themselves are never enough for me, I must have the desire to read them. I'm not a hermeneutist.

> *And this time you could bring back from Peking nothing except an article on the "neuter"* . . .

In China, I found absolutely no possibility of erotic, sensual, or amorous interest or investment. For contingent reasons, I agree. And perhaps structural ones as well: I mean in particular the moralism of the regime there.

> *You speak of "wisps of the art of living": the art of living is also the way people eat, food as an aspect of culture.*

As a cultural object, food means at least three things to me. First, the aura of the maternal model, nourishment as it is considered and prepared by the mother: that is the food I like. Second, from that home base, I enjoy excursions, digressions toward the new and unusual: I can never resist the temptation of a dish endowed with the prestige of novelty. And finally, I'm particularly sensitive to conviviality, to the companionship of eating together, but only if this conviviality is on a small scale: when the company becomes too numerous, the meal becomes tiresome, and I lose interest in the food, or else I overeat from boredom.

> *You didn't really answer my question a while ago. What did you mean when you wrote that money rather than sex was the formative problem of your life?*

Simply this, that my childhood and adolescence were spent in poverty. That there was often no food in the house. That we had to go buy a bit of pâté or a few potatoes at a little grocery on the rue de Seine, and this would be all we'd have to eat. Life was actually lived to the rhythm of the first of the month, when the rent was due. And I had before me the daily spectacle of my mother working hard at bookbinding, a job for which she was absolutely unsuited. Poverty, at the time, had an existential contour that it perhaps no longer does, in France, not to the same extent . . .

> *And yours was a bourgeois family, bourgeois in its origins, at least.*

A bourgeois but completely impoverished family. There was thus a symbolic effect that intensified the real poverty, an awareness of having materially come down in the world, even though the family had managed to maintain some of its former standards of living. I remember, for example, the small crises at the start of each school year. I didn't have the proper clothes. No money for school supplies. No money to pay for schoolbooks. It's the small things, you see, that mark you for a long time, that make you extravagant later on.

> *Is that where your oft-proclaimed aversion to the petite bourgeoisie comes from?*

It's true that I've used that term in my books; I use it less these days, because one can become tired of one's own language. In any case, it's undeniable: there is a kind of ethical and/or aesthetic element in the petite bourgeoisie that both fascinates and displeases me. But is that really so original? It's in Flaubert. Who will admit to being a petit bourgeois? Politically and historically, the petite bourgeoisie is the key to the century, the rising class, the one we see all around us, at any rate. The bourgeoisie and the proletariat have become abstractions, while the petite bourgeoisie is everywhere, even among the bourgeois and the proletarians, what's left of them, anyway.

> *Then you no longer believe in the proletariat, in its historic mission, and all that that entails politically?*

I'm saying that there was a time when the proletariat *could be seen*, but this time has passed: in France, it was when the proletariat was galvanized by anarcho-syndicalism and the socialist tradition of Proudhon, but nowadays this tradition has been replaced by Marxism and regular trade unionism.

> *Were you ever a Marxist?*

"To be a Marxist": what does the verb "to be" mean in this expression? I've already explained my position here. I "went over" to Marxism rather late, encouraged by a dear friend who has since died, and who was a Trotskyite. So that I joined up without ever having been a militant, and via a dissident group having nothing to do with what was already being called Stalinism. Let's just say that I've read Marx, Lenin, Trotsky. Not all their works, of course, but I've read some of them. I haven't reread them for a while now, except here and there a text by Marx.

> *Do you read a text by Marx as you would a text by Michelet, Sade, or Flaubert? A pure system of signs, engendering pure enjoyment?*

Marx could be read in this way, but not Lenin, or even Trotsky. And yet I don't think one could read Marx simply as one would read any other writer, one couldn't ignore the political effects, the subsequent inscriptions through which the text exists so concretely.

*Your attitude is somewhat like that of Lardreau, Jambet,
or Glucksmann . . .*

I know Glucksmann, we've worked together, and I like what he
does. As for *L'Ange*, I haven't read it, but I've heard about it.
You understand—I feel very close to these positions and yet I
must keep at an incalculable distance from them. For reasons of
style, I suppose. Not a style of writing, but style in general . . .

*What I mean is, unlike so many others in your position,
you haven't any "political itinerary" behind you . . .*

It's true that my written work contains no political discourse in
the thematic sense of the word: I don't deal with themes that are
directly political, with political "positions." The reason is that I
can't manage to get excited over politics, and these days a discourse that is not impassioned can't be heard, quite simply. There's
a decibel threshold that must be crossed for discourse to be heard.
And I don't cross it.

You seem to regret this.

Politics is not necessarily just talking, it can also be listening.
Perhaps we lack a practice of political *listening* and *attention*.

*If one had to select a label for you, "left-wing intellectual"
would just about do.*

It would be up to the left to say whether it considers me to be
among its intellectuals. As for myself, it's fine with me, providing
that the left is understood not as an idea but as an obstinate
sensibility, a way of perceiving reality. In my case—an inalterable
foundation of anarchism, in the most etymological sense of the
word.

A rejection of power?

Let's say an extreme sensitivity to its ubiquity—power is every-where—and to its endurance—it is perpetual. It never gets tired, it goes on and on, like a calendar. Power is plural. I thus have the feeling that my private war is not with power but with powers, wherever they are. This is perhaps what makes me more "leftist" than "on the left"; what complicates things is that I haven't the "style" of the left.

> *Do you think that a "style" or a refusal of "style" is sufficient to set a political course?*

On the level of the individual, a political course is set existentially. For example, power is not only what oppresses, what is oppressive, it's also what depresses: wherever I'm depressed, there's power at work somewhere.

> *And today, in 1977, you're not depressed?*

Depressed, but not particularly indignant. Until now, what might be called the leftist temperament was determined in relation to focal points that were not programs but important themes: anti-clericalism before 1914, pacifism between the wars, then the Resistance, and then the war in Algeria . . . Today, for the first time, things are different: there's Giscard, who is after all a rather feeble crystallizing agent, or a "Common Program" that I don't really see as the rallying point for political feeling, even if it is a good program. What seems new to me in the current situation is that I can't find any touchstone for guidance.

> *Is that why you accepted Giscard's luncheon invitation?*

That's something else. I went out of curiosity, a taste for hearing things, a bit like a myth-hunter on the prowl. And a myth-hunter, as you know, must hunt everywhere.

> *What did you expect from this luncheon?*

To discover if Giscard spoke in any other language besides that of a statesman. Obviously, in order to find that out, one has to hear him speak as a private person. I did in fact receive the impression of someone who knows how to talk about his experience at one remove, in a secondary or reflexive discourse. What was interesting to me was to notice an "unhooking," an "uncoupling" of languages. As for what he said, it was obviously a political philosophy articulated on a completely different culture from that of a leftist intellectual.

Did you find him charming as a person?

Yes, insofar as I seemed to be watching a very successful grand bourgeois in his native element.

What did you talk about?

He did most of the talking. Perhaps he was disappointed—or pleased—at having to refine his image: but we made him talk much more than we talked ourselves.

The left didn't particularly approve of this luncheon . . .

I know. There are, even on the left, people who substitute facile indignation for difficult analysis: it was shocking, incorrect; it's just not done to chat with the enemy, to eat with him. One must remain pure. It's all part of the left's "good manners."

Have you never been tempted to return to your Mythologies *of twenty years ago, adding more work in a leftist direction, toward the new mythologies of the left?*

In twenty years the situation has obviously changed. There was May 1968, which liberated, opened up language on the left, at the price of imparting a certain arrogance at the same time. Above all, in a country where 49 percent of the people voted on the left, it would be surprising if there hadn't been a shifting, a disguising of social mythology: myths follow the majority. Why, then, do I delay describing this new mythology? I will never do so unless the left itself supports such an undertaking. *Le Nouvel Observateur,* for example . . .

> *One mythology among others: is it obvious to you that Giscard is indeed "the enemy"?*

What he represents, the men who are behind him and have pushed him into his present position of power, yes. But there is a historical dialectic that might arrange things so that one day, perhaps, he will be less of an enemy to us than someone else . . .

> *So in the end, if you do have a political stance, it's somewhat like Descartes's provisional morality, it's a constantly temporary, minimal, minimalist politics . . .*

The idea of a minimal position interests me and often seems to me to be the least unjust. As far as I'm concerned, the minimal in politics, the point of no compromise, is the problem of fascism. I belong to a generation that knew what it was and that remembers it. On that point, my commitment would be immediate and absolute.

> *Does that mean that below that limit, which is after all pegged rather high, all things are equal, and political choices are indistinguishable from each other?*

The limit isn't set as high as all that. First, because fascism comprises many things; let me specify that to me fascism means any regime that not only prevents one from speaking but above all *obliges* one to speak. And then fascism is the constant temptation of power, its natural element, what comes in through the back door after it has been tossed out the front. The limit is quickly reached . . .

Can a political minimalist still anticipate, still desire revolution?

It's strange: revolution is a pleasing image for everyone, and yet it's certainly a terrible reality. Of course, revolution might remain an image, and one could desire that image, militate for it. But it is more than an image, there are incarnations of revolution in the world. And that, you see, is what complicates the problem, after all . . . As for those societies where revolution has triumphed, I would call them "disappointing." They are the site of a major disappointment that makes many of us unhappy. These societies are disappointing because the state has not withered away . . . In my case, it would be demagogic to speak of revolution, but I would willingly speak for subversion. I find it a clearer word than revolution. It means: to come up from underneath so as to cheat with things, to divert them from their assigned paths, from their intended destinations.

Isn't "liberalism" also an acceptable minimal position?

There are two liberalisms. One is almost always—deep down—authoritarian, paternalistic, on the side of good conscience. And then there is a liberalism that is more ethical than political, for which reason there ought to be another name for it. Something like a profound suspension of judgment. A complete nonracism applied to any kind of object or subject, which would go, let's say, in the direction of Zen.

That's an intellectual's idea?

It's most certainly an intellectual's idea.

There was a time when intellectuals considered themselves to be the "salt of the earth" . . .

For my part, I'd say that they are more like the refuse of society. Waste in the strict sense, i.e., what serves no purpose, unless it's recuperated. There are regimes that do try in fact to recuperate the refuse we represent, but, fundamentally, waste is useless. In a certain sense, intellectuals are useless.

> *What do you mean by "waste"?*

Organic waste proves the *passage* of the matter it contains. Human waste, for example, attests to the digestive process. Well, intellectuals attest to a passage of history of which they are in a way the waste product. The intellectual crystallizes, in the form of refuse, impulses, desires, complications, blockages that probably belong to society as a whole. Optimists say that an intellectual is a "witness." I'd say that he's only a "trace."

> *Then you're saying that the intellectual is completely useless.*

Useless, but dangerous; every strong regime tries to keep the intellectual in line. The danger he presents is symbolic in nature; he is treated like an illness under observation, a bothersome supplement one keeps in order to confine within a controlled space the fantasies and exuberances of language.

> *And of what passage are you the waste product?*

Let's just say that I'm doubtless the trace of a historical interest in language; and also the trace of many fads, fashions, neologisms, buzzwords.

> *You mention fashion: does that mean what's in the wind? In other words, do you read your contemporaries?*

In fact, I generally read very little. That's not a confession, it's obvious from my writings. I have three ways of reading, three kinds of reading material. The first consists in *looking over* a book: I receive a book, I hear things about it, so I look it over; this is a very important kind of reading that is never talked about. Like Jules Romains, who wrote scholarly treatises on paroptical vision in the blind, I would suggest that there is a type of information connected with this first type of reading that is fluid and haphazard, but it functions all the same: para-acoustical information. My second way of reading applies to my work: a course to prepare, an article, a book—well, here I read books, from beginning to end, taking notes, but I read them only in terms of my work, they *go into* my work. And the third type of reading is my bedside reading, usually the classics . . .

You didn't answer my question . . .

My "contemporaries"? I put almost all of them in the first category: I "take a look at" them. Why? It's hard to say. Probably because I'm afraid of being seduced by material too close to me, so close that I wouldn't be able to transform it. I don't see myself reworking Foucault, Deleuze, or Sollers . . . It's too close. It arrives in a language that is too contemporary, absolutely contemporary.

Are there any exceptions?

A few. Once in a while a book impresses me very much and filters into my work, but it's always somewhat by accident. Moreover, whenever I seriously read a contemporary book, it's always long after its publication, never while it's popular. When everyone is talking about it, there's too much noise, I don't feel like reading it. I read Deleuze's *Nietzsche*, for example, and *L'Anti-Oedipe*, but always some time *after* they first came out.

And then there's Lacan, to whom you often refer, after all.

I don't know about "often." Mostly, in fact, when I was working on A *Lover's Discourse*. Because I needed a "psychology," and only psychoanalysis can provide one. And it was there, at that precise point, that I often came across Lacan.

Lacanianism or the Lacanian "text"?

Both. The Lacanian text as such interests me, it's a text that mobilizes things.

Because of the wordplay?

No, in fact. That's what I'm the least sensitive to; I see what it means, but I stop listening. The rest, however, I often like very much. To go back to Nietzsche's typology, Lacan is at bottom that rather rare mixture of "priest" and "artist."

Is there a relation between the imaginaire, *that central theme in your work, the image-repertoire, and Lacan's* imaginaire?

Yes, they're the same thing, but I'm sure I deform this theme by isolating it. I have the impression that the image-repertoire is almost the poor relation of psychoanalysis. Trapped between the real and the symbolic, it seems underrated, at least by the psychoanalytic vulgate. My next book, on the other hand, will be an affirmation of the image-repertoire.

Do you read your books? What I mean is, do you reread them?

Never. I'm too afraid. Either of thinking that they're good and that I won't be able to do as well, or of finding that they're bad and regretting having written them.

Do you know who does read your books? For whom do you write?

I think one always knows to whom, for whom one speaks. There is always, where speech is concerned, a definite audience, even if it is heterogeneous. Whereas what defines the absolute singularity of writing is that it is really the zero degree of allocution. The place exists, but it's empty. One never knows who will fill this space, for whom one is writing.

*Do you sometimes have the feeling of writing for pos-
terity?*

Frankly, no. I can't imagine that my oeuvre, my texts, will be
read after my death. I literally do not *imagine* it.

*You say "oeuvre." Are you conscious of writing an
"oeuvre"?*

No. Moreover, I instinctively changed "oeuvre" to "texts": I'm
not conscious of creating an oeuvre. I write each piece as it comes.
Through a mixture of obsessions, of tactical continuities and
detours.

*Are there any "oeuvres" that have been constructed in
any other way?*

Perhaps not. I don't know.

*What is certain, in any case, is that you often write, like
Valéry, "on demand."*

Often, yes, but to tell the truth, less and less. When it's a *writing*
commission, things work fairly well, whether it's a preface for a
book, an introduction to a painter, an article . . . In
short, things work out well enough if it's my writing that
is commissioned. On the other hand, when the request is for a
dissertation, when I have to discuss a certain subject, for example,
then things run into trouble. And when I let myself agree to these
requests, I become quite unhappy about it.

*Which explains the extremely fragmentary character of
what you write . . .*

It's like a proclivity. I'm moving closer and closer to the fragment—I enjoy its savor, and I believe in its theoretical importance. To the point, by the way, that I'm starting to have trouble
writing texts of a certain length and continuity.

Even though your work is fragmented and subject to the contingency of commissions, it is still traversed, unified by a few major themes . . .

There are themes. The image-repertoire, for example. The indirect. *Doxa.* Also the theme of anti-hysteria, even if it has evolved only recently. But I repeat that they are themes.

Do you mean that they're not philosophical "concepts"?

No. They are concepts. But they are metaphor-concepts, functioning like metaphors. And if what Nietzsche says is true, if concepts do have, as he says, a metaphorical origin, then it's at this origin that I situate myself. And so my concepts don't have that rigor usually conferred by philosophers.

What is most striking in your books is not so much the absence of rigor as it is the wild, unruly nature of your conceptual appropriations or importations.

"Wild" is the right word. I follow a somewhat piratical law that doesn't always recognize original property. Not at all from a spirit of contestation, but from the immediacy of desire, from greed, in a way. It's because of greed that I sometimes seize on the themes and words of others. I never complain, by the way, when someone "takes" something from me.

So that the unity of your work resides less in its themes than in this kind of operation?

Exactly. Movements and operations rather than themes or concepts. For example, "shifting." The shifting of images. The shifting of the meaning of words. Or the recourse to etymology. Or again the deformation, the anamorphosis of concepts. A whole series of methods, of procedures for which I should perhaps have tried to establish a nomenclature in *Roland Barthes.*

What is the aim of these procedures? Do they even have a specific aim, independently of their pure exercise?

I'm looking for a writing that doesn't paralyze the other, the reader. And that won't be too familiar, either. That's the difficulty: I would like to arrive at a writing that would be neither paralyzing nor overly "friendly."

You used to say that you were looking for "grids" through which to apprehend and appropriate reality . . .

I don't think I ever talked about grids. In any case, if I have one, it can only be literature. A grid that I carry around with me just about everywhere. But I think that it's quite possible to drive reality from cover, as a friend of mine puts it, without a "grid"! And that is the whole problem of semiology: in the beginning it was a grid, and I myself tried to make it into one. But when it had become a grid, it didn't turn up anything else at all. So I had to go elsewhere, without repudiating semiology, of course.

In speaking of your books, people who don't like you talk about a superstition, a sanctification of writing . . .

I'm not against sanctification. Lacan said not long ago that true atheists are very rare. The sacred is always somewhere . . . So let's just say that for me it turned out to be writing. Let me repeat: it is very difficult not to sanctify anything. Sollers is the only one I know of who has brought it off. Perhaps. He may have a secret somewhere, like the blasphemy of Saint-Fond was for Sade. In any case, as for me, I definitely sanctify the bliss of writing.

Language is also spoken language—theatrical language, for example.

My relations to the theater are rather complicated. As a meta-phorical energy, it's still very important to me: I see theater everywhere, in writing, in images, etc. But as for going to the theater, seeing plays, that doesn't really interest me anymore, I hardly go at all now. Let's say that I'm still sensitive to theatricalization, and that is an operation in the sense I mentioned a little while ago.

An operation you recognize in the language of teaching.

The teacher-student relationship is something else again. It's a contractual relationship that is also a relationship of desire, of reciprocal desire implying the possibility of disappointment and therefore of realization. I could be provocative and say: a contract of prostitution.

This year you are joining the Collège de France. Do you think the nature of this teaching relationship will be changed in any way?

I don't think so. I hope not. In any case, I have always had an "idyllic" relation to teaching within the framework of my seminars. I have never lectured except to subjects who have chosen me, who come to listen to me, and on whom I have not imposed myself. These privileged conditions are also, by definition, those of a course at the Collège.

Except that a seminar implies dialogue, and a course implies soliloquy . . .

That's not necessarily as important as one might think. There's a distressing prejudice that claims that everything in a teaching relationship belongs to the one who speaks, while nothing belongs to the one who listens. Whereas things happen on both sides, in my opinion. Listening must not be censured, in the name of speech. To listen can be active enjoyment.

In other words, no obligatory relation of power?

There is of course the question of power within discourse, in all discourse, and I talk about this in my inaugural address. As for the rest, I don't think we need to be in a hurry to eliminate courses in favor of false dialogues that often turn into psychodramas. And the soliloquy can certainly be thought of as a kind of theater, even a fraudulent, fluid, and uncertain theater, where a subtle game between speech and listening is played out. A soliloquy is not necessarily magisterial; it can be "loving."

Art Press, May 1977
From an interview conducted by Jacques Henric

A Lover's Discourse

Roland Barthes has written a new book, A Lover's Discourse.
*What does Barthes feel is his role in current intellectual debate?
Why, today, a book on the lover's discourse? Is there an autobio-
graphical element? What is the relation between writing and ethics?*

> *Roland Barthes, it seems to me that since* Writing Degree
> Zero, *since* Mythologies, *and with each succeeding book,
> it becomes more and more difficult to categorize you as
> an author. If you were to look back over your past work,
> how would you describe your place in the recent history
> of ideas and intellectual movements? And what do you
> feel is your current role in these debates?*

One of the figures in my book, among the fragments of the lover's
discourse, of *a* lover's discourse, is a figure bearing a Greek name,
the adjective applied to Socrates. Socrates was described as being
atopos, "site-less," unclassifiable, Unique. It's an adjective that
I apply instead to the beloved, so that, as the amorous subject
represented in the book, I am unable to see myself as *atopos,*
being instead someone quite banal, with a well-thumbed dossier.
Without taking a position on the idea that I'm unclassifiable, I
should admit that I've always worked by fits and starts, in phases,
and that there's a kind of motor in me, which I explained somewhat in *Roland Barthes*: the paradox. When a collection of opinions and positions seems to be hardening into a precise social

situation, then I immediately want—on my own and without
thinking about it—to go elsewhere. And it's in this that I could
recognize myself as an intellectual, whose function it is always
to go elsewhere when things begin to "jell." As for the second
part of your question, what role I see myself as playing nowadays,
I don't see myself at all as someone who strives for originality,
but as someone who always tries to speak for a certain marginality.
What is a bit difficult to explain is that with me this championing
of marginality is never ostentatious. I prefer to work quietly. It's
a marginality that still maintains aspects of a certain courtesy, a
certain tenderness—why not?—a marginality that cannot be assigned a well-defined label from the current intellectual stockpile.

> *You often assert an explicit and apparently contradictory
> double preference: on the one hand, you proclaim your
> interest in modernity (the introduction of Brecht in France,
> the New Novel,* Tel Quel *. . .); on the other hand, you
> like to talk about your traditional tastes in literature. What
> could be the profound coherence behind these choices?*

I don't know if there is a profound coherence behind them, but
you've touched on the heart of the matter. My situation has not
been as cut and dried as you make it out to be, and for a long
time I felt torn in an almost inadmissible manner between my
different predilections, or between what I would call—because I
prefer to define things in terms of conduct rather than taste—my
evening reading material, which is always a classical book, and
my work during the day, when, in fact, without any hypocrisy,
I feel completely in agreement on a theoretical and critical level
with certain modern works. I kept this contradiction somewhat
hidden, and it was only with *The Pleasure of the Text* that I claimed
the right to avow certain tastes for literature of the past. And as
always when one permits oneself to announce a preference, a
theory is not far off. I am trying more or less to construct the
theory of this taste for the past. I use two arguments: first, a
metaphor. According to Vico's image, history proceeds in a spiral,
and things of the past return, but obviously not in the same place;

thus, there are tastes, values, behavior, "writings" of the past that may return, but in a very modern place. The second argument is linked to my work on the amorous subject. This subject develops mainly in a register that, since Lacan, is called *l'imaginaire*, the image-repertoire—and I recognize myself as a subject of the image-repertoire: I have a vital relation to past literature precisely because this literature provides me with images, with a good relation to images. For example, the narrative, the novel, forms a dimension of the image-repertoire that existed in "readerly" literature. In admitting my fondness for this literature, I claim the rights of the subject of the image-repertoire insofar as this subject is in a way disinherited, crushed between those two great psychic structures that have claimed most of modernity's attention: neurosis and psychosis. The subject of the image-repertoire is a poor relation of those structures, because he is never either completely psychotic or completely neurotic. You see that, while militating discreetly for this subject of the image-repertoire, I can give myself the alibi of work that is actually quite far along, something like one form of tomorrow's avant-garde, with a touch of humor, of course.

> *When modernity becomes the discourse of hegemony, of stereotypes, don't you decide, in your own way, to keep your distance? Isn't it somewhat provocative to talk about "love" today, just as it was yesterday, in the midst of structuralism, to defend "the pleasure of the text"?*

Doubtless, but I don't experience this as tactical behavior. It's just that I find it very difficult, as you remarked, to put up with stereotypy, the elaboration of small collective languages, a phenomenon quite familiar to me through my work in teaching, in the student milieu. I'm exposed on all sides to these stereotyped languages of marginality, the stereotypy of nonstereotypy. I can hear them being invented. At first they can be enjoyable, but in time they become a burden. For a while, I don't dare make my escape, but finally, often because of some chance occurrence in my personal life, I find the courage to break with these languages.

The archetype of love-as-passion

> *Let's talk, if you will, about* A Lover's Discourse: Fragments. *To avoid possible misunderstandings, would you explain the title?*

I'll have to give you a short history of the project itself. I have a seminar at the École Pratique des Hautes Études, and as you know, a few of us are at work on the concept of discourse, discursiveness, a concept distinct from the idea of language in general or in particular. This is discursiveness in the larger sense, the enveloping flow of language as an object for analysis. A little over two years ago, I decided to study a certain type of discourse, what I presumed to be amorous discourse, and it was understood from the beginning that the amorous subjects would come from what is called love-as-passion, romantic love. I decided to conduct a seminar that would be the objective analysis of a certain type of discursiveness. I then chose a tutor text and analyzed the amorous discourse of that work, not the work itself. I chose Goethe's *Werther*, which is the very archetype of love-as-passion. But during the two years of this seminar I became aware of a double movement. First of all, I realized that I was projecting myself, by reason of my past experience, my life, into certain of the figures under study. I was even mixing figures from my own life in with those of *Werther*.

The second observation was that the participants in the seminar were also projecting themselves very strongly into what was being said. Under these conditions, I decided that when the moment came to move from the seminar to a book, instead of writing a treatise on amorous discourse, which would have been a kind of lie (I no longer aspired to any claims of scientific generality for my work), I should on the contrary write the discourse of a lover myself. There was an about-face. Of course, Nietzsche's influence was at work here, even if I did deform it a great deal; I'm thinking in particular of what Nietzsche tells us about the need to "dramatize," to adopt a method of "dramatization"—which for me had the epistemological advantage of prying me away from metalanguage. Since *The Pleasure of the Text* I have not been able to put up with "dissertating" on a topic. So I fabricated, feigned the discourse of a lover. The title is quite explicit and it is constructed intentionally: the subject of the book is not *the* amorous discourse, it's the discourse of *a* lover. Who is not necessarily myself. Speaking frankly, there are elements from my experience, elements from *Werther*, or books I have read: culture, mysticism, psychoanalysis, Nietzsche . . . There are also elements from conversations with friends, who are very much a presence in this book. The result is thus the discourse of a subject who says *I*, who is thus individualized on the level of the utterance, but the discourse is nevertheless a composed, feigned, or, if you prefer, a "pieced-together" discourse (the result of montage).

> *But still, who does say "I" in these fragments?*

You see, the one who says "I" in the book is the *I* of writing. That's really all that can be said. Naturally, I can be lured into saying that I'm the subject—but then I offer Flaubert's reply: it's me, and it isn't me. It is no more Roland Barthes, if you'll permit a comparison springing perhaps from infatuation, than it is Stendhal putting a character through his paces. That's why the book is rather novelistic. Moreover, the relationship between the author and the character on stage is fictive, novelistic.

> *Indeed, certain "fragments" are truly the beginnings of narratives. A story begins to take shape, but is immediately interrupted. I often asked myself while reading these very successful, very "written" sketches, why doesn't he continue them? Why not a real novel? A real autobiography?*

That will come later, perhaps. I've been flirting with that idea for a long time. But, with this particular book, the reason why the stories never become established as such must be seen in doctrinal terms, I would say. My vision of the lover's discourse is essentially fragmented, discontinuous, fluttering. These are episodes of language swirling around in the mind of the ena-

moured, impassioned subject, episodes suddenly interrupted by
some circumstance or other, jealousy, a rendezvous that doesn't
work out, some unbearable anxiety, at which moment these tag
ends of monologues are broken up, and we go on to another
figure. I was careful to preserve the radical discontinuity of this
linguistic torment unfolding in the lover's head. That is why I
cut the work up into fragments and put them into alphabetical
order. I absolutely did not want the text to seem like a love story.
I'm convinced that the well-constructed love story, with a beginning, an end, and a crisis in the middle, is the way society hopes
to persuade the lover to be reconciled with the language of the
Other, by constructing his own narrative, in which he plays a
role. I feel that the unhappy lover is not even able to benefit from
this reconciliation, and that he is not, paradoxically, within a
love story; he's in something else that closely resembles madness,
because it's not for nothing that we say someone is madly in love,
and the story is simply impossible from the lover's point of view.
That is why I constantly tried to break up the construction of any
story. At one point I even thought about opening the book with
a figure that would serve as an initiation: love-at-first-sight, en-
amoration, ravishment; I thought about it for a long time and
finally decided against it, because I couldn't be certain that even
love-at-first-sight was chronologically the first figure, because it's
entirely possible that the *coup de foudre* is really a kind of after-
thought, something the lover tells himself later. So my book is
a discontinuous text that protests somewhat against the love story.

Writing for the beloved

> *What do you mean when you write: "I am beside the
> writing"?*

First, a digression: I noticed that there were two types of amorous
subject. The one in French literature from Racine to Proust is a
jealous lover, a paranoiac. There is another lover who is not
much in evidence in French literature but who has been admirably celebrated by German Romanticism, particularly in the
lieder of Schubert and Schumann (which are mentioned in my

book). This type of love-as-passion, while not excluding jealousy, is not focused on it, being instead a much more effusive feeling of love, directed toward fulfillment. The essential figure here is the Mother. One of the figures in my book concerns the desire, the temptation, the impulse that the lover often seems to have—and this is confirmed by books—to create, or paint, or write for the beloved. I try to explain the profound pessimism one may feel on that particular plane, since the lover's discourse cannot become writing except at the price of vast transformations and losses.

My profound feeling is that the lover is a marginal being, which explains in a way my decision to publish this book, to give voice to a marginality all the more insistent today in that it isn't even within fashionable marginality. A book on the lover's discourse is much more kitsch than a book on drug addicts, for example.

> *Doesn't it take a certain courage to talk about love as you do, in the face of the invading wave of psychoanalytical discourse?*

In my book there is indeed a relation to psychoanalytical discourse that I would call "interesting," because this relation evolved even as I was working on the seminar and the book. You're perfectly aware that if we look at culture today—this is also one of the propositions of the book—we see no important language that is able to deal with the feelings of love. Among these major languages, psychoanalysis has at least attempted descriptions of the state of being in love; there are some in Freud, Lacan, in the work of other analysts. I had to use these descriptions, they were topical, they cried out to me, they were so pertinent. I emphasize them in the book because the lover I put on stage is a subject from today's culture, who thus knows a few things about psychoanalysis and applies them to himself, in an untutored fashion. But as the feigned discourse of the lover continued to spin itself out, it developed as an affirmation of values, of love as an order of affirmative values that resists all attack. At that point, the amorous subject can only part company with analytical discourse insofar as it certainly talks about the feeling of being in love, but always in a deprecatory fashion, in the end, trying to persuade the lover to reintegrate a certain normality, to separate "being in love" from "loving" and "liking," etc. Psychoanalysis supports an image of normality in love that is in fact the image of the couple, even of the married couple . . . So my relation to psychoanalysis in this book is quite ambiguous; it's a relation that uses psychoanalytical descriptions and ideas, as usual, but uses them a bit like the elements of fiction, which is not necessarily credible.

Writing as a morality

> *I have never had such a strong impression that writing is deeply involved with ethics as I did while reading this book. You insisted on this point in your inaugural address at the Collège de France. I would like you to say something about this . . .*

That is a wonderful question. But I don't have a clear understanding of the relationship between writing and ethics, and I can only tell you that, to me, the writing of this book is somewhat unusual. Given the subject, I was obliged to protect this book. In order to protect this discourse spoken in the name of "I," which is a risk, after all, my greatest protective weapon was pure language. I would even say, precisely, syntax. I felt to what extent syntax can protect a speaker. It is a double-edged weapon, because it can often be—it often is—an instrument of oppression, but when the subject is unprotected, disadvantaged, and alone, syntax protects him. This book is rather syntactical, not very lyrical, without any grand neologisms, but great attention is paid to the outline of sentences. At such a moment, writing functions in a way as a morality, the models for which should be sought in agnosticism, skepticism, moralities that are not rooted in faith.

> *What is the title of your course program at the Collège de France?*

I've begun a series of courses on "Living Together," intended to explore certain small utopian groups. Not communes like we had after the hippie movement, but the utopias of affective communities whose members would in fact live together but each in his own rhythm, what Oriental monks used to call idiorhythmics. I've centered the courses quite a bit on the notion of idiorhythmics.

[. . .]

I feel that I will be returning to properly literary material in my courses now, but I always reserve the right to digress and, as you correctly noted, to open up an ethical vanishing point within writing. Because, in the end, "living together" is an ethical problem.

I'm sure that if I'm working on a specific literary form next year, ethics will be part of the picture.

If I were a philosopher, and if I wanted to write an important treatise, I would call it a literary study. Under the guise of literary analysis, I would try to liberate an ethics, in the broadest sense of the word.

Playboy, **September** 1977
From an interview conducted by Philippe Roger

The Greatest Cryptographer
of Contemporary Myths
Talks about Love

Roland Barthes doesn't like to be considered a guru, which seems to be the fashion these days. He prefers to be called a semiologist, a critic, an essayist. And yet there is a "Barthes phenomenon" that goes beyond the importance and diversity of his published works. Almost all his books have enjoyed exceptional success: after their initial notoriety as controversial bestsellers, they have settled down to become classics.

Roland Barthes has just been elected to the Collège de France, and he has already returned to the fray. His latest provocation? He dares to talk about love. And at a time when it is sexuality (not to mention pornography) that brings in the money, everyone is talking about his new book, A Lover's Discourse. *Roland Barthes, who has also written a* Fashion System, *could very well be one of those people who are setting tomorrow's trends today.*

We asked the critic Philippe Roger, an expert on libertinage *who has just published* Sade: la Philosophie dans le Pressoir, *to interview Barthes for the readers of* Playboy.

The subject of love is old-fashioned, of course. But with books like A Lover's Discourse, *perhaps the springtime of love will return.*

Roland Barthes, you have just published A Lover's Discourse. *Do you think that this is the kind of serious work
a professor at the Collège de France should be doing?*

No, you're right. Now, if I had said or written: "the sentiment
of love," that would have been a bit more respectable, because
it contains echoes of something important in nineteenth-century
psychology. But everyone uses the word "love," it's in all the
popular songs and always has been. So, obviously, to talk about
"love" like that is not respectably professorial behavior.

*It's a very personal book, but there is one major reference:
Goethe's* Werther, *which prompted the famous wave of
suicides "à la Werther." Goethe's book was published in
1774; are there no other great novelists of love today?*

There are descriptions of the feelings of love, of course, but the
novel rarely describes a *passion*. At least I can't think of any that
do.

Is love old-fashioned?

Yes, no doubt. Love is out of date in intellectual milieux. From
the point of view of the intelligentsia, the intellectual milieu that
nourishes me, in which I live, and that I love . . . I had the
feeling of writing something rather old-fashioned.

And outside this intellectual milieu?

There is also a popular attitude expressed in remarks, pleasantries,
broad jokes that denigrate the lover, who is assumed to be a kind
of lunatic, a madman. But it should be said that the greatest
attacks on love are those mounted by the "theoretical languages."
Either they ignore love completely, as do political or Marxist
languages, or they speak about it with subtlety, but in a deprecatory fashion, in the manner of psychoanalysis.

What is this "depreciation" affecting love today?

Love-as-passion (the love I'm talking about) is almost "frowned upon," it's considered to be an illness from which the lover must recover, and no enriching aspects are attributed to it any longer.

> *Who could this "underrated" lover be, now that we can no longer recognize him by his "Werther costume," the famous blue suit and yellow vest? How do you recognize him?*

I will answer treacherously that I wrote the book in order to be able to recognize him! So that I would receive letters and confidences that would allow me to think that there are more people in love than I thought . . .

> *And if they don't write you?*

Then they don't recognize themselves from the outside. Because in modern urban life there are no longer any poses of the pathetic lover.

> *By these "poses" you mean the balcony scene, for example? "Juliet lives on the twenty-fifth floor, there are no more Romeos . . ." That was in a recent anti-love song.*

Exactly. The balcony scene is gone. But we no longer have even the morphology of the lover's features, his expressions, his behavior; in the nineteenth century, there were hundreds of lithographs, paintings, engravings representing the lover. Now we can no longer recognize a lover in the street. We have no way of knowing if the people who surround us are in love or not. Because, if they are, they're certainly putting up a good front.

> *To accompany your lover, there is the "beloved object." Why this curious expression, the "beloved object"?*

It's a question of principle: being in love is a unisex situation, like unisex jeans and haircuts these days. This is quite important, I think.

> *Do you feel that heterosexual and homosexual lovers are*
> *in love in the same way?*

I think that exactly the same *tonality* can be found in a man who loves a woman or a man, and a woman who loves a man or a woman. And so I was careful to de-emphasize the sexual difference. Unfortunately, French is not a language that makes this kind of thing very easy. "The beloved object" has the advantage of being an expression that doesn't take sides on the sex of *whom one loves.*

> *But doesn't "object" also contrast with "subject"?*

Yes. The beloved is inevitably an object, is not experienced at all as a subject. "Object" is the right word, because it indicates the depersonalization of the beloved.

> *One doesn't love the other as a person?*

That is the great enigma of love. Because this depersonalized object becomes at the same time the person par excellence, incomparable to any other, what psychoanalysis calls the unique object.

> *Would it, then, be more correct to say that one loves an*
> *image?*

Assuredly. One is never in love with anything *but* an image. Love-at-first-sight, what I call "ravishment," happens through an image.

> *Through a "real" image? Through a photograph in* Play-
> boy?

One might well ask. But I would say no, after all. Because the ravishing image is alive, in action.

> *Like the image of Charlotte cutting pieces of bread and butter for her brothers, in* Werther . . .

Yes. I would prudently add that passion knows no boundaries. A person can fall hopelessly in love with a photograph, but in general, the *coup de foudre* does not strike from an image completely out of context: the image must be "in situ."

> *And there we have your "ravished" lover . . . That's what a poll taken last year called "true love." And an impressive majority of the French public said they "believed in it," and thought it lasted throughout life. What does your lover think of that?*

He would answer "yes," of course, on the question of "true love." But a "lifelong" love? I don't know. That implies an optimism that doesn't belong in the lover as I presented him. To him, the expression "lifelong" has no meaning. He is within a kind of temporal absolute. He doesn't parcel out time along the entire estimated length of his life . . .

> *Suffering plays a major role in the figures described in this subject's love life. There's so much suffering that one has the impression the lover doesn't try to avoid it at all.*

True, he assumes suffering and unhappiness as a kind of value. But not at all in a Christian sense. On the contrary: as an unhappiness that is completely blameless.

> *How does he react to this unhappiness?*

He would tend to *accept* the suffering, while rejecting all guilt.

> *Then the unhappiness of love is inevitable?*

Yes, I think so. Or rather, I would say that the feeling of love is defined precisely like that: because suffering is inevitable. But one can always imagine that the feeling will change . . .

One would cease being in love?

That's the biggest problem, on which the book comes to a halt. Common sense tells us that there comes a time when one must uncouple "being in love" from "loving." One puts aside "being in love," with its cortege of traps, illusions, tyrannies, scenes, difficulties, even suicides . . . In order to attain a more serene feeling, more dialectical, less jealous, less possessive.

You just mentioned jealousy. In novels, as in life, no doubt, the lover's most spectacular suffering is caused by jealousy. But not in your book . . .

Yes, you noticed, that cardinal figure of passion is given short shrift in my book. I even thought about eliminating it . . .

Because you don't know much about it?

On the contrary. But it's a feeling that is not deeply rooted in my life, even though it's atrociously painful to experience. I really don't have any ideas about jealousy beyond the usual ones. And it's the only figure in the book for which I didn't provide a personal definition. I simply copied out a dictionary definition, because it was perfect. Jealousy: "A sentiment born in love and produced by the fear that the beloved prefers someone else." Of all the figures, this one seems to me the most banal.

Is everyone jealous?

I would say—and here I'll trot out some big words—that it's a phenomenon of anthropological breadth. There is no being in the world who hasn't experienced waves of jealousy. And I don't think it's possible to be in love, even in the lax and relaxed manner we may ascribe to young people today, without finally, at some point, being touched by jealousy.

> *Then you're skeptical about these attempts at "unpossessive" love?*

Yes. Many of my friends are younger than I am. I'm often astounded by what seems, at first glance, an absence of jealousy in their relations. And I tell myself that in similar situations I would be terribly jealous. I'm amazed, I admire them very much for sharing sensuality, sexuality, communal property, seemingly without huge problems. But that is only a first impression. If one watches them more closely, one sees that even they experience feelings of jealousy.

In fact, a lover who would not be jealous—I was going to say he would be a mystic par excellence, but I can't say that, because there are some wonderful texts where the mystic reveals a certain jealousy, in regard to God or other people. A lover who would not be jealous would be, literally, a *saint*.

> *Failing that, if I may say so, can one love several people at the same time?*

I think that one can, for a while, anyway. One can . . . and I even think that it's a *delicious* feeling, to use a classical word. Yes, it's a delicious sentiment, to bathe in an atmosphere of love, of generalized flirtation—giving "flirtation" a certain strength . . .

> *Only for a while?*

Yes, I don't think the freedom that comes from spreading oneself thinly, as it were, can last very long . . . because there comes a moment, for the lover, when things "crystallize."

> *And that's the end of "flitting about"?*

Yes, from the moment the lover is absorbed by passion, flirting is a thing of the past. The other's flirting makes him suffer horribly. And he himself hasn't the heart for it anymore.

> *That's the tyrannical relation you were talking about . . .*

Right. The lover feels dominated, captivated, possessed by the beloved. But, in reality, the one who loves also exerts a tyrannical power over the one who is loved. It's not funny to be loved by someone who is in love . . . I suppose . . .

> *Then there is no love without combat, the marshaling of forces, battles, victories, defeats?*

The lover struggles against being enthralled, but he fails. He realizes with humiliation, and sometimes with delight, that he is completely enthralled by the beloved image. And in his better moments, moreover, he suffers greatly from his enslavement of the other, he tries not to tyrannize the beloved.

> *Which is what you call the "non-will-to-possess." Is that the solution?*

Yes. The *ideal* solution is to place oneself in a state of the non-will-to-possess, which is a notion borrowed from Oriental philosophies. "Not to possess" the beloved, to let desire circulate freely. At the same time, not to "sublimate": to master desire in order not to master the other.

> *This is, then, if not a program, at least a proposal?*

Yes, it's a proposal. A utopia, perhaps . . .

> *Toward a new amorous world . . .*

Yes, that's it.

> *But this new amorous world would be something com-*
> *pletely different, I suppose, from the "liberated sexuality"*
> *everyone was talking about ten years ago. It would seem*
> *that there is a reaction nowadays against those ideologies,*
> *that there is a certain distrust of desire. Would you situate*
> *your book in this current, or countercurrent?*

Yes, in a way, I do see it as part of this trend. The common
factor is that being in love permits a distancing of sexuality.

> *And of desire?*

There is desire in the feeling of love. But this desire is diverted
toward a diffuse sexuality, toward a kind of generalized sensuality.

> *What would you say about eroticism in this relation?*

It's not simple to talk about eroticism that is, let's say, "successful."
Put that in quotation marks, because this success depends on each
subject. There are no recipes. A "successful" eroticism is a sexual
and sensual relationship with the being one loves. It happens,
after all. And when it does, it's something so beautiful, so good,
so perfect, so dazzling, that at that moment eroticism itself is a
kind of access to a transcendence of sexuality. Sexuality remains
within experience, and the greater the eroticism, the more acute
the experience. But there is a sentimental surplus value, which
means that eroticism is completely detached from all pornography.

> *Would you say that* In the Realm of the Senses *is a film*
> *about love?*

Yes, I think so. I wasn't particularly receptive to it, perhaps, for
personal reasons, but it's a beautiful film. A perfect example of
the *film d'amour*.

> *In your book, you contrast the lover with the*
> *"cruiser" . . .*

Yes, those two types of "discourse," in the larger sense, should be contrasted with each other. The practices of cruising don't coincide at all with the quite ascetic practices of the lover, who doesn't scatter himself through the world, remaining instead imprisoned with his image.

But isn't the lover also a cruiser?

Yes, precisely. There are cruisers who cruise to find *someone* to be in love with. That is even the typical case. In homosexual milieux, at any rate, where cruising is quite extensive, one can cruise for years at a time, often in an unavoidably sordid fashion, given the kinds of places one must frequent, with in fact the invincible idea that one will find someone with whom to be in love.

In contrast to Don Juan, whose pleasure was to be found "entirely in change," and who passes ceaselessly from country to country, from woman to woman . . .

To me, in fact, Don Juan is the model cruiser, with his famous list of conquests: "a thousand and three." That's the cruiser's slogan. You know, cruisers exchange notes constantly. And their conversations always boil down to lists . . .

Aside from lovers and cruisers, there are the ones who have settled down, the sistemati . . .

Yes. I was talking one day with a friend who told me that the Italian for "settled down," in the sense of "married," was *sistemato.* I thought it was interesting that instead of saying "So-and-so has settled down," "So-and-so is married," one could imagine him "systemized," caught in a system . . .

But to say that people have "settled down," isn't this cruiser talk?

I hadn't thought about that. Yes, perhaps. Because in fact the
cruiser and the lover are both equally distant from married people.
They're both on the margin in relation to the established couple.
Both excluded.

> *In your book, in any case, it's more the couple that is
> excluded . . .*

Yes, that's very true. I did have a "figure" on union, at the end.
But, why not say so, I didn't have any personal experience of this
type of union. And so I didn't have the language to describe it.
But that's not taking a stand on the subject.

> *Does the lover think in terms of a couple?*

I think that the couple is always on the horizon. The book's point
of view was that of a lover who is not loved. But he constantly
thinks about being loved, of course, and thus about being part
of a couple. I would even say that he wants nothing else.

> *At the other end of the scale, there are those referred to,
> depending on one's vocabulary, as "deviants" or "per-
> verts." They, like the married couple, are absent from
> your book. Your lover sometimes seems to be speaking
> in their place.*

No. The lover does not speak by proxy for other deviants, for an
essential reason: he is a deviant in relation to deviants. In the
sense that he is less demanding, less contentious . . . and less
glorious. In relation to the problems of homosexuality, there is
an important consequence: if one is talking about a homosexual
(male or female) in love, the important term isn't "homosexual"
but "in love." I refused to proffer a homosexual discourse. Not
because I refuse to recognize homosexuality, not through censure,
or prudence, but because a lover's discourse is not any more
related to homosexuality than it is to heterosexuality.

> *The lover is thus a deviant in relation to "deviants,"*
> *deviant in relation to "those who desire." But aren't they*
> *at each other's throat?*

I don't think so. I think they're off on different planets. Which isn't particularly cheerful either . . .

> *Venus for the désirants, and lovers on the moon: That's*
> *what gives them that silly look, perhaps. As you wrote:*
> *"What is more silly than a lover?" . . . What makes him*
> *silly?*

It's because he is situated in what I call "dis-reality." Everything that the world calls "reality," he experiences as illusion. Everything that amuses others, their conversations, their passions, their indignations, none of that seems real to him. His personal "reality" is his relation to the beloved, and the thousand incidents that affect it—exactly what the world considers to be his "madness." Because of this very reversal, he feels himself imprisoned by a bitter maladjustment. And he does in fact behave in many ways that seem idiotic in the eyes of common sense.

> *The lover is asocial, also apolitical. You write more spe-*
> *cifically that he no longer "gets excited" over politics.*
> *But isn't this a way of saying that he doesn't engage in*
> *politics anymore, that it no longer counts for him?*

No, that nuance is intentional. Because this is something I feel very deeply. A person functions on several wavelengths. He may continue to receive political waves, but what he no longer understands is how anyone can be passionately interested, "invested" in them. He isn't "depoliticized" in the sense that he isn't fundamentally indifferent to what happens politically, but he has established a hierarchy within himself, and he finds it extraordinary that anyone could get "all worked up" over such things.

> *It's tempting to contrast yesterday's "impassioned revo-*
> *lutionary" with your "relaxed lover," relaxed along the*

*lines of a certain liberalism . . . Would you agree with
this opposition?*

Yes, I would. The lover is himself the site of a fierce investment
of energy, and he therefore feels himself excluded from other
investments of a differing nature. The only human being with
whom he could feel complicity would be another lover. After all,
it's true that lovers understand each other! But a political militant
is, in his fashion, in love with a cause, an idea. And this rivalry
is unendurable. On either side. I don't think a political militant
could easily put up with someone madly in love . . .

*I still see an ambiguity here. Is your lover really so "in-
tractable," "unsalvageable," and in this sense, subversive? Or is he rather, for any system, quiet and inoffen-
sive?*

He's a marginal being. But, as I said, modest, retiring. His marginality is invisible, not obstreperous. In this sense, he is truly
"unsalvageable."

*But you say this yourself: every other night, on the tele-
vision, someone's saying "I love you." There is thus a
"promotion" of love by the media. How could mass culture be pushing "love" if it's asocial and dangerous?*

That's a more difficult question. Why does mass culture focus so
much on the problems of the amorous subject? What are really
being staged in these cases are *narratives* of *episodes*, not the
sentiment of love itself. The distinction is perhaps a subtle one,
but I insist on it. This means that if you put the lover in a "love
story," you thereby *reconcile* him with society. Why? Because
telling stories is one of the activities coded by society, one of the
great social constraints. Society tames the lover through the love
story.

*If I understand you correctly, your lover is subversive,
but* La Marquise des Anges *is conformist?*

That's precisely it. And that's why I took Draconian precautions so that my book *would not be* a "love story." So that the lover would be left in his nakedness, as a being inaccessible to the usual forms of social recuperation—the novel in particular.

> *Your book is not the work of a novelist; it's a semiologist's book. And a lover's book. Isn't that a rather bizarre being, a "semiologist in love"?*

Absolutely not! The lover is the natural semiologist in the pure state! He spends his time reading signs—he does nothing else: signs of happiness, signs of unhappiness. On the face of the other, in his behavior. He is truly a prey to signs.

> *So the proverb is a lie: love is not blind . . .*

Love is not blind. On the contrary, it has an unbelievable power to decipher things, which is related to the paranoid element in every lover. You know, a lover combines bits of neurosis and psychosis: he's tormented and crazed. He sees clearly—but the result is often the same as if he were blind.

> *Why?*

Because he doesn't know where or how to make signs stop. He deciphers perfectly, but he's unable to arrive at a definite interpretation, and he's swept away by a perpetual circus, where he'll never find peace.

> *Here is a question I've been wanting to ask you from the beginning: This lover's book, were you in love when you wrote it?*

[Smile.] That's a question I've refused to answer so far. Well . . . let's say that the book is based in large part on personal experience; in large part also on reading, on conversations with friends. As for my contribution, the personal knowledge I drew on is not that of one particular experience. These states of mind, movements, contortions are the inheritance of several previous love affairs. Having said that—why not admit it?—there was a crystallizing episode. Let's say that I conceived the book as a way to keep from losing myself, from lapsing into despair. I wrote it, things having formed themselves into a dialectic on their own . . .

Two necessary stages?

I would not have been able to write with the distance of style, of phrasing, if I hadn't managed to see things in a dialectical fashion . . .

It's not necessarily the end of a real-life experience that pushes one toward writing?

I would say that the desire to write such a book is fueled by two different moments. Either at the end, because writing has a marvelous power of pacification: or at the beginning, in a moment of exuberance, because one thinks one will write a book of love— that it will be given, dedicated to the beloved.

So, then, the lover who speaks is really you, Roland Barthes?

My answer may seem to be a pirouette, but it is not. The subject that I am is not unified. This is something I feel profoundly. To then say "It's I!" would be to postulate a unity of self that I do not recognize in myself.

Allow me to rephrase my question: For each figure in the book, one after the other, do you say: "There I am"?

Well! . . . When I conducted a research seminar on this same topic, I took into account figures that I had not experienced myself, figures taken from books . . . But, obviously, that's what was cut from my book. Yes, I definitely have a personal relation to all the figures in the book.

> *Roland Barthes, one often has the impression, contem-*
> *plating this "structural portrait" of the lover, that you*
> *wish not only to describe but also to convince. Could*
> *we say that it's a book that is modestly militant on behalf*
> *of all lovers?*

Militant? You're issuing a small challenge there . . . My book
implies certain values.

> *And a moral?*

Yes, there is a moral.

> *And that would be?*

A morality of affirmation. One should not let oneself be swayed
by disparagements of the sentiment of love. One should affirm.
One should dare. Dare to love . . .

Réforme, September 2, 1978
From an interview conducted by Jacqueline Sers

On the Subject of Violence

During the late-summer holidays, many of those themes that haunt public opinion and the newspapers all year long quietly slip from view. One of these themes is violence. Because we hear so much about violence, and because what we hear is often poorly understood, Présence Protestante *has prepared a television round-table on this subject. Jacqueline Sers has asked Roland Barthes—writer, critic, professor—to decorticate this word "violence," as he did so artfully and delightfully with other words in his book* Mythologies.

> *Quite graciously, you told me that you would be happy to be interviewed by* Réforme . . . *Why?*

For sentimental reasons. I had a Protestant childhood; my mother was a Protestant, and I was quite familiar with Protestantism during my adolescence. Protestantism interested me, it raised questions in me, and I took part in it. Then I drew away from it. But I always kept a sentimental bond, perhaps more with Protestants than with Protestantism. Perhaps it was because of that feeling of benevolence one always has toward a minority . . .

> *Putting aside all those definitions of celebrity, who is Roland Barthes?*

I've participated in many types of intellectual activity: the theory of meaning, literary and social criticism . . . But if there is a word that would truly define what happens within me, and not within my writings, it would be the word "philosopher," which does not refer to a degree of competence, because I have had no philosophical training. What I do within myself is philosophize, reflect on my experience. This reflection is a joy and a benefit to me, and when I'm unable to pursue this activity, I become unhappy, because I am deprived of something important to me. Philosophizing? It belongs perhaps more to the ethical order than to the metaphysical one . . .

A good look at this word reveals that it is completely irregular, an unusual word that creates a kind of panic of responses in us.

It's a word that is understood differently by many different people, and it covers very different things: one may think violence means something quite specific, but the more one thinks about it, the more it means. That is a first difficulty, on an intellectual and analytical order; this word lends itself to dissertation, because it is already firmly embedded in the vast paperwork of the judicial system. Mass culture itself has provided us with all sorts of ways of looking at this word.

The second difficulty is of an existential nature. Violence threatens our bodies: therefore, we usually react to it with rejection, refusal, but there are perhaps beings who accept and assume violence, even finding a kind of exaltation in it. Violence is not a simple thing.

The third difficulty: it's a word that poses problems of conduct on the level of states, organizations, groups, individuals. And here we feel quite at a loss. It's a problem as old as the world itself: how do we control violence, except with more violence?

This kind of impasse finally develops a religious dimension. The difficulties are immense, and we must accept the fact that we are, in a way, impotent before this word. It is an insoluble word.

> *Why did you refer to a religious dimension apropos of the word "violence"?*

There is not one of the world's great religions, in the East or the West, that has not dealt with the problem of violence within a general metaphysical conception, either by assimilating violence into evil, or by assimilating it on the contrary into the forces of right, in certain more archaic religions. The fact that religion addresses this problem therefore implies conversion in order to deal with violence on the particular terms of each religion. If one wishes to discuss it in secular terms, then another key must be found. One must choose one's key to discuss violence.

> *If the word is insoluble, as you said, then there is no key, in secular terms?*

The word is equally insoluble in the temporal religious domain! That it may be spiritually soluble is possible, even certain, but that's not for me to say.

But to return to the plane of intellectual analysis, we must keep in mind that there are several types of violence.

There is the violence residing in all constraint of the individual by the group. This is why one may say that there is a violence of the law, of laws, a violence of the police, the state, of what is right: in certain cases, justice presents itself as a limitation or surveillance of violence, but only by instituting in its turn a violence that, while noncorporal, is still the violence of constraint. This is a theme that should be remembered, because it has been considered in both political and cultural terms by thinkers such as Sorel, Walter Benjamin, not to mention Marx. And the implications there can be widespread: experiencing the constraint of a norm can be felt as a confrontation with violence. But it's a diffuse violence, dry, polite . . .

There is the violence that concerns individual bodies: sometimes it consists in limiting bodily freedom, an incarcerating violence; sometimes it is the bloody violence of wounds, assassinations, murders. It is obviously this particular violence that commands our attention at present, in our streets . . . the violence of criminals, anarchy, even war.

We must distinguish between these different circles of violence, because there is in general a mechanism whereby we respond to one type of violence only through a second, more extensive type of violence.

For example: the violence of the state may be answered by bloody insurrection. And thus a kind of unending system is set up; it is the nature of violence to be perpetual, it is self-engendering . . . Banal as this realization is, how can we escape from it?

> *Doesn't the word "violence" have two meanings: a destructive violence, a sign of death, and at the same time an impulse of aggressivity, creativity, a force of life?*

Even though this may seem paradoxical, I would make a distinction between the noun "violence" and the adjective "violent." There are in fact conditions, actions, or choices that may be violent in a positive way or, rather, violent *and* positive: creative passions, creative radicalism! But this is included only in the adjective, when it is merely the attribute of another end. Violence in itself appears when the attribute, which was in the adjective, becomes the essence . . .

A particularly thorny problem is presented by violence claiming to be in the service of a cause or an idea. For my part, I find it difficult to accept giving doctrinal alibis to violent and destructive behavior. I agree with these simple words of Castellion, a Calvinist of the sixteenth century: "Killing a man is not defending a doctrine, it is killing a man." In this, Castellion differed from Calvin in Geneva. Castellion's words represent, I would say, what is stubbornly literal, when going by the letter—saying that *killing a man* cannot be disguised as *defending a doctrine*—does not kill but preserves life. To interpret the letter—to say that killing a man is defending a doctrine—seems indefensible to me, in the face of life.

In the current state of affairs, one problem demands consideration: the relationship between violence and power. All power inescapably contains violence. Joseph de Maistre said: "All sovereignty is absolute by nature. Whether it be placed on one or on several heads, whether it be divided, organize its powers how you will, there will always be in the last analysis an absolute power that will be able to do evil with impunity, that will thus be despotic from this point of view in the strongest sense of the term, and against which there will be no other rampart than that of insurrection." If one wishes to separate oneself from violence, one must accept the thought of nonpower, in current social terms, a way of thinking of the absolute margin. If one is against violence, one must manage to have an ethic, strong in itself, outside power, and one must not put oneself in a situation where one will participate in power.

Finally, I ask myself this question: Can one be against violence only in part, that is, under certain conditions, allowing for exceptions? Can one hedge with nonviolence? I ask this question, and I ask it of myself. I sense that you want to offer certain objections or qualifications, which are also mine. But I answer you with a question: Can one begin to evaluate the contents of violence, and its justifications?

In fact, there are two ethical attitudes: either one gives oneself the right to judge the contents of violence, to retain certain contents and condemn others, which is generally what the world does; or else violence is perceived by the body as intolerable, from which moment one refuses all alibis and makes no compromises over nonviolence, but this is an excessive attitude, assumed only within the limit zones of personal morality.

> *Your answers are quite pessimistic, they don't seem to offer a way out. But is there one?*

I don't see our present world society opting for a general resolution of the problem of violence. The world appears hopeless at the level of general organization: states are proliferating, and each state multiplies its forces of constraint, its power. Socialist solutions appear to be completely blocked: so the past fifty years have shown us, to our intense dismay. A world without violence seems a utopia, and imagining such a world is no longer even pleasant, so to speak, since the distance between this utopia and reality is so overwhelming.

The subject who lives in such a society is obliged to fall back on individual solutions and behavior.

> *Is that a solution born of despair?*

Not necessarily! For two hundred years, we have been conditioned by philosophical and political culture to valorize collectivity in general.

All philosophies are philosophies of collectivity, of society, and individualism is frowned upon. There is no longer or very rarely a philosophy of nongregariousness, of the person. Perhaps this singularity itself should be assumed, not lived as a kind of de-valorization, or humiliation, but effectively reconsidered in a philosophy of the subject. One shouldn't be intimidated by this morality of the collective superego, so widespread in our culture with its values of responsibility and political engagement. One should perhaps accept the scandal of individualist positions, even though all this would have to be clarified, of course.

> *What you say doesn't seem scandalous to me. Must we not first "be" before we can "be with"?*

I assure you, it's a scandal for every thought and theory since Hegel! Any philosophy that tries to free itself from these collective imperatives is extremely unusual and, I would say, carries a bad trademark.

> *And you, Roland Barthes, is that what you yourself think?*

As for me, I'm trying, bit by bit, to free myself from everything that is thus imposed upon me intellectually. But slowly . . . One has to give this transformation time . . .

Elle, **December 4, 1978**
From an interview conducted by Françoise Tournier

A Few Words to
Let in Doubt

Admired—or vilified—by intellectuals, which is to say by a minority, Roland Barthes might very well have continued his successful academic career outside the glare of publicity if he hadn't published, last year, a book that has been enjoying considerable popularity: A Lover's Discourse.

Roland Barthes's vast culture, his tireless desire to explore the word as sign and the sentence as structure, to shift them, to probe until they finally reveal what speaking means, coupled with the exacting writing of this amateur pianist and painter who selects from his word palette precisely what is needed to convey the right color, the correct note—all these qualities distinguish this great writer, who two years ago was offered the Chair of Literary Semiology at the Collège de France, in recognition of his innovative textual and linguistic criticism.

Semiology is the science of signs, and for Barthes, signs are everywhere. Everything is language. The problem is that all language ends by entrapping thought and intelligence. Words become snares engendering mental stereotypes. Denouncing this danger, Barthes calls on intelligence to reverse a certain disenchantment in our society, which now more than ever needs to revise its received ideas.

> *You say that we must always be on the lookout today for signs that are the forerunners of tomorrow. Can we not*

already discern a resurgence of anti-Semitism? A certain
return to Romanticism? And a nostalgia for the sacred,
evidenced in the proliferation of sects?

The future can never be predicted in a pure state. But all readings
of the present, in fact, lead us to anticipate a future filled with
fear and menace. Like all racism in each country, each civilization, each mentality, latent anti-Semitism is still alive in petit-
bourgeois ideology. In France, happily, it is not supported by
political decisions on a large scale. But anti-Semitic and racist
temptation is present in the press and in conversations. The fact
that it is reality on the ideological level obliges intellectuals to
maintain a strict vigilance. They have a positive role to play here.
The absolute rule is to watch what is said on all levels and on
all occasions, so that the idea of a separate Semitic reality is never
accredited. It is absolutely necessary that language must constantly
erase that horrible phantom.

The appeal of Romanticism is more ambiguous. Romanticism
comprises forces of creation, the exaltation of a desire for indi-
viduality, and resistance to rationalist systematics, and all that
may be very positive. But Romanticism can carry the myth of
anti-intellectualism, and even a certain risk of anti-Semitism. We
should not forget the Germany of post-Romanticism.

As for the sacred, it comprises all the ambiguity of the religious.
I am convinced that humanity cannot live without the sacred,
the symbolic. But there are risks: obscurantism on the level of
sects, and the assimilation of the sacred by political power.

In the face of all these dangers, I think that what is just and
right—hope, in other words—is always to be found in the margin,
so to speak. Combat at the level of the individual. I mean that
Romanticism and the sacred should be lived marginally and in-
dividually. Because when a value becomes established within a
society as gregarious as ours, that value becomes aggressive.

There is talk, aggressive talk, as you say, of "liquidating"
the great thinkers, and a general desire to return to "com-
mon sense." Now, we haven't reached the point of an

> *intellectual Gulag, but haven't you noticed, for some*
> *time now, a distinct fascist trend?*

You're right to link the risk of fascism to this way of thinking. But we should safeguard the proper meaning of words, the better to fight. There are, of course, fascist elements in language, discourse, conversations, the press, elements that spread and begin to seem sinister. There is definitely an anti-intellectual bias, and the intellectual does serve as a scapegoat, along with the Jew, the pederast, the black. Intellectuals have been periodically put on trial in France since Romanticism by "common sense," by vulgar conformist opinion, by what was called in Greece the "right opinion," i.e., what the majority is supposed to think. The petite bourgeoisie, a class majority, is dangerous: caught between the proletariat and the bourgeoisie, it has always wound up rallying to strong and fascist regimes. In France there is incontestably a historic growth of the petite bourgeoisie. It's the rising class, reaching for power. And, in great measure, it has attained power.

As for the supposed liquidation of great thinkers by popular opinion, it's a feeble practical joke to decree that there are "master thinkers"—which is not at all certain—the better to pronounce their death sentence. The slightest dialectic, the slightest subtlety, frightens vulgar minds so intensely that, in order to defend their stupidity, they call in common sense to stamp out all nuance.

> *Do you think that there are two types of intelligence, as*
> *is commonly believed: the mathematical and the literary?*

It all depends on the degree of development of mathematics and literature. There is a first level where there are two types of aptitude, or inaptitude, for these two languages. I think that there is a certain real opposition there. But on a second level, when mathematics and literature are more advanced, the barriers fall, and there are interactions, crossovers.

There is an enormous wealth of imagination in mathematics; there are important models of logical thought, thought of a very lively kind, focused solely on forms, without consideration of contents. Literature is very much interested in all this. There is a growing movement in literature toward forms of mathematical thought. At a certain point, mathematics and literature come together.

What would the end of all myths mean to you? The end of creativity and imagination?

I believe that the decay of myths and religions is caused by history, which wears out values, sometimes quickly, sometimes slowly. At present, there is an acceleration of the wearing-out process, a shift in the intensity and duration of humanity's great phantasms. But, and I say this with conviction, myths are absolutely necessary to societies, to keep them from tearing each other apart. Myths should not be considered alibis for reality, however; they should be experienced as art, which is not a realm of falsehood and errors, as people think. Art points out error, making it less dangerous.

Have you ever considered writing a sequel to Mythologies, *which you published twenty years ago? The portrait you gave of* Elle *in your book is now out of date. Rose-tinted glasses may once have colored all our observations, but we took them off after 1968, and these days we often deal with rather serious subjects.*

I'm not a great reader of magazines, but I think that *Elle* has in fact changed quite a bit. On the level of a magazine like *Elle*, good journalism has a task that somewhat reflects everything we've been talking about. Good journalism should definitely help its readers to look at society in a critical and unprejudiced manner. The transformation of *Elle* is obviously related to the growth of feminine consciousness. And the important thing, for women, is not to have a strong voice—which is sometimes what feminist movements claim—but to have the right voice. A voice that welcomes subtlety.

You say that the French are proud of having had Racine but don't regret not having had Shakespeare. Would love,

> *in this context, be a garden in the French manner, formal
> and well organized? Where is our wild and rustic garden
> in the English manner: love-as-passion? Has it never been
> a part of our heritage?*

The great French classics described love-as-passion with the accent on jealousy. To be blunt, paranoia. Whereas the Germans,
Heine, for example, emphasized the pain instead, the nostalgia,
the effusiveness of such a love, and it is this that is in fact rather
foreign to the French tradition. France had a few difficulties with
Romanticism, which can be felt in the French attitude toward
love.

> *And divine love? What would be the result of applying
> to the Gospels and their language of prayer the same
> critical decipherment you brought to bear on Balzac's
> Sarrasine?*

Bossuet said, in a decidedly pugnacious manner, that there is no
prayer that is not articulated, formulated in language. Here he
was attacking Fénelon and the mystics who claimed that pure
prayer is outside language, in the realm of the ineffable. Mysticism has always represented the most difficult experience of language, which is what makes it so fascinating. Could there be a
structuralist analysis of the Gospels? I would say yes. I have made
two short analyses of texts from the Old and New Testaments,
but it's impossible to get very far along, because structuralist
analysis describes only forms, and remains on this side of the
religious message. The text is many-layered, like a *mille-feuille*:
meanings are superimposed like layers of puff pastry. And as far
as the Gospels are concerned, this type of work would indeed be
necessary. It would allow us, after having examined all the levels
of textual organization, to return to the letter of the text, without
the letter killing the text.

> *In* The Fashion System, *you say that fashion doesn't
> exist, except as a system of meaning. Do you mean by
> that: "Tell me how you dress, I'll tell you who you are"?*

Fashion is a code, a language. And there is a complicated relationship between language as it is coded and the manner in which the subject speaks it. A relationship between competence—knowing how to speak the language, knowing the code—and performance—what one does when one speaks. Fashion is precisely that, which is what allowed me to describe it as a language. There is a personal way of speaking this language that obliges you to say personal things in an artificial code. Fashion obliges you to say what you think you are, what you want to seem, with a language used by everyone. And I would say that this is the very definition of the human condition. Man is condemned to "speak" himself with the language of others. Look at women's fashion for the last fifty years: the changes reflect very different erotic ideals. I think fashion is too cultural, you see, to ever be able to liberate the body. On the other hand, I think fashion is progressive when it attempts to develop aristocratic values of taste. When it tries to imagine forms and colors, models and silhouettes that keep a certain relation to the great plastic experiences of humanity—a relation to art, quite simply.

And the art of living. That was what won you over in Japan. Do you think there is a national art of living that comes before any individual art of living?

An art of living may be social. For example, the bourgeois art of living, which is not unpleasant, in France. Or an art of living may be national. I have often dreamed about setting up on paper, in the form of descriptions, a kind of synthetic art of living that would bring together all the best features of *l'art de vivre* from extremely different civilizations.

In our industrial society, isn't amateurism a liberating approach to the art of living?

Absolutely, because it emphasizes the production of a work, and not the work as product. We belong to a civilization of the product, however, where it has become subversive to take pleasure in producing something. There are amateur painters who find an immense joy in painting, and this joy is something very important. But "common sense" treats amateurism with a certain commiseration. Or even a kind of fear. The fear that amateurism creates marginal types. And therefore subversives.

Your new way of perceiving things, of reading between the lines—isn't that highly subversive?

I think it would be very pretentious of me to think that I am subversive. But I would say that, etymologically speaking, yes, I try to subvert. To come up underneath conformity, underneath an existing way of thinking, in order to shift it a little. Not to revolutionize things, but to shake them up a bit. To unstick them, make them a bit more mobile, to let in doubt. I always try to discomfit what is supposedly natural, what goes without saying.

Les Nouvelles littéraires, February 6–13, 1979

An Extremely Brutal Context

I am an essayist. I have written neither novels nor plays: I have never created fictional characters. In certain essays, of course, I have approached the fictive, but only as a category. I admit to being tempted these days to write something that could be related to the novel, but this temptation does not extend to plays for the theater. The professional world of the theater is a very difficult, very irregular world; everything there is played out in an extremely brutal context, and in record time.

On the level of a text's survival, this idea of time is quite disturbing. The brutality of theatrical creation is doubtless partly responsible for its sensual pleasure and worth. It must be very exciting to see one's text pass into the body of the actor, into his gestures, in that kind of immediate realization. But the French theatrical machine is based on a very harsh economic system: there is a struggle with, or against, money. Perhaps someday I'll come up against the temptation of writing dialogues. But then I would find it difficult to create the remainder, the body of a story or an intrigue, even if today's theater can get along without such things. It has happened that portions of a written text like *A Lover's Discourse* have been brought to the stage. As an author, I found this very interesting. It showed me what happens to a "silent" text when it passes into the actor's voice and breathing, it showed me what becomes of punctuation once it enters the actor's body, where commas become pauses, or gestures. At that moment, I wanted to write dialogues "intended" for the theater. If I were to write a play, by some miracle, I feel that it would be a very literary text. I would be reacting against a certain contemporary theater that entirely sacrifices text to dramaturgy.

In the essays I have written, which concern literature and not the theater, I have often struggled against the limitation of a textual reading to one definite meaning. But as soon as a dramatic spectacle is involved, I require a strong, unique meaning, some moral or social responsibility. Because I am still faithful to the ideas of Brecht, so important to me when I was a theater critic.

Lire, **April** 1979
From an interview conducted by Pierre Boncenne

Roland Barthes on Roland Barthes

The works of Roland Barthes—fifteen books or so, some of them quite well known: Writing Degree Zero, Mythologies, *and recently,* A Lover's Discourse—*are distinguished first of all by their diversity: they include critical studies of Michelet and Racine as well as a methodical analysis of fashion language, or even an astonishing piece on Japan,* Empire of Signs. *This polyvalence goes deeper than mere appearance. Instead of seeking to construct a system of thought, Roland Barthes has always made his way across different fields of knowledge, moving serenely from one theory to another, taking an idea from Marx, for example, in order to put it to the test in linguistics or vice versa. And if, when the opportunity arose, he stopped long enough to construct an analyzing apparatus, "semiology," he started to leave it behind the day it threatened to become too rigid and exclusive a framework of interpretation.*

Roland Barthes's itinerary, despite its detours, driftings, and side trips, presents one constant element: a particular attention to language. On the one hand, he denounces linguistic oppression, the frozen expressions of common sense, the "it goes without saying," or stereotypes (and where there are stereotypes, or even better, stupidity, Roland Barthes arrives on the run). But, on the other hand, he celebrates the extraordinary possibilities of jubilation and the explosion of meaning provided by a centuries-old activity: literature. And it is this Roland Barthes, the lover of literature, to whom the following questions were addressed, the Barthes who has just published a collection of articles devoted to his friend the writer Philippe Sollers, whose literary experiments are considered "avant-garde" by some, soporiferously "unreadable" by others. But there is also the Roland Barthes whose latest works—in particular A Lover's Discourse—*seem to be drawing closer and closer to literature through their style, to such an extent that today one hears more about Barthes the writer than about Barthes the critic. How does he feel about this? What is he working on now, this professor at the Collège de France who claims he has arrived at the age designated in Latin by the term* sapientia, *which he translates as "no power, a bit of knowledge, some wisdom, and as much spirit as possible"? Or, to greatly simplify things: a structuralist today, a novelist tomorrow? Roland Barthes has agreed to answer our questions, on his place in the intelligentsia, his opinion on avant-garde literature, and to reply in passing to those who accuse him of speaking jargon. One last observation: we should remark on the indefinable balance, in his voice and demeanor, between real tolerance, extreme sensitivity, and discreet hedonism. Perhaps these are the things that create what used to be called* courtesy, *and which Roland Barthes, in his way, brings back into fashion.*

> *I should like to begin this interview by asking what you think an interview is, or should be . . .*

The interview is a rather complex activity, if not to analyze, at least to evaluate. Generally speaking, I don't enjoy interviews, and at one point I wanted to stop giving them. I had even decided upon a kind of "last interview." And then I realized that this was an excessive attitude: the interview belongs, to put it casually, to an inescapable social game, or, to put it more seriously, to a solidarity of intellectual work between writers and the media. There are certain interlocking events that must be accepted: if one writes, it is in order to be published, in the end, and when one is a published writer, one must accept what society wants from books and what it does with them. Consequently, one agrees to be interviewed, while trying not to overdo it.

Now, why don't I enjoy interviews? The basic reason has to

do with my ideas on the relationship between speech and writing. I love writing. I love speech only within a very specific framework, one that I establish myself, for example in a seminar, or in a course. I'm always uneasy when speech is used somehow to repeat writing, because then I have an impression of uselessness: I could not say what I want to say any better than by writing it, and to repeat it by talking about it tends to diminish it. That is the essential reason for my reticence. There is another reason that has more to do with the mood of an interview: I don't think this will apply to you, but very often, you know, in interviews for the major media, a somewhat sadistic relationship is established between the interviewer and the interviewee, where it's a question of ferreting out some kind of truth from the latter by asking aggressive or indiscreet questions to get a reaction out of him. I find the rudeness of these maneuvers shocking.

What I've just said doesn't answer one of the possible interpretations of your question: What purpose does an interview serve? I only know that it's a rather traumatic experience that provokes in me an "I have nothing to say" response, a more or less unconscious defense. Someone who writes, and even someone who speaks, must struggle against the constant threat of aphasia (it should be understood that chattering or logorrhea is one form of aphasia). All that has to do with the rightness of writing and speech, or, to use a pedantic word, "homometer," where there is a correct metric relation between what one has to say and the way one says it. Your question brings to mind a general study that has yet to be made, one that I have always wanted to take as the subject of a course: a vast schematic analysis of the activities of contemporary intellectual life.

Is that why one of your projects for books in Roland Barthes *is entitled* Ethology of Intellectuals?

Exactly. One meaning of "ethology," in French, is animal behaviorism, the study of the habits of animals. In my opinion, the same work should be done on intellectuals: a study of their activities, courses, seminars, conferences, interviews, etc. As far as

I know, no one has ever deduced the philosophy of the modern intellectual's way of life.

> *The tape recorder on the table between us embarrasses, even disturbs, today's intellectuals very much. And you?*

It's true that the tape recorder bothers me a bit, but, as that strange expression goes, "I take it upon myself." A tape recorder doesn't let you read its erasures. In writing, you can cross things out immediately, which is marvelous. And there is a code in speech with which one can cross out something that has just been said: "No, I didn't mean that," etc. With the tape recorder, there's such profusion in the tape that it's hard to correct oneself, and speaking becomes a riskier business.

> *The tape recorder has also been considered a threat to writing, and therefore to literature.*

Les Nouvelles littéraires published a dossier on this subject containing the testimony of young writers who seemed completely relaxed vis-à-vis the tape recorder. As for myself, a writer from a different generation, I'm still fascinated by the classic mastery of language, and thus the possibility of criticizing language as I produce it is very important to me. Once again, it's the problem of nature. A human body mediated by manual writing is different from a human body mediated by the voice. The voice is an organ of the image-repertoire, and with the tape recorder one can obtain an expression that is less censored, less repressed, less subject to internal laws. Writing, on the contrary, implies a kind of legalization and the function of a rather harsh code brought to bear in particular on the sentence. A sentence is not the same with the voice and with writing.

> *So you don't use a tape recorder. What about the type-writer?*

I always write my texts by hand because I cross out a lot. After that, I have to type them up myself because there's a second wave of corrections at that point, which are always made in the direction of ellipsis or elimination. This is the moment when what has been written, which remains very subjective in the graphic appearance of manual writing, becomes objective: it's not yet a book or an article, but thanks to the typewritten characters, there is already an objective appearance to the text, and this is a very important stage.

> *In 1964, when you published your* Critical Essays, *and again in 1966, in* Critique et Vérité, *you affirmed that the critic is a writer. But recently, in 1977, at the Conference at Cerisy held in your honor, you declared: "There is a journalistic offensive that consists in making me into a writer."*

That was a witticism, of course, rigged up on purpose. I would very much like to be a writer, and I have always wanted to be one, without making any value judgment, because for me writing isn't a promotion list, it's an occupation. I was simply noting with amusement that my little social image has been changing for some time now, from that of a critic to that of a writer. What I have written in the past few years has contributed to this change in perception, which I do not regret. It is true, however, that one's image in society is always the object of concerted efforts, and that's why I spoke of an offensive, insofar as one is well aware of how this social image is built up and often changed independently of oneself.

> *But why this offensive, in your opinion?*

If I were still the rationalist I used to be in part, I would say: because French intellectual society today needs writers. There are empty spaces, and I have certain qualifications that fill the bill.

> *You are now a professor at the Collège de France, one of our most prestigious institutions. Yet there is a theme that returns insistently in your work, even in your in-*

augural address at the Collège: you say you are an "un-
certain subject," or an "impure subject" in relation to
the university, in particular because you never passed the
agrégation *teaching examination.*

It's obvious that this is still a very important subjective theme for me. I've always had a strong desire to belong to the university, a desire originating in my adolescence at a time when the university was very different. I was not able to join the university through the normal channels, if only for the reason that I was ill with tuberculosis each time I was due to go on to the next stage. The first time I was ill I was unable to prepare for the École Normale Supérieure, as I would have liked to do, and then I had a relapse when it was time to prepare for the *agrégation* exam. My career proves that I always held on to the idea of belonging to the university, but I belonged to it—which was lucky for me—through marginal institutions that were able to accept me without the diplomas usually required: the Centre National de Recherche Scientifique, the École Pratique des Hautes Études, and now the Collège de France. These institutions are marginal for reasons of style, but also for an objective reason that was not well understood when I spoke of it in my inaugural address: the Collège de France and, in large part, the École Pratique des Hautes Études do not grant diplomas. Thus, one is not enmeshed in a power system, and that creates an objective marginality.

And are you finally satisfied with this slight displacement
vis-à-vis the university?

From the professional point of view, I have had the best life I could have, since I was welcomed—even at the cost of some dispute—into the university system I had always wanted to join, but welcomed into rather marginal institutions, outside the power structure. I'm not forgetting that at the Collège de France, the function of which is rather difficult to explain to an outsider, there are contradictions between very innovative ideas and an incontestable aristocratism.

I've often noticed in bookstores that your books are never displayed together in one place but are classified instead under linguistics, philosophy, sociology, or literature. Does this ambiguous classification correspond in fact to your approach?

Yes, and if we go beyond my individual case, I think it corresponds to an effort of intermixture that began some time ago. Sartre, in particular, was a great polygraph: philosopher, essayist, novelist, playwright, and critic. It was doubtless at that point that the status of the writer began to become more fluid, approaching and eventually being identified with the status of the intellectual and the professor. There is nowadays a kind of peremption or suppression of the traditional writing genres, but this protean situation has not been closely followed by the publishing business, which still needs and relies on traditional classifications.

Even if one judges that he failed, Sartre at least tried to construct a comprehensive system, which does not seem to have been one of your ambitions. What was it in Sartre you found so important?

First of all, if it's true that Sartre, with a philosophical puissance that I do not possess, tried to produce a complete system of thought, I would not say that he failed. In any case, no grand philosophical system succeeds on the scale of history: at some point it becomes a vast fiction, which it always was originally, moreover. I would say that Sartre produced a great philosophical fiction that was incarnated in different writings and that managed to take the form of a system. What was important to me in Sartre was what I discovered after the Liberation, after my stay in a sanatorium, where I read mostly classical and not modern works. Sartre brought me into modern literature. With *Being and Nothingness*, but also with some other books that I find very beautiful; they have been somewhat forgotten and ought to be rediscovered: *Esquisse d'une théorie des émotions* and *L'Imaginaire*. And of course, above all, his *Baudelaire* and *Saint Genet*, which I consider to be great books. After that, I read less Sartre, I fell off a bit.

> *When you spoke of a science of literature, at a given moment, it was as an impossible model, a science that will never exist?*

In the sentence to which you refer, I wrote: "The science of literature . . . (if it exists one day)." What is important is the parentheses. Even during a time when I was much more resolutely pro-science, I didn't believe in a science of literature. Now, of course, I believe in it even less. But scientific, positivistic, or rationalistic attitudes should be explored. As for myself, I'm finished with all that now. Why shouldn't others continue literary analysis in a formalist direction, if they want to? It bothers me a bit, but I understand it quite well.

> *In what sense did you write: "Have I not reason to consider everything I have written as a clandestine effort to reintroduce one day, freely, the theme of the Gidean 'journal' "?*

Reading Gide's oeuvre was very important for me as an adolescent, and what I loved more than anything else was his *Journal*. It's a book that has always fascinated me by its discontinuous structure, its "patchwork" quality spread out over more than fifty years. Everything goes into Gide's *Journal*, all the iridescence of subjectivity: books, acquaintances, reflections, even foolishness. That's what intrigued me, and that's how I've always wanted to write: in fragments. Then why don't I keep a diary? It's a temptation that comes to many of us, and not only to writers. But it raises the problem of the "I" and of sincerity, a problem that was perhaps easier to resolve in Gide's time—one that he solved quite well, in any case, with a masterly directness—and that has become much more difficult today after the transformation of psychoanalysis and the passage of the Marxist bulldozer. One can't take up a past form again as if nothing had happened in the meantime.

You write in "fragments." Isn't the term "fragment" am-
biguous, giving the impression that they are small pieces
of a whole, a complete edifice?

I understand your objection. But I could give you a specious
answer by saying that this whole does exist, that writing is in fact
never anything but the rather poor and skimpy remains of the
wonderful things each person has inside himself. What ends up
as writing are erratic little clumps of ruins when compared to a
complicated and splendid *ensemble.* And that is the problem of
writing: how to put up with the fact that the great flood I have
within me leads in the best of cases to a rivulet of writing. I myself
get along best by not appearing to construct a complete whole
and by leaving plural residues in plain sight. That is how I justify
my fragments.

Having said that, I am very strongly tempted these days to write
a long, continuous work, something nonfragmentary. (Once more,
the problem is typically Proustian, since Proust spent half his life
producing only fragments, and then all at once, in 1909, he
began constructing that oceanic flood, *Remembrance of Things*
Past.) I find the temptation is so great that my course at the
Collège de France is based on this problem, via a wealth of related
detours. I'm interested in what I call the "novel" or "making a
novel," not in a commercial sense but because it would be a kind
of writing that would no longer be fragmentary.

Were you really surprised by the success of A Lover's
Discourse?

Sincerely, yes. I almost kept back this manuscript, because I didn't
think it would interest more than five hundred people; that is,
five hundred subjects who would have some affinity for this type
of subjectivity.

At the Cerisy conference, you stated that A Lover's Discourse *was successful because you had worked so care-*
fully on the writing. For no other reason?

That was an after-the-fact justification that is not necessarily false: it was perhaps the work on the writing of the book that permitted a transcendence of the extreme particularity of its subjectivity. Because, don't forget, after all, that the book concerns a very particular type of lover, belonging more or less to the tradition of German Romanticism, which might lead one to expect considerable resistance from the French public, especially the intellectuals. As for the book's success, of course I wonder about it, but in a way I could really not have imagined before. And that is what is so fascinating in "the craft of writing," as Pavese said: in the end, you never know what will happen. You drive yourself crazy trying to learn and anticipate what will happen, quite simply because one needs a loving response when one writes. But to no avail: you'll never know, and this is where marketing savvy is irrelevant.

Do you think very much about your readers?

More and more. Through the very fact of having abandoned a scientific point of view, even a strictly intellectual point of view, I am necessarily anxious to obtain not a wider public but affective responses from a certain public. And so I ask myself questions about style, clarity, simplicity. Which isn't always easy, since form isn't on one side and content on the other: to express oneself simply is not enough, one must also think and feel simply.

Has the success of A Lover's Discourse *changed your writing?*

There might be a kind of aftereffect. When one writes, one thinks a good deal about how the text will be received, and I may indeed be remote-controlled by the desire to renew a simple relation such as the one I had, it seems, with this book. But I'm very prudent, because that sort of experience shouldn't make one complacent.

You have just published a new book: Sollers écrivain. *In this book, which is really a collection of articles, you claim the right to practice an "affectionate criticism,"*

> not to separate your reading of Sollers from your friend-
> ship for him. Since all criticism is more or less affec-
> tionate, I don't see who might seek to deny you this right.

It's better to affirm it. I've known Sollers for a long time, I have
very strong ties of intellectual affection with him, and I don't
think they should be separated from the way I talk about his work.
I always repeat that Michelet greatly valued a historical distinction
to which he had given almost mythological names: on one side,
there was the "Guelph mentality," the mentality of the scribe,
the legislator, or the Jesuit, a dry and rationalistic spirit; and on
the other side, the "Ghibelline mentality," a feudal and Romantic
spirit, the devotion of men for each other. I myself feel more
Ghibelline than Guelph: in the end, I always want to defend men
more than ideas. I have affectionate intellectual ties to Sollers,
and I defend him overall as a personality and an individual. You
say that all criticism is affectionate. Yes, very often, and I'm glad
to hear you say it. But this should be carried even further, almost
to the postulation of a theory of affect as the motive force of
criticism. A few years ago, criticism was still a very analytical
activity, very rational, subject to a superego of impartiality and
objectivity, and I wanted to react against this approach.

> Without going into great detail, let's say that Sollers's
> texts, along with other avant-garde texts, present the reader
> with what has become familiar as the problem of read-
> ability or unreadability.

It's true that one can't deal with the complexities of readability
within the framework of an interview. But let me say first of all
that there is no objective criterion, broadly speaking, of readability
or unreadability. I would also say that readability is a classic
scholastic model: to be readable is to be read in school. But if
one were to observe the vibrant groups in society, the lively expressions that people use, all that subjectivity expressed in our daily
and urban life, there would certainly be many that would seem
unreadable to us, that might very well be popular ones. Finally,
I hypothesize that if texts like those of Sollers are considered

unreadable, the problem is that one hasn't found the correct rhythm for reading them. That particular aspect of the question has never been seriously considered.

For many readers, unreadability is quite simply a synonym for boredom.

Well, that's it: perhaps if one read certain texts more slowly, one would be much less bored. With authors like Alexandre Dumas, one must read very quickly or be faced with deadly boredom. Authors like Sollers, on the other hand, must be read at a slower rhythm, all the more so in that his project of the subversion and transmutation of language is closely tied to linguistic experiments. Here I'm almost handing you an argument I would not be able to get out of: when confronted with so-called unreadable texts, one begins to see those that are good or bad, roughly speaking.

Because the criteria of taste are also changed, but we don't know at all what they are. Why does one text sound better than another? We don't know. But we should be patient, because all these things form a kind of marquetry of the lively and diverse culture now coming into being.

In the meantime, the old criterion or myth of clarity is still on the job.

I myself have had a lot of trouble because of this myth, since I am often accused—as I was just recently—of writing obscure jargon. I don't think that clarity is a good myth, however. We are realizing more and more that form and content cannot be separated, and that clarity doesn't mean very much. But one may opt either for an aesthetics of false clarity or for subjectivity through some kind of revived classicism that may seem like an avant-garde attitude in literary history. Personally, my work is absolutely not parallel to Sollers's adventurous texts, and these days I'd like to attain an ever-greater simplicity of language. Which doesn't preclude sensitivity to the liveliness of Sollers's approach.

> *You who hate stereotypes so much, don't you find after*
> *all that there are some real beauties in the avant-garde?*

Definitely. There are stereotypes of nonstereotypy, there is a conformity of unreadability. What am I using as proof? I'm going to
use a slightly out-of-date criterion, a very kitsch formula: the
"suffering" of the writer. To me, suffering isn't slaving a whole
day over one page but rather the fact that the entire life of someone
like Sollers is visibly fascinated, agitated, and almost crucified by
the need to write. That is why Sollers's unreadability is hard-won
and why it will doubtless one day cease to be perceived as unreadable.

> *If I'm following you rightly, your interest in avant-garde*
> *texts like those of Sollers doesn't turn you away from*
> *more classical texts, texts with stories and characters . . .*

Of course not. My subjectivity requires this classicism. And if I
were to write such a work, I would give it a very strong classical
appearance. I would thus not be very avant-garde, in the current
sense of the expression.

> *In* Sollers écrivain *you refer to the "crisis of represen-*
> *tation" in painting, the passage from figurative to abstract*
> *art. Why has that crisis of representation been finally*
> *accepted by the public in the case of abstract painting*
> *but poorly received when it comes to literature?*

That is a fundamental question to which I can give only a general
answer. The difficulty comes from the fact that the basic material
of literature is articulated language, and that this material is in
itself already significative: a word means something even before
it is used. As a result, undoing all the procedures of analogy,
figuration, representation, narrativity, description, and so on, becomes much more difficult in literature since one must struggle
with a material that is already significative. Given this framework,
we encounter an ethical question: Should one struggle or not?

Should one struggle to wear out meaning, destroy it, transmute it, to attain through words another zone of the body that is not tied to syntactical logic—or should one turn away from this struggle? I think that the answers to these questions can only be tactical ones, and that they will depend on the way one judges our current historical situation and the combat at hand. It seems to me that this has been the meaning of our entire conversation. As for myself, and this is an absolutely personal point of view, I think that the moment has perhaps arrived to struggle less, to militate less on behalf of texts, to fall back a bit to regroup our forces. Tactically, I envision a slight withdrawal: less deconstructing of texts and more playing at readability (even through traps, feints, tricks, or ruses); in short, less struggling with the semantic givens of language. But again, don't forget that a cultural period is made up of several concomitant tactical efforts.

> *In* Le Nouvel Observateur, *you recently wrote: "Nothing says that Kuznetsov is a 'good' writer. I would even say that he is not, no more than is Solzhenitsyn . . ." You don't think Solzhenitsyn is a "good" writer?*

He isn't a "good" writer *for us*: the formal problems he has resolved are a bit fossilized in relation to us. He is not responsible for this—and for good reason—but there is a gap of some seventy years of culture between us. Our culture is not necessarily better than his, but it's there, and we can't renounce it, renounce everything that has happened in French literature since Mallarmé, for example. And we cannot judge someone who writes, let's say, like Maupassant or Zola, in the same way as we do one of our writers of today. Although I don't know foreign literatures very well, I have a quite acute and selective relation to the maternal tongue, and I truly love only what is written in French.

> *In the beginning of* Sollers écrivain, *you say: "The writer is alone, abandoned by the old classes and the new. His fall is made all the more grave in that he lives in a society where solitude itself, en soi, is considered a fault." Why such a pessimistic statement?*

Quite simply, because there has been a terrible disenchantment in the intellectual class since 1945, a political disenchantment caused by certain world events, such as the Gulags, Cuba, and China. Progressivism is a very difficult attitude for an intellectual today. Which explains the appearance of the "new philosophers" who, in various ways, have manipulated this historical pessimism and established the death of progressivism, for the time being.

> *And you write in* Roland Barthes*: "In a given historical situation—a situation of pessimism and rejection—it is the entire intellectual class that, if it does not become militant, is virtually given over to dandyism."*

Yes, everything that effectively consists in assuming an extremely marginal position becomes a form of combat. Once political progressivism is no longer simple or even possible, one must fall back on ruse and devious attitudes. Because at that point the principal enemy becomes what Nietzsche called the "gregarity" of society. And it becomes inevitable that there will be states of solitude unlike any we have hitherto known. This is why the writer, today, is fundamentally and transcendentally alone. Of course, he has access to the press and publishing industries, but that doesn't alleviate the very great solitude of creation. Today writers are not sustained by any identifiable social class, not by the grande bourgeoisie (supposing that it still exists), or by the petite bourgeoisie, or by a proletariat, which is, culturally, petit-bourgeois. The writer is within a marginality so extreme that he cannot even benefit from the kind of solidarity that exists between certain types of minorities or people on the margins of society. A writer is terribly alone now, and that is what I wanted to examine through the example of Sollers.

> *But you, you don't feel isolated within the same solitude?*

No, because I decided several years ago to cultivate a kind of "affectivity" in my relation to a certain public. Each time I find this affective response, therefore, I am no longer alone. If I were fighting for a particular idea of literature, I would doubtless be quite alone. But since I have changed the tactical significance of my activity, in my writing as well as in my courses, the reward is different, in a way.

> *Do you feel that there is now a certain anti-intellec-tualism in the air, an anti-intellectualism that has made you one of its targets, through a recent pastiche?*

Definitely. In reality, anti-intellectualism is a Romantic invention. It was the Romantics who began to cast suspicion on intellectual things by dissociating the head and the heart. After that, anti-intellectualism was passed on by political episodes, like the Dreyfus affair. And since then French society, in contradiction to its taste for prestige, has periodically had fits of anti-intellectualism. Without pushing this analysis, we might say that current anti-intellectualism is linked to the reshuffling of social classes. In France, to use traditional terms, there is an undeniable petit-bourgeois thrust in our institutions and culture. The intellectual thus becomes a kind of scapegoat, since he uses a language from which people feel cut off. We always return to language, and to the curse of the division of human languages, to the fact that we cannot produce a unitary language except in an artificial fashion. The regrowth of anti-intellectualism is centered on problems of expression, and it's in this sense that I recently served as a scape-goat. Because of *A Lover's Discourse,* I was one of the most "writer-like" of our small group of intellectuals, and thus one of the most well known to the general public. In that way, the "hermetic" intellectual could be selected as a target for criticism, and many people would have a good idea of what was meant.

> *This is not the first time that the work of Roland Barthes has been the subject of a broadside denouncing his language and style of expression. In 1963, when he was a standard-bearer of new crit-icism, which championed an analysis of the internal structure of texts instead of a reliance on vague psychology, Roland Barthes published a work on one of our great classics:* On Racine. *A few months later, Raymond Picard, a professor at the Sorbonne and a Racine specialist, published a pamphlet entitled* Nouvelle Cri-

tique ou Nouvelle Imposture. *Roland Barthes answered in 1966 with* Critique et Vérité. *When I asked him about the possible similarities between Picard's pamphlet and Burnier-Rambaud's pastiche, Roland Barthes made it clear that he thought the pastiche was indeed "a Picard operation more than ten years later, with the difference that the theater of operations has changed: because I am better known, they have moved from the arena of the university to that of the media. But in the end the problem remains the same, a problem tied to language."*

> *At the Cerisy conference, you mentioned that you were surprised that interviewers never ask you about your book on Michelet, which you called "the least talked-about of my books, and yet the one I like the best." I should like to end this interview by asking you why you like this book . . .*

That's quite a trap you've set for me! But it's true, I admit that I find the thematics of this book rather well done. And then, Michelet remains somewhat of an innovator, because he's a historian who really introduced the human body into history. Of course, he can be faulted on all sorts of scientific points, he committed many historical errors. But the entire *Annales* school of history, and the "living history" school of Georges Duby, Emmanuel Le Roy Ladurie, and Jacques Le Goff, recognizes what history owes to Michelet, who reexamined and rethought the body within history, with its suffering, its humors, blood, physiologies, and foods. And it was Michelet who founded the ethnology of France by moving away from chronology in order to look at French society the way ethnologists study other societies.

> *And somewhat in the manner of Michelet rethinking the body in history, you also are becoming more and more attentive to the savor of knowledge and things.*

Somewhat, yes. For that, I take the detour of subjectivity. Let's say that I'm taking more responsibility for myself as a subject.

Le Monde-Dimanche, **September 16, 1979**
From an interview conducted by Christine Eff

Dare to Be Lazy

Doing nothing. Watching the grass grow. Floating along the stream of life. Every day a Sunday . . . Roland Barthes talks about the delights of idleness.

How would you analyze laziness, that key item in student mythology?

Laziness is not a myth, it's a fundamental and quasi-natural given in a scholastic situation. Why? Because school is a structure of constraint, and idleness provides a way for a student to foil this constraint. A class necessarily involves a repressive force, if only because things are taught there that may not interest the adolescent. Laziness can be a response to this repression, a subjective tactic to take charge of one's boredom, show that one is aware of it, and thus, in a way, to "dialectize" it. This is an indirect response, not an overt protest, because a student hasn't the means to confront these constraints directly; by turning away, the student avoids a crisis. In other words, a student's idleness has a semantic value, it belongs to the classroom code, to the student's natural language.

If you look at the etymology of the word, you notice that *piger,* the Latin adjective (the French word *paresse* comes from *pigritia*), means "slow." This is the saddest, most negative face of laziness, which is to do things, but poorly, against one's will, to satisfy the institution by giving it an answer, but an answer that dawdles.

In Greek, on the other hand, the word for "lazy" is *argos,* a contraction of *a-ergos*, quite simply: "who doesn't work." Greek is much more frank than Latin.

We may already glimpse the possibility of a certain philosophy of laziness in this little etymological debate.

I was a high-school teacher for only one year. My conception of scholastic laziness is not drawn from that experience, but rather from my memories of life as a student. I sometimes spontaneously return to scholastic laziness in metaphorical form in my present life, which in principle has nothing in common with that of a schoolchild: often, confronted by boring or irritating tasks, such as mail, manuscripts to read, and so on, I rebel and tell myself that I just can't get everything done, like a student who can't do his homework. At such moments, laziness is experienced painfully, insofar as it is a painful experience of the will.

> *What place do you assign—or must you concede—to idleness in your life, in your work?*

I'm tempted to say that I leave no place in my life for idleness, and that that itself is an error: I feel that there is something missing, something wrong there. I often get myself into situations where I have to struggle to get things done. When I don't do them, or at least while I'm not doing them (because the work does generally get done), that is a laziness that imposes itself on me, instead of the other way around.

Obviously, this shameful laziness doesn't take the form of "not doing anything," which is the glorious and philosophical form of laziness.

At one time in my life, I used to allow myself a bit of this euphoric idleness, this giving in to laziness, which I would indulge in after my nap, until around four or five in the afternoon. I would relax and take orders from my body, which was then rather sleepy, not very energetic.

I didn't try to work, I just did as I pleased.

But this was life in the country, during the summer. I did a little painting, puttered about, as many Frenchmen do. But in Paris I'm more caught up in the need to work and the difficulty of working. Here I let myself go in that form of passive laziness, the distraction, the repetition of diversions one creates for oneself: making a cup of coffee, getting a glass of water . . . In completely bad faith, moreover, since instead of welcoming any distraction coming from the outside, I get very irritated with the person who causes it. I disagreeably endure phone calls or visits that, in fact, disturb only work that is not being done.

Aside from these diversions, I'm familiar with another form of painful laziness, which I would invoke in the name of Flaubert, who called it his "marinade." This means that you throw yourself on the bed or sofa and "marinate." You don't do anything, your thoughts whirl around, you're a bit depressed . . . I often have these "marinades," very often, but they never last long, fifteen or twenty minutes . . . Then my courage picks up again.

In fact, I think that I'm unhappy at not having the freedom and the power to do nothing. There are moments when I would really like to rest. But, as Flaubert said, "What do you want me to rest at?"

I'm unable to put any idleness into my life, still less any spare time. Aside from friends, I have only work or a rather grumpy laziness. I've never particularly cared for sports, and I'm too old for them now, in any case. So what do you want someone like me to do if he decides to do nothing?

Read? But that's my work. Write? Again, work. That's why I'm fond of painting. It's an absolutely gratuitous activity, corporal, aesthetic after all, and truly restful at the same time, real laziness, because there's no pride or narcissism involved, since I'm just an amateur. It's all the same to me whether I paint well or badly.

What else? Toward the end of his life, in Switzerland, Rousseau made lace.

One could raise the question of knitting, without too much irony. Knitting is the very gesture of a certain idleness, except if one is caught up in the desire to finish a piece of work. But conventions forbid men to knit.

Things were not always like that. Fifty or a hundred years ago, men commonly did crewelwork, but that's no longer possible these days.

Perhaps the most unconventional and thus the most literally scandalous thing I ever saw in my life—scandalous for the people watching, not for me—was a young man seated in a subway car in Paris who pulled some knitting out of his bag and openly began to knit. Everyone felt scandalized, but no one said anything.

Now, knitting is the perfect example of a manual activity that is minimal, gratuitous, without finality, but that still represents a beautiful and successful idleness.

We should also consider what idleness is in modern life. Have you ever noticed that everyone always talks about the right to leisure activities but never about a right to idleness? I even wonder if there is such a thing as *doing nothing* in the modern Western world.

Even people who lead a life completely different from mine, a more alienated, difficult, laborious life, when they have free time, they don't do "nothing," they always do something.

I remember this image . . . When I was a child, an adolescent, Paris was different. It was before the war. It was hot in the summer, hotter than it is now, at least it seems that way to me. In the evening, when it was hot, you'd often see the Parisian concierges—there were a lot of them, they were an institution—bring chairs out in front of the doors, in the street, and they'd just sit there, doing nothing.

It's an image of idleness that has disappeared. I don't see it anymore . . . In modern Paris, there aren't as many gestures of idleness. The café is, after all, a kind of laziness with spin-offs: there are conversations, an "appearance" of activity. This is not true idleness.

These days, idleness probably consists not in doing nothing, since we're incapable of that, but in cutting time up as often as possible, in diversifying it. That's what I do on my small scale when I introduce diversions into my work. I cut up time. It's a way of becoming lazy. And yet I aspire to a different kind of laziness.

I always marvel at the simplicity of this Zen poem, which could be the poetic definition of the particular idleness I dream about:

> *Sitting peacefully doing nothing*
> *Springtime is coming*
> *and the grass grows all by itself.*

And what is more, the poem presents an admirable anacoluthon, a break in grammatical construction. The one who is sitting peacefully is not the subject of the sentence, it isn't Springtime that is sitting down. This break in construction, intentional or not, clearly indicates that in a situation of idleness the subject is almost dispossessed of his consistency as a subject. He is decentered, unable even to say "I." That would be true idleness. To be able, at certain moments, to no longer have to say "I."

> *Wouldn't a lover be the one who most desires such idleness?*

The idleness sought after by the lover is not only "doing nothing," it is above all "deciding nothing."

In the fragment of *A Lover's Discourse* entitled "What is to be done?" I said that the lover, at certain moments, tries to arrange "a little corner of sloth" in the perpetual tension of passion.

In fact, the lover I tried to describe is constantly wondering about what he should do: Should I telephone? Should I go to the rendezvous? Should I stay home?

I remarked on the fact that the "What is to be done?"—that fabric of deliberations and decisions that perhaps makes up our lives—resembles the Buddhist karma, the interlocking causes that constantly oblige us to act, to respond. The opposite of karma is nirvana. And so, when one is suffering a great deal from karma, one may postulate or fantasize a kind of nirvana. Idleness then takes on a dimension of annihilation.

True laziness would be at bottom a laziness of "not deciding," of "being there." Like dunces, who are at the bottom of the class and have no other attribute except being there.

They don't participate, they aren't excluded, they're just there, period, like bumps.

That's what we sometimes long for: being there, deciding nothing. There is a Taoist precept on idleness, I think, on "doing nothing" in the sense of "moving nothing," determining nothing.

We might also recall certain temptations of Tolstoyan morality, insofar as one might wonder if one didn't have the right to be idle when confronted by evil. Tolstoy answered yes, and said that to do nothing was best, since one should not answer evil with more evil.

Needless to say, this morality is now completely discredited. And if we were to carry things even further, idleness might appear as an important philosophical solution to the problem of evil. To not answer. But once again, modern society does not get along very well with neutral attitudes, and it finds laziness intolerable, as if it were itself, in the end, the chief evil.

What is terrible about idleness is that it can be the most banal, stereotyped thing in the world, the most thoughtless behavior, just as it can be the most thoughtful.

It can be a natural aptitude, but also a conquest.

> *This thoughtful idleness, wouldn't that be what Proust calls* le Temps perdu?

Proust's attitude toward a writer's work is something quite particular. His masterpiece is constructed, if not on, at least in the company of, a theory of involuntary memory, of the rising to the surface of memories and sensations. This free-flowing remembrance obviously involves a kind of idleness. To be idle, within that particular perspective, is—to use the Proustian metaphor— to be like the madeleine that slowly dissolves in the mouth, which, at that moment, is idle. The subject allows himself to disintegrate through memory, and he is idle. If he were not idle, he would find himself once more in the domain of voluntary memory.

We might turn to another Proustian image: the Japanese paper flowers, tightly folded, that blossom and develop in water. That would be idleness: a moment of writing, a moment of the work.

And yet, even for Proust, writing was not a lazy activity. Proust uses another metaphor to designate the writer, a metaphor of labor. He says that he writes a work as a dressmaker sews a dress. That implies an incessant, meticulous, plundering, constructive, tacking-on activity, like Proust's. Because, after all, he was perhaps idle for the first half of his life (if then!), but afterward, when he shut himself away to write *Remembrance*, he was not idle, he worked constantly.

In the end, there would be two periods in writing. At first, there would be a time for rambling around, one might almost say cruising around, cruising for memories, sensations, incidents that are allowed to flourish. Afterward, there would be a second time, a time of writing at one's desk (for Proust, writing in bed).

But I really believe that, in order to write, one must not be lazy, and that is precisely one of the difficulties of writing. To write is a pleasure, but a difficult pleasure at the same time because it must span zones of very hard work, with the risks that that entails: the longings and threats of idleness, the temptations to abandon work, fatigues, revolts. Just an hour ago I was busy taking notes on Tolstoy's private diary. He was a man obsessed by the rules of life, the blocking out of schedules, the moral problem of not being lazy. He constantly writes down his failings. It's an interminable struggle, a truly diabolical struggle. And in fact, if one is fundamentally lazy, or if one has decided to become lazy, which is perfectly conceivable and quite defensible, then one cannot write.

> *Are there rituals of sloth, or is Sunday a day like all the others?*

It's time to say that there are as many forms of idleness as there are professions, perhaps as many as there are social classes. And although Sunday may be the established compartment for idleness, it's obvious that a teacher's Sunday isn't the same as the Sunday of a workman, a bureaucrat, or a doctor.

But aside from this sociological problem, there is the historical problem of the weekly day of rest, whether it's Sunday, or Saturday, or Friday, according to different religions . . . I mean, the problem of ritualized idleness.

In very codified societies, like Victorian England, for example, or in Orthodox Judaism, the day of rest was and is marked by rites forbidding certain actions. The rite anticipates this desire to do nothing. But it seems, unfortunately, that as soon as people are obliged to submit to this rite of interdiction, they suffer from "doing nothing."

Since this idleness is imposed from the outside, it becomes torture. This torture is called boredom.

Schopenhauer said: "The social representation of boredom is Sunday."

As a child, I found Sunday rather boring. I don't really know why, but I think that children often think of Sunday as a boring day. There's no school that day, and school, even if it is a mixed experience for children, is a social and affective environment . . . and rather entertaining.

Now that I am no longer a child, Sunday has become once more an auspicious day for me, a day on which all those social demands that fatigue me during the week—mail, phone calls, appointments—are suspended. It's a happy day, because it's a blank day, a silent day on which I can laze about, be free. Because the votive form of modern idleness, after all, is liberty.

Le Nouvel Observateur, December 10, 1979
From an interview conducted by Jean-Paul Enthoven

For a Chateaubriand
of Paper

Well, what does Chateaubriand mean to you?

In my life, in my cultural memories, Chateaubriand—as he is
for everyone—was first of all the author of selected excerpts, those
descriptions of moonlit scenes, or American wilderness landscapes. These *official* pages are not without beauty, but I don't
think that we can find much pleasure in them . . . These are
generally the pages used to fill out a certain mythology of the
Romantic hero, but they are not really representative of an oeuvre
that goes far beyond them. In this respect, I think that Chateaubriand has become an exemplary victim of our teaching system,
because as a result of the scholastic impoverishment to which he
was subjected—and the *withdrawal* of sympathy that has en-
sued—he is now little read in France.

> *You had already read enough of his work to want to write
> a preface for the* Life of Rancé . . .

Indeed, I had to discover this sumptuous and austere book to
understand that Chateaubriand was not merely the diligent champion described in schoolbooks. In the *Life of Rancé* I found a
profound, grave, and powerful man, and it was perhaps in thinking of that Chateaubriand that I began to really read the *Mémoires
d'outre-tombe* a few months ago. And I was astounded . . .

The *Mémoires* became my bedside reading for several weeks; each evening I would hurry to return to them, because the language is inconceivably, breathtakingly beautiful. Even more, this beauty provides effects of suspense: one longs constantly to learn more, to find once again the enchantment of a certain phrase, and so you are drawn on by your reading . . .

> *Is the beauty of his language enough for you?*

Behind the language there is a complex and contradictory Chateaubriand, there is a morality, and a real political philosophy.

> *The political thought of* La Monarchie selon la Charte *or* Le Génie du Christianisme?

Here I'm speaking only of the *Mémoires d'outre-tombe*. I find *Le Génie* boring. In speaking of his political views, I was alluding to something greater than a simple constitutional dissertation. In politics, Chateaubriand has a kind of grandeur, a nobility, a quality of soul. He would never have been able to speak the cynical words of Joseph de Maistre: "One has done nothing against opinions as long as one has not attacked the people who hold them." Chateaubriand remains loyal, even toward those he criticizes the most. Think of his portrait of Charles X.

> *And Chateaubriand's vanity, his lies . . .*

They don't bother me. They belong to his "self," which protects him, in the end, from baseness. Nietzsche speaks of this "antique sovereignty of the self," which Chateaubriand exemplifies beautifully . . . What is essential, in my reading, is the nobility I perceive in him, a nobility that seems to enjoin him never to consent to pettiness, even in the world of politics in which he moves, a world so predisposed to paltriness.

> *Would you like to have written a biography of Chateaubriand?*

I have often wanted to write a biography, but I admit I never thought of Chateaubriand. The life of a German musician, perhaps, if I had been a good Germanist . . . In any case, there is now a definitive biography of Chateaubriand: George Painter's book . . .

> *What do you think of Painter's biographies, their meticulous research and* mise en scène?

I was very impressed by his Proust, because Painter was the first to rehabilitate "Marcelism," a real interest in the private life of Proust himself and no longer simply in the characters of his novel. On the other hand, I was disappointed in Painter's book on Gide . . . As for his recently published *Chateaubriand,* it's hard for me to say anything; the first volume—the only one published yet—covers his life until 1793. Now, the Chateaubriand who interests me is the writer in his old age. I willingly admit that Painter has a certain genius for biography. His work is always lively, well done. But . . .

> *But?*

. . . I wonder if the very logic of the genre at which he excels doesn't forbid him access to what makes Chateaubriand a unique figure: his style, his language. In addition, French is not Painter's mother tongue, and I wonder what can be derived from a close study of Chateaubriand that doesn't emphasize the mystery of his language, what makes him unique. In France today there is not a crisis of language—because words always manage to survive— but there is a *crisis of love for language.* Without a sensitive evaluation of that crisis, without that love of language, how could one understand the modernity of such a prodigious syntactician and lexicologist as Chateaubriand?

> *Would you then say that it is the rhetoric rather than the anecdotal content that contains the truth of the* Mémoires d'outre-tombe?

That is not really the question. But since Chateaubriand talks to us about his life and times in a language of such jubilation—which he must have greatly enjoyed writing, and which we so enjoy reading—I don't think this language can be passed over without analysis.

> *Fine, let's talk about this language, about its mystery; don't you sometimes have the impression that Chateaubriand can become an enormous machine of "sonorous inanity," that he willingly lapses into facility, like those too-gifted composers who pull out all the stops at the same time?*

I don't agree. To me, in the *Mémoires d'outre-tombe*, Chateaubriand is a miracle of equilibrium and measure, because there he possesses a knowledge of the *mot juste*, the right word used without exaggeration: for example, when he describes Mme Récamier "in a white dress on a blue sofa," it's simple, and perfect. And elsewhere this language never fails him in the description of his destiny, between two worlds, it never fails him for his old age . . .

Once again, it's this language that permits him to transform poetically such barren subjects as boredom, of which he speaks so well, thereby changing it into *something else.* And then, it's his language that allows him to maintain, to express, the nobility that remains at all times his inflexible choice . . .

> *What do you mean by nobility?*

An absence of calculation, of meanness, a spirit of generosity and, I would say, of hospitable welcome—all qualities absent from today's political discourse, an absence that bothers me. Of course, this nobility goes along with a certain moral and chivalrous *presentation*, but his sentences remain simple, and what they say is often very true. It makes you nostalgic.

> *You're ascribing to Chateaubriand an innocence and*
> *loyalty that he doesn't always seem to have dis-*
> *played . . .*

My Chateaubriand is first of all his oeuvre, his books: a Chateaubriand of paper, and it's indeed possible that my Chateaubriand doesn't resemble the one in biographies. It doesn't interest
me very much to confront this paper Chateaubriand with the
man of flesh and blood whom Painter calls back to life.

> *It is generally said that in France the eighteenth century*
> *was intelligent, whereas the following century was more*
> *or less devoted to stupidity. It would seem that you think*
> *Chateaubriand was an exception . . .*

The "intelligence" ascribed to the eighteenth century and denied
the nineteenth belongs in general to a reactionary mythology à
la Maurras. One has only to *read* the *Mémoires* to see how *in-*
telligent they are: he says magnificent things about the French
and their political "psychology." Remember this passage of his
about Napoleon: "Daily experience inclines the French instinctively to power. They do not love liberty at all, equality alone is
their idol. And equality and despotism share secret connections.
In these two respects. Napoleon sprang from the heart of Frenchmen militarily inclined toward power and democratically in love
with the average." Isn't this the very truth of our obsession with
putting everyone on the same level? So you see, Chateaubriand—
the one whose body is made of paper—moves me by this dignified
lucidity that always forces him to tell the truth, *despite everything.*
Chateaubriand was often disappointed but always lucid, anxious
to describe things as they were; this is why he was, even more
than a politician, a writer in possession of a system of ethics. And
thus a writer for our times . . .

Le Matin, **February 22, 1980**
From an interview conducted by Laurent Dispot

From Taste to Ecstasy

A book by Roland Barthes is always an event. Camera Lucida
appears under the patronage of three publishers at once, a rare
phenomenon. Roland Barthes is not a photographer, but he speaks
here about an art that interests him, as it does all of us today.

> *Susan Sontag and Michel Tournier have also recently*
> *published books on photography. Is this a coincidence?*

There does seem to be a kind of "theoretical boom" in photography, in fact. People who are not technicians, historians, or
aestheticians are becoming interested in it. They're only closing
what was a scandalous gap: photography is an integral part of our
civilization, there is no reason not to reflect upon it, as we do
on painting and film. Whether this will please photographers
remains to be seen. Because, although they are trying to gain
acceptance for photography as a serious art, they show a certain
distrust of the "intellectualization" of their art . . . In any case,
photography is not taught in the universities, except for pioneering
experiments such as that of the University of Aix-Marseille, which
three months ago accepted a doctoral proposal from Lucien Cler-
gue; the ad hoc center (this is significant) was set up . . . in the
Chemistry Department! As if photography were still dependent
on its heroic beginnings, as far as the university is concerned.

> *Why* Camera Lucida, *when Tournier calls his camera*
> *"a little box of night"?*

I wanted to play on the paradox and a reversal of the stereotype. But it does have a symbolic reality: I try to say that what is terrible about a photograph is that there is no depth in it, that it is *clear evidence* of what was there.

Your book is a "note," and yet it creates concepts . . .

It was with sincere modesty that I called it a "note" in the subtitle, because it's a short book, with no encyclopedic pretensions. It's just barely a thesis, a proposition. But on the other hand, I'm quite conscious of the *particularity* of my position, which is on the edge of this scientific field . . . One must define one's terms whenever one writes a work of analytical reflection, and I chose two Latin words that simplified things. *Studium* is the general, cultural, and civilized interest one has in a photograph. It's what corresponds to the photographer's work: he tries to please our *studium*, our . . . taste, in a way. Thus, all photos of reality in general have a sense of *studium*.

But I noticed that certain photographs touched me more sharply than their general interest warranted, through details that captivated me, surprised and awakened me in a rather enigmatic fashion. I called that element the *punctum*, because it's a kind of point, a sting, that touches me sharply.

A "pleasure of the image" after the "pleasure of the text"?

The first part of my book could have been called that. But I then begin a more painful reflection on an episode of mourning, on grief. I try to discover and explain what causes this painful impression: the violence of "what was there." This is "photographic ecstasy": certain photographs take you outside of yourself, when they are associated with a loss, an emptiness, and in this sense my book is symmetrical to *A Lover's Discourse*, in the realm of mourning.

Le Photographe, February 1980
From interviews conducted by Angelo Schwarz (late 1977)
and Guy Mandery (December 1979)

On Photography

Barthes is one of the men who will leave his mark on our time. From Mythologies *to* A Lover's Discourse, *Roland Barthes's analyses of different elements and aspects of society are talked about, imitated, sometimes mocked, but never ignored. His influence on the intellectual life of France is undeniable.*

Here are some of his thoughts on photography and the role it plays in modern society.

> ANGELO SCHWARZ: *Photography is now commonly defined as a language. Isn't this definition confusing, in a way?*

To call photography a language is both true and false. It's false, in the literal sense, because the photographic image is an analogical reproduction of reality, and as such it includes no discontinuous element that could be called *sign*: there is literally no equivalent of a word or letter in a photograph. But the statement is true insofar as the composition and style of a photo function as a secondary message that tells us about the reality depicted and the photographer himself: this is *connotation*, which is language. Photographs always connote something different from what they show on the plane of *denotation*: it is paradoxically through style, and through style alone, that photographs are language.

> *As Baudelaire already observed, photography is closely linked to an industrial process. Could we, then, define*

> *it as a system of writing strongly conditioned by this
> industrial process?*

Film and photography are pure products of the Industrial Revolution. They're not part of a heritage, a tradition. That makes
them extremely difficult to analyze: we should invent a new aesthetics that can deal with both film and photography by differ-
entiating them, whereas in reality there is a cinematographic
aesthetics that functions on the basis of stylistic values of a literary
kind. Photography hasn't benefited from this transference, appearing instead as a kind of cultural poor relation for whom no
one wants to claim responsibility. There are few great texts of
intellectual quality on photography. I don't know of very many.
There is Walter Benjamin's essay, which is good because it is
premonitory. There are forthcoming books by Susan Sontag and
Michel Tournier. The photograph is a victim of its superpower;
since photography has the reputation of literally transcribing reality or a slice of reality, no one ever thinks about its real power,
its true implications. We have a double perspective on photography that is always either excessive or erroneous. A photo can
be thought of as a purely mechanical and exact transcription of
reality, which is photo reportage, or family pictures in certain
cases. This is obviously excessive because even a straightforward
news photograph implies some consideration, some ideology behind the shot. Or else, at the other extreme, a photo can be
thought of as a kind of substitute for painting; this is what is called
an art photograph, which is another exaggeration, because it's
evident that a photo is not art, in the classic sense of the term.

> *There are theories of film—why is there no theory of
> photography?*

I think that we are victimized by cultural stereotypes. Film immediately took its place in culture as an art of fiction, of imagination. Even though the first cinematographic works in the period of the Lumière brothers were records of reality (*Train Arriving
in Station, Workers Leaving the Factory*), the true development
of film has been a fictional development. As an activity (or a

technique) opting for the security of a simple recording of reality, photography has not been able to enjoy such a development. Society has repressed what it thought was only a technique, while unblocking what it took to be an art.

You wrote recently that there was something in common between the work of a writer and that of a photographer. But what are the flagrant historical differences between these two activities?

They were born at different times, they have different signifiers; I'm not quite sure what the signifiers of photography are. I have no experience as a photographer, I don't know what it's like to take photographs. I am a pure consumer of photographed products. It's obvious that photography and writing don't use the same material. The writer works with words, pieces of material that already have meaning, but photography is not a language, it doesn't deal with pieces of material. There's an obvious difference.

How can it be that photography, in your own words, is foreign to both art and the "illusory naturalness" of the referent?

A photograph is caught between two dangers. It can mimic and copy art, which is a coded form of culture, but it cannot copy as well as painting, because its referent, the object it photographs, is experienced as real by someone looking at the photo. There's a very strong constraint there, which is why photography cannot be an art like painting.

But, on the other hand, the photographed object is illusively natural because in reality this referent is selected by the photographer. The camera's optical system has been chosen from among other possible systems inherited from Renaissance perspective. All that implies an ideological choice in relation to the object represented. In short, a photo cannot be a pure and simple transcription of the object that presents itself as natural, if only because a photo is one-dimensional; and besides, photography cannot be

an art, because it copies mechanically. That is the double misfortune of photography, and any photographic theory would have
to start from that difficult contradiction.

> *The photographer is said to be a witness . . . Of what,*
> *would you say?*

You know, I'm not a partisan of realism in art, or a supporter of
positivism in the social sciences. I would therefore say that the
photographer bears witness essentially to his own subjectivity, the
way in which he establishes himself as a subject faced with an
object. What I say is banal and well known. But I would greatly
emphasize this aspect of the photographer's situation, because it
is generally repressed.

> *Is a grammar of the image possible?*

In the strict sense of the word, a grammar of photography is
impossible, because there is no discontinuity (of sign) in a photograph. At the most, one might be able to establish a lexicon of
connotative signifieds, especially in commercial photography. If
photography is to be discussed on a serious level, it must be
described in relation to death. It's true that a photograph is a
witness, but a witness of something that is no more. Even if the
person in the picture is still alive, it's a moment of this subject's
existence that was photographed, and this moment is gone. This
is an enormous trauma for humanity, a trauma endlessly renewed.
Each reading of a photo, and there are billions worldwide in a
day, each perception and reading of a photo is implicitly, in a
repressed manner, a contact with what has ceased to exist, a
contact with death. I think that this is the way to approach the
photographic enigma, at least that is how I experience photography: as a fascinating and funereal enigma.

> GUY MANDERY: *You are about to publish a book with*
> *photographs; can you tell us what it's about?*

It's a modest book, done at the request of *Cahiers du cinéma*, which is publishing a series of books on film; they left me free to choose my own subject, however, and I chose photography. My book will disappoint photographers.

I say this not from coquetry but from honesty. Because my book is not a sociology, or an aesthetics, or a history of photography. It's more like a phenomenology of photography. I consider the phenomenon of photography in its absolute novelty in world history. The world has existed for hundreds of thousands of years, there have been images for thousands of years, since the cave paintings . . . There are millions of images in the world. And then, all at once, around 1822, a new type of image appears, a new iconic phenomenon, entirely, anthropologically new.

It's this newness that I try to examine, and I place myself in the situation of a naïve man, outside culture, someone untutored who would be constantly astonished at photography. This is why my text might disappoint photographers, because this sustained astonishment obliges me to ignore their photographically sophisticated world.

How is the book organized?

I look at several arbitrarily chosen photographs and I try to reflect on them, to see what my consciousness tells me about the essence of photography. This is a phenomenological method, an entirely subjective one. I tried to find out why certain photographs moved me, intrigued me, pleased and concerned me, and why others did not. There are thousands of photos that say absolutely nothing to me. You have to be blunt about it.

It doesn't make any difference whether they're newspaper or so-called artistic photographs?

No. I chose to be guided by my *pleasure* or my *desire* in regard to certain photographs. And I tried to analyze this pleasure or desire, which brought back certain reflexes of semiological analysis. I tried to analyze what it was in certain photos that involved me, clicked with me, produced a kind of shock in me that was not necessarily the shock of the subject depicted. There are traumatic news photos in newspapers and magazines that perhaps command high prices because they are traumatic, but they don't affect me at all. On the other hand, there are some rather anodyne reportage photos that can suddenly strike a chord in me, affect me. That is what I tried to analyze. Then I noticed that, by being guided by my pleasure, I was certainly getting results, but I was not able to define what it was that radically opposed photography to all other types of images. Because that was my intention. And so at that point . . .

. . .But I don't want to go into detail because my book involves a bit of intellectual suspense, and I don't want to ruin the effect. In any case, at this stage I decided to consider a private photograph, in relation to a recent personal loss, the death of my mother, and it was in reflecting on a photograph of her that I was able to formulate a certain philosophy of photography, which puts into relation photography and death. This is something that everyone feels intuitively, even though we live in a world of living photographs, lively images. That is the philosophy I tried to explore and formulate. I won't say any more about it, it's all in the text. Obviously, I concentrated on photographs of people rather than landscapes, and I don't deny that I postulated a certain "promotion" of private photography. I think that in contrast to painting, the ideal future of photography lies in private photography, images that represent a loving relationship with someone and possess all their power only if there was a bond of love, even a virtual one, with the person in the photo. This is all played out around love and death. It's very Romantic.

> *What does the book look like? What photographs did you select?*

The photographs I chose have an essentially argumentative value. They are the ones I used in the text to make certain points. The book is, thus, not an anthology. I wanted to show not the best picture, or even my favorite picture, from each photographer's work, but simply the photo I needed to illustrate my argument.

But I did of course try to use pictures that are beautiful in themselves.

>   *What was the corpus from which you made your selections?*

It was very narrow, a few albums and magazines. I used the *Nouvel Observateur Photo* a great deal.

There are many old photographs, because I think that the golden age of photography was at its beginnings, its heroic period. But more contemporary photographers like Avedon and Mapplethorpe are also represented. There are some great photographers whose work I like very much who are not represented. The photographs in my book simply correspond to moments in the text.

>   *What place does photography have in your work in general? Do you use it as a tool to cull information about society?*

One thing I truly enjoy working at is showing a relation between text and image. I have always found an intense pleasure in such work. I love to write captions for pictures. I did this in my book on Japan, in my *Roland Barthes*, and I have just completed such work in *Camera Lucida*. What I love is the relation of the image and the text, a very difficult relation but which thereby provides truly creative enjoyment, the way poets used to enjoy working on difficult problems of versification.

The modern equivalent is to find a relation between text and images.

I should also say that if I chose photography as the subject of my book, I did so, in a way, *against* film. I realized that I had a positive relation to photographs, I love to look at them, whereas I have a difficult and somewhat resistant relation to film. I don't mean that I never go to the movies, but in the end, paradoxically, I put photography above cinema in my little personal pantheon.

>   *Nowadays, photography is being recognized as an art . . .*

. . . The game isn't over yet. I would say rather that every photograph is answerable to art, except (paradoxically) art photographs.

> *Socially, in any case, photography is well on the way to being recognized as art. Nevertheless, it has a very special, very close relation to reality. Would you agree that photography is a bridge between art and non-art?*

Yes, that's quite true. I don't know if it's a bridge, but it's certainly an intermediate zone. Photography displaces, shifts the notion of art, and that is why it takes part in a certain progress in the world.

Le Nouvel Observateur, **April 20, 1980**
From an interview conducted by Philip Brooks, which was published almost a
  month after Barthes's death

The Crisis of Desire

What does it mean to be an intellectual in France today?

Gide, who at first supported Soviet Russia before becoming a
critic of the regime, and who took a stand on colonialism as well,
was one of the last to play the traditional role of the intellectual
who also remains a great writer. Now, writers are somewhat in
the background; there really aren't any more great writers, properly
speaking. After Gide there were still Malraux and Aragon . . .
Instead of a new wave of great writers, there came the massive
invasion of intellectuals; in other words, professors. There's even
a real intellectual caste. And what is threatening is the considerable development of the media, television, radio, the press,
which pass on anti-intellectual attitudes. In fact, if France becomes a petit-bourgeois country, intellectuals will lose their identity more and more. They will be obliged either to seek refuge
in obscure publications, as today's poets do, or to install themselves as intellectuals within the media themselves—which is in
part the approach of the "new philosophers," intellectuals who
have decided: "We're not going to let ourselves be constantly
manipulated by the media; we're going to gain entry to the media
by using their own methods, and by changing our language so
that it will be more understandable to more people." Personally,
I'm not attacking this position, which I find perfectly defensible.
The "new philosophers" try to publicize the problems raised by
their intellectuality: liberty, morality, everything in the world that
calls for debate.

Why, in contrast to many French intellectuals, have you never been a militant yourself?

At the end of the last war, I was intellectually quite fascinated by Sartre and the theory of commitment. This was during my adolescence, or rather my youth. But I was never a militant, and it would be impossible for me to be one because of my personal attitude toward language: I don't like militant language. Of course, after the events of 1968, militancy became more overt, but no one doubts that a communist is a militant. And I think the same goes for a leftist. There is a very stereotyped leftist discourse that is thereby unacceptable to me—as language. A newspaper like *Libération*, which is very well done and which I like a great deal, purveys a type of discourse with the same themes, the same stereotypes. I always view problems in terms of language. That's my particular limit. An intellectual cannot directly attack the powers that be, but he can inject new styles of discourse to make things change.

Is that why intellectuals are interested in trends?

Yes, fashion is a privileged vantage point for observing how society functions. It's fascinating and cruel, because you see things that are in fashion one year but must revamp themselves the following year to catch up with new trends. The rapid pace of fashion is not favorable to myth, which needs time to install itself, gain strength, take on traditions. Fashion goes too fast. We no longer experience the passage of history, but the acceleration of incidental history. It is therefore precisely in militant discourse that one now finds myths, because it is a fixed and immobile discourse. There is a very strong mythology today, even in *Libération*. Police fallibility, for example, is becoming a leftist myth. There are others: ecology, abortion, racism. I don't mean that these problems don't exist. It's just that they have now practically become contemporary myths.

> *It seems that you are sometimes seen in a very Parisian nightclub called the Palace. What do you think of a place like that?*

I'll give you a general answer. My point of view is perhaps affected by my age, by nostalgia, but I think that the present generation doesn't know very much about desire. Lots of activities go on that don't really seem to be activities of desire. And when a person is afflicted by a lack of desire, it's almost a sickness, not at all in the moral sense, but almost in the physical sense of the term. A man without desire atrophies. The crisis and malaise of civilization we hear about today is perhaps a crisis of desire.

There is a loss of desire in the milieux where taboos are on the wane. You might think it would be quite common to see two boys kissing on a Saturday night at the Palace—there's no rule against it. But it never happens. New prohibitions have sprung up—I'm talking about a relatively emancipated class of intellectuals, students, artists, people in fashion and the theater; if you were to move into more rigid social classes, you'd find very strong prohibitions, operating through myths of masculinity, virility—and these new inhibitions come from fashion. I know that one evening, at the Baths, two men started dancing, and a girl said to them: "Oh no, no one does that anymore." So she wasn't protesting against the fact that they were boys dancing with each other, but because it wasn't the style anymore!

> *Then a new conformity is taking shape these days. Why do you think the protest movement has failed?*

The historical phenomenon that seems to have been growing for ten years now is the problem of "gregarity"—a Nietzschean word. People on the margins of society flock together, become herds, small, it's true, but herds just the same. At that point I lose interest, because conformity reigns in every herd. Current history is a drifting toward gregarity: regionalisms, for example, are little gregarities trying to build themselves up. I now believe that the only truly consistent marginalism is individualism. But this idea should be taken up again in a new way.

Are you optimistic about individualism?

No, not really. Because anyone who lived his individualism in
a radical fashion would have a tough life. There are possibilities,
however, for the rebirth of individualism that would be more
radical and enigmatic than the petit-bourgeois variety. Even if
it's just "thinking" my body until I realize that I can think nothing
but my own body—this is an attitude that runs up against science,
fashion, morality, and so on.

But how can one live like that?

You can only do it by cheating, by clandestine behavior, un-
dogmatic, nonphilosophical behavior—by cheating, I can't find
another word for it.

Is this a protest against power?

Yes, and the only one that no power can tolerate: protest through
withdrawal. Power can be affronted through attack or defense,
but withdrawal is what society can assimilate the least.

A Lover's Discourse *is part of this struggle, in a way.*

Not really. The book is the portrait of an image-repertoire, of my
image-repertoire. It's true that the sentiment of love in this particular genre, a rather Romantic feeling, is experienced by the
lover as a separation from society, experienced both as the right
to be in love and the difficulty of being in love in the real world.
Well, I was able to write the book, I was lucky. Matters had
resolved themselves—more or less!
    I said that A *Lover's Discourse* would be "the most widely read
and most quickly forgotten" of all my books, because this book
reached a public that is not really mine, after all. And with my
next books, *Camera Lucida* above all, I will probably go back to
my public, which is a much smaller one. Because A *Lover's
Discourse*, although not very marked by intellectualism, was rather
"empathetic": one can project oneself into it not from the basis

of a cultural situation but simply from being in love. My next books will probably be written from a more intellectual standpoint. But I don't know, I really can't speak for the future.

Haven't you ever wanted to write a novel?

Yes, sometimes I feel like writing something at greater length, changing my manner. But I'm afraid of being boring. And I'm afraid of being bored. Writing allows you to jettison some of your image-repertoire, which is quite a paralyzing force, rather mortal and funereal, and writing allows you to communicate with others, even if this communication is complicated. You know, as para-Lacanian analysis says, my body is my imaginary prison. Your body, the thing that seems most real to you, is doubtless the most phantasmatic. Perhaps it is even only phantasmatic. One needs an Other to liberate the body, but things become very difficult, and the result is all of philosophy, metaphysics, and psychoanalysis. I can push my body to its own limits only with an Other, but this other also has a body, an image-repertoire. This Other may be an object. But the game I enjoy most is when there really is an Other around me, in the precise sense of the term. I'm not at all inclined toward politics, history, or sociology. If I had lived a hundred years ago, I would have been a psychologist. I would have practiced what was then called psychology, with no complexes. I would have enjoyed that very much.

What makes you continue to write?

I can only answer with grand, almost grandiloquent reasons. One must play on the simplest words. Writing is creation, and to that extent it is also a form of procreation. Quite simply, it's a way of struggling, of dominating the feeling of death and complete annihilation. I'm not talking about a belief that as a writer one will be eternal after death, that's not it at all. But, despite everything, when one writes one scatters seeds, one can imagine that one disseminates a kind of seed and that, consequently, one returns to the general circulation of *semences*.

Biography

November 12, 1915	Born in Cherbourg, to Henriette Binger and Louis Barthes, midshipman
October 26, 1916	Death of Louis Barthes in combat, in the North Sea
1916–24	Childhood in Bayonne. Elementary school
1924	Family moves to Paris, rue Mazarine and rue Jacques-Callot. Henceforward, all school holidays spent in Bayonne, with paternal grandparents
1924–30	Lycée Montaigne
1930–34	Lycée Louis-le-Grand. Baccalaureates: 1933 and 1934
May 10, 1934	Haemoptysis. Lesion in the left lung
1934–35	Fresh-air cure in the Pyrenees, at Bedous, in the Aspe Valley
1935–39	Sorbonne: license in Classics. Foundation of the Groupe de Théâtre Antique
1937	Exempt from military service. Foreign language assistant during the summer in Debreczen (Hungary)
1938	Voyage to Greece with the Groupe de Théâtre Antique
1939–40	Teacher at the new *lycée* in Biarritz
1940–41	Assistant and teacher at Lycée Voltaire and Lycée Carnot, Paris. Graduate degree in Greek tragedy
October 1941	Relapse of pulmonary tuberculosis
1942	First sojourn at the Sanatorium des Étudiants, Saint-Hilaire-du-Touvet, Isère

1943	Convalescence at the Post-Cure on rue Quatrefages, Paris. Last of the license examinations (grammar and philology)
July 1943	Relapse in the right lung
1943–45	Second sojourn at the Sanatorium des Étudiants Began studies for the medical preliminary examination, with the intention of specializing in psychiatric medicine. Relapse while still at the sanatorium
1945–46	Treatment at Leysin, at the Clinique Alexandre, Sanatorium Universitaire Suisse
October 1945	Extrapleural pneumothorax, right lung
1946–47	Convalescence in Paris
1948–49	Assistant librarian, then professor at the French Institute of Bucharest, and reader at the University of Bucharest
1949–50	Reader at the University of Alexandria (Egypt)
1950–52	At the Direction Générale des Relations Culturelles, teaching division
1952–54	Officer of Instruction at the Centre National de Recherche Scientifique (lexicology)
1954–55	Literary adviser at Éditions de l'Arche
1955–59	Research attaché at the Centre National de Recherche Scientifique (sociology)
1960–62	Chairman of Section VI of the École Pratique des Hautes Études (economic and social sciences)
1962	Director of Studies, École Pratique des Hautes Études ("Sociology of Signs, Symbols, and Representations")
1976	Professor at the Collège de France (Chair of Literary Semiology)
November 1978	Death of Henriette Barthes, his mother
February 25, 1980	Roland Barthes is struck by a van outside the Collège de France
March 26, 1980	Death of Roland Barthes